Must Goals

Must Goals

The Art and Science of Authentic
Goal-Setting for Lasting Change

STEPHEN RUE

Award Winning, Best Selling Author

The MUST Personal Development Book Series
The Personal Development Experience™

MUST BOOK PRESS
COPYRIGHT © 2026 Stephen Rue
All rights reserved.

"I AM SMART TO ACT™ Goals Method is a trademark of Stephen Rue. © 2025.
All rights reserved. Unauthorized use is strictly prohibited.

Must Goals
The Art and Science of Authentic Goal-Setting for Lasting Change
Introducing the "I AM SMART TO ACT™ Goals Method

FIRST EDITION

ISBN: 979-8-9935336-6-7   Hardcover
ISBN: 979-8-9935336-7-4   Paperback
ISBN: 979-8-9935336-8-1   Ebook

Disclaimers:

This book is for educational and informational purposes only and is not intended to provide medical, mental health, psychological, therapeutic, financial, tax, or legal advice. It is not a substitute for professional diagnosis, treatment, or counsel from a qualified provider.

Readers should consult with a licensed physician, mental health professional, attorney, financial advisor, or other appropriate professional regarding their individual circumstances before acting on any information contained in this book. If you are experiencing significant emotional distress, thoughts of self-harm, or a mental health crisis, contact a qualified mental health professional or emergency services in your area immediately. If you are in immediate danger, call your local emergency number right away.

The "I AM SMART TO ACT™" referenced in this book is distinct and is not affiliated with, sponsored by, or the same as any vendor or registrant using the S.M.A.R.T. GOALS trademark or brand for their own materials.

"Achievement without authenticity yields empty victories. Before we pursue goals, we must look inward—because only those aims that reflect our deepest identity can ever lead to genuine fulfillment and lasting success."

—Stephen Rue

Dedication

To my family—whose love, example, and encouragement continue to shape my journey. Your strength and support are the foundation of all I achieve.

With gratitude for the visionaries in goal setting—mainstream authors, speakers, academics, and scientists—whose insights have advanced the art and science explored in these pages.

May this work serve and inspire all who seek to grow, achieve, and uplift others through purposeful goals.

CONTENTS

Introducing the "I AM SMART TO ACT™" Goals Method............xi
Introduction xvii
How to Use This Book.. xxv
Quick Start Guide.. xxix

PART ONE
EXPLORATION: FOUNDATIONS
OF IDENTITY FOR AUTHENTIC GOALS

Chapter 1: Must Potential: Awakening Your True Capacity 5
Chapter 2: Must Mindset: The Mental Foundation of
  Authentic Goals 15
Chapter 3: Must Core Beliefs: Aligning Goals With Inner Truths....28
Chapter 4: Must Core Values: Aligning Goals with What
  Matters Most 48
Chapter 5: Must Personal Narrative: Shaping Your Story for
  Authentic Goals 71
Chapter 6: Must Standards: Elevating Your Benchmarks for
  Authentic Success 91
Chapter 7: Must Purpose: Defining Your Why for Authentic
  Goals... 101
Chapter 8: Must Identity Map (My "I AM")............................... 117

PART TWO
IMPLEMENTATION: CREATING MUST GOALS AND ACTIONS FOR RESULTS

Chapter 9: The Bridge: From "I AM" to Implementation 125

Chapter 10: Unlimited Goal Ideation: Dreamstorming for Possibilities 129

Chapter 11: Must Goal Setting Foundations 141

Chapter 12: Must Health & Vitality Goals – The Energy of Excellence 163

Chapter 13: Must Relationship Goals – Building Meaningful Connection 180

Chapter 14: Must Career & Professional Development Goals 196

Chapter 15: Must Financial Well-Being Goals: Creating Abundance Through Alignment 213

Chapter 16: Must Personal Growth Goals: Becoming Your Next Self 224

Chapter 17: Your Spiritual and Peace of Mind Goals 234

Chapter 18: Your Community & Legacy Goals 244

Chapter 19: Measuring Progress and Implementing Systems: Tracking and Achieving Must Goals 253

Chapter 20: Must Actions in the Must Zone: Turning Goals into Momentum 261

Chapter 21: Achieving Goals Through Must Habits 272

Chapter 22: Tenacity, Perseverance & Grit 284

Conclusion: The Must Goal-Setting Journey Towards Becoming 313

About the Author 317

Connect and Grow Together: Stay in Touch with Me and Our Must Book Community 319

How to Stay in Touch with Me 321

Key Must Concepts (At a Glance) 323

References & Ongoing Research Updates 331

Thank you, and Next Steps 335

INTRODUCING THE "I AM SMART TO ACT™" GOALS METHOD

The **"I AM SMART TO ACT™" Goals Method** is an original framework created by Stephen Rue and introduced here for the first time. It builds on the trusted foundations of classic SMART goals while integrating identity, alignment, and authentic meaning at every step. The result is a system that helps you craft clear, actionable goals that are fully aligned with who you truly are.

"**I AM SMART TO ACT**™ Goals Method
is a trademark of Stephen Rue. © 2025.
All rights reserved. Unauthorized use is strictly prohibited.

Why "I AM SMART TO ACT™"?

For decades, SMART goals—Specific, Measurable, Achievable, Relevant, and Time-bound—have provided a proven structure for achievement. However, real, lasting change begins not with what we want, but with who we are. The **"I AM SMART TO ACT™"** Goals Method places your identity, values, and personal narrative at the center of every goal, so each outcome reflects your story, purpose, and unique potential.

How This Method Works

Every goal in this book uses the I AM SMART TO ACT™ framework. Begin by affirming your "I AM"—your authentic self—and walk each goal through the following steps:

I AM: The Identity Foundation

- **I – Identity**

  Root your goal in your true self and unique strengths by beginning with an "I am…" declaration that reflects who you are becoming.

- **A – Aligned**

  Ensure your goal aligns with your Must identity, as defined by your mindset, core beliefs, core values, enhanced personal narrative, standards, and purpose.

- **M – Meaning**

  Focus on outcomes that express your Must purpose, not just what seems impressive or expected.

SMART: The Classic Structure

- **S – Specific**

  State precisely what you want and how you will pursue it.

- **M – Measurable**

  Track your progress with concrete, visible actions and clear indicators of success.

- **A – Achievable**

  Set goals that stretch you beyond your comfort zone while remaining realistically attainable.

- **R – Relevant**

    Prioritize what truly matters in your current season and life context.

- **T – Time-bound**

    Add a deadline and milestones to create urgency, focus, and momentum.

TO ACT – Turning Your "I AM" Into Action

- **TO – Take Ownership**

    Accept full responsibility for this goal. Own the choices, habits, and adjustments required—no blaming, no waiting for perfect conditions.

- **ACT – Aligned Consistent Steps**

    Commit to small, repeatable actions that match your Must identity. Action is how your "I AM" and your SMART goal become visible in your daily life.

TO ACT reminds you that action is required. Goals only come alive when you consistently act in alignment with who you are and what you must become.

Example: **I AM SMART TO ACT™ Must Goal**

I – Identity: I am a present, energetic parent who leads my family with love and strength.

A – Aligned: This goal supports my Must Values of health, family, and service.

M – Meaning: Having steady energy allows me to show up fully for my children and my purpose.

S – Specific: I will walk 8,000 steps a day, at least 5 days per week.

M – Measurable: I'll track my steps in a simple app and mark each completed day on my calendar.

A – Achievable: I'll begin with 10–15 minute walks after dinner and add time as my stamina improves.

R – Relevant: Building my energy is essential for my current season of parenting and work.

T – Time-bound: I will follow this plan for the next 30 days, then review and adjust.

TO – Take Ownership: I accept full responsibility for planning my walks and protecting this time.

ACT – Aligned Consistent Steps: I will schedule my walks on my calendar, prepare my shoes in advance, and treat each walk as a vote for the parent and person I am becoming.

What Makes This Method Different

The **I AM SMART TO ACT™ Goals Method** honors the scientific rigor of the original SMART approach while elevating it. Instead of starting with tasks and metrics, you begin with identity, beliefs, and meaning. This is more than a technique; it is a transformational practice for becoming your authentic potential. Each goal becomes a daily act of self-leadership, not just another item on a checklist.

Evolution: From SMART to I AM SMART TO ACT™

Building on classic goal frameworks, the I AM SMART TO ACT™ Goals Method starts with "I AM" and connects each goal directly to your values and evolving story. This approach goes beyond mechanics by rooting every objective in alignment and purpose. Your goals become both a plan and a living expression of who you are choosing to be.

To apply this method effectively:

- Write your goals down.
- Make them specific and measurable.
- Review them regularly.
- Ensure they clearly express who you are and who you are becoming.

This combination creates maximum clarity, motivation, and sustainable success.

How to use this in the rest of the book

You'll see the **I AM SMART TO ACT™ Goals Method** woven throughout this book and applied in every life domain. In later chapters, you'll often be invited to "write this as an **I AM SMART TO ACT™ Must Goal**." When you need a refresher, return to this section as your manual—it contains the complete framework you can reuse for any goal.

INTRODUCTION

Have you ever felt a quiet stirring of potential—a sense you could become something more, but without a clear path forward? Many people sense untapped possibilities yet struggle to bring them into focus.

My own journey began with that same tension. For a long time, I believed potential was a nice word reserved for other people. Early memories—my mother's encouragement, my father's absence—fed a mix of self-doubt and longing. Achievement helped on the surface, but it did not touch the emptiness underneath.

The turning point came not in a moment of triumph, but in a morning of honest reflection. I looked in the mirror and saw someone who had weathered storms but was still adrift.

That realization changed everything. Our struggles do not just wound us; they reveal where our deepest commitments live. When I embraced my potential, I moved from limitation to purpose. That shift—from protecting myself to becoming who I was meant to be—became the heartbeat of this book. In the pages ahead, you will learn how to make a similar shift.

This book is an important anchor in the Must Book Personal Development Series. It will show you how to set and achieve goals in every area of your life, each one arising from your authentic self—your core identity and personal narrative—rather than being imposed from outside.

You will learn to elevate every life domain—health, relationships, career, finances, personal growth, spirituality, and community—so you thrive with proper balance and meaning, not just isolated accomplishments.

Why This Structure?

This book is structured to help you achieve lasting results. Each chapter builds on the previous one, introducing key principles and practical strategies to help you overcome internal barriers, develop lasting habits, and accomplish the goals that matter most in every part of your life. At its core, the Must system is a deep personal commitment to living and achieving as your true self.

THE POWER OF MUST: REDEFINING OUR COMMITMENT

Before setting meaningful goals, it is vital to understand the root of their power: the word **Must**.

Must is not external pressure; it is your most authentic, non-negotiable values guiding each action. Here, real goals reflect your identity—your deepest values, your highest standards, and your true self, directing your choices. In this book, your real goals are not checklists, but authentic extensions of self.

Throughout **Must Goals**, you will turn this inner Must into measurable achievement—connecting identity with action, belief with behavior, and purpose with consistent follow-through.

You will:

- Clarify your Musts across every life domain.
- Align your beliefs, values, standards, and purpose with the goals you pursue.
- Build habits and systems that turn identity- and purpose-anchored goals into daily action.
- Develop the resilience, focus, and grit to stay faithful to your Must through resistance and change.

To further strengthen your **Must Goals** and ensure maximum motivation, begin each goal declaration with "I must..." to express your deepest desires and commitment in the present, positive tense. Framing Must Goals with "I must..." (for example, "I must have creative fulfillment" rather than "I wish I were not bored") turns vague wishes into focused, value-driven intention. This practice transforms generic desires into empowered commitments, anchoring each Must Goal not only in your core identity but also in conscious, actionable choice. You create momentum and clarity by focusing on what you want to build, not what you hope to avoid.

This is the art and science of goal-setting for success.

This is the power of Must.

EXPLORING, IMPLEMENTING, AND INTEGRATING THE BUILDING BLOCKS OF GOAL SETTING MASTERY

It is essential to understand how this book is structured and why each section builds intentionally on the last. Each part moves you forward in clarity, commitment, and alignment, guiding you from the inner work of mindset transformation to the outer work of applied achievement.

This is your goal-setting blueprint for a flourishing life, built on three integrated phases: Exploration, Implementation, and Integration. Think of them as three dimensions of success—discovering who you are, executing what matters most, and embodying your purpose in every dimension of life.

Part One: Exploration — The Foundations of the Must Mindset

Transformation begins with awareness. In this opening phase, you will explore the essential building blocks that form the foundation of your goal-setting success: Mindset, Beliefs, Values, Personal Narrative, Standards, and Purpose.

Each of these elements is interconnected. Together, they shape how you see yourself, what you believe is possible, and what you commit to achieving. Before lasting outer success can occur, your thoughts, emotions, and decisions must align with your true self.

Exploration helps you uncover your inner blueprint—your authentic why. It invites you to reflect on your defining experiences, reveal hidden limitations, and reframe them as sources of strength. In doing so, you awaken your sense of possibility and clarify what you must become and what you must do to live authentically. This is where you begin to design your goals not from pressure or comparison, but from alignment—with who you are meant to be.

Part Two: Implementation — Turning Insight into Action

Once the groundwork is laid, we move into transformation through deliberate and focused action. This is where clarity meets commitment. Implementation is about translating your values and beliefs into systems of action. You will learn specific tools and strategies—such as the Must Zone, goal-formation templates, habit systems, visualization practices, and accountability frameworks—that turn your vision into measurable progress.

Here, we go beyond theory. You will set clear goals in each area of your Circle of Life: health, relationships, career, finances, growth, spirituality, and community. Setting specific, challenging goals leads to better results than vague intentions. Must Goals go further—grounding specificity not only in metrics but in meaning, identity, and alignment. Through guided exercises and reflection, you will develop and prioritize the Must Goals that have the most significant impact on your journey.

In this phase, you will discover that goals are not merely targets—they are commitments. The Must Zone becomes the environment where your actions are fueled by discipline, belief, and purpose. The principles of Implementation will help you create consistent habits, stay focused under pressure, and turn obstacles into stepping stones toward your success.

This is your roadmap for total alignment—personally, professionally, spiritually, and emotionally. The journey is not about becoming someone new; it is about returning to who you were always meant to be and aligning every area of your life with that truth. The path begins now.

Part Three: Integration — Living Your Must

Exploration gives you clarity. Implementation gives you systems and action. Integration is where everything comes together in the real world.

In this phase, you will deepen your understanding that goals are not tasks to complete but commitments you embody. You will strengthen your tenacity, persistence, and grit; learn how to navigate common obstacles; and weave your **Must Goals** into the daily rhythm of your relationships, work, and community.

Here, your goals stop being a project and become a way of living.

The Must Inside-Out Flowchart: From Identity to Outcomes

Every authentic transformation begins within. This framework reveals how inner alignment becomes outer achievement—how identity gives rise to mindset, beliefs, and purpose, which in turn shape goals, habits, and results. Each layer builds on the one before it, turning who you are into what you do and, ultimately, what you become.

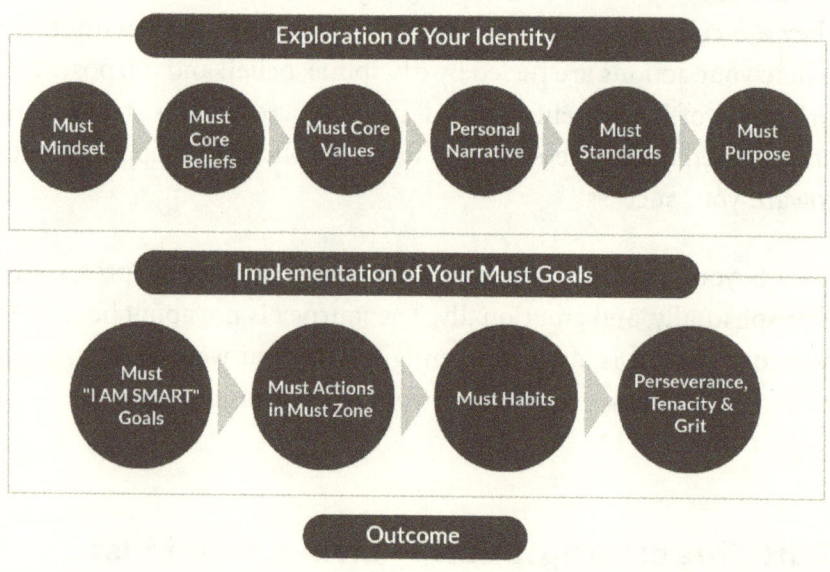

Copyright © 2025 Stephen Rue
All rights reserved.

Identity → Mindset → Beliefs → Values → Personal Narrative → Standards → Purpose → Goals → Must Actions in the Must Zone →Habits → Tenacity, Perseverance & Grit → *Outcomes*

© 2025 Stephen Rue. All rights reserved.

This Flowchart is the backbone of this book. Each chapter will walk you through one link in this chain, and by the end, you will create your own **Must Alignment Map** that connects identity, beliefs, values, narrative, standards, and purpose directly to your goals, habits, and outcomes.

By the end of this book, you will have not only learned the art and science of authentic goal-setting—you will have embodied it. Specifically, you will:

- Define your Must Mindset—the mental foundation that transforms intention into identity, where motivation becomes consistency and effort becomes devotion.

- Identify and reprogram limiting core beliefs that quietly shape your choices, replacing self-doubt with empowering truths that align with who you are becoming.

- Clarify your Must Core Values, Standards, and Purpose so every goal you pursue flows naturally from the deepest parts of your authentic self.

- Set and achieve Must Goals—objectives that are not just SMART but sacred, fueled by meaning, measured by alignment, and sustained by identity.

- Build Must Habits and Must Micro-Goals that turn alignment into action—daily, repeatable behaviors that keep you anchored when enthusiasm fades.

Along the way, you will also strengthen your perseverance and grit—not as raw willpower, but as a natural expression of living from your **Must**.

Ultimately, sustainable motivation arises from autonomy, competence, and relatedness—the pillars of Self-Determination Theory. Sustainable motivation grows when your goals support your independence, growth, and relationships.

Your life is calling. Your goals await. Let's begin.

HOW TO USE THIS BOOK

Two Paths, One Purpose

There are two ways to experience *Must Goals: The Art and Science of Authentic Goal-Setting for Lasting Change.*

Both will move you toward alignment and action—but the pace and depth are yours to choose.

Path One: Quick Start — Immediate Action

If you're ready to get moving now, this path gives you traction on Day One.

Begin with **the Quick Start** Guide in the opening section.

You'll define one *Must Goal*, translate it into a *Micro-Goal*, and start building the daily habits that bring it to life.

This path is designed **for momentum and measurable progress.**

It's ideal if you want to jump in, apply the framework immediately, and experience quick wins that build confidence and consistency.

Once you've established your first Must Goal and gained momentum, you can choose one of the two following steps:

1. Return to the earlier chapters for deeper alignment and reflection.
2. Or move directly into **Part Two: Implementation**, where you'll explore the advanced mechanics—the *art and science*—behind effective goal creation, habit design, and long-term execution.

The Quick Start is your entry point into results; the later chapters are where those results mature into mastery.

Quick Start Summary

- Begin with the *Quick Start Guide*
- Set one *Must Goal* aligned with your highest priority using the I AM SMART TO ACT™ Goals Method
- Implement the *Micro-Goal + Must Habit* process
- Track your progress using the downloadable templates at *MustGoals.com/Resources*
- Continue into **Part Two: Implementation** when you're ready for deeper mechanics, advanced frameworks, and sustained mastery

Purpose: Momentum

Focus: Action, traction, and immediate results

Path Two: Deep Alignment Journey — Transformational Process

If you're seeking lasting transformation—not just productivity but purpose—this is your path.

The Deep Alignment Journey invites you to move through the book in sequence, layer by layer, uncovering the architecture of your authentic self.

You'll explore how your **Mindset, Beliefs, Values, Personal Narrative, Standards, and Purpose** create the inner alignment from which all meaningful goals arise.

Each chapter includes reflection prompts, micro-assignments, and integration practices that help you design a life built on what truly matters.

By the time you reach the Implementation phase, your goals will no longer be something you chase—they'll be the natural expression of who you've become.

Deep Alignment Summary:

- Start at **Part One: Exploration** — The Foundations of the **Must Mindset.**
- Move through each building block—Mindset to Purpose—in sequence.
- Complete the exercises, reflections, and Activation Moments in each chapter.
- Proceed to **Part Two: Implementation** to convert clarity into consistent, measurable results.
- Use the downloadable *Must Alignment Map* and Weekly Review Template to integrate what you've learned into your daily rhythm.

Purpose: Transformation.

Focus: Identity, alignment, and mastery.

Whichever Path You Choose

Both paths lead to the same destin*ation—living from your* Must.
One begins with action; the other begins with awareness.

STEPHEN RUE

Choose the path that best fits your current season of life… and remember, you can move fluidly between them.

Your journey is not about doing more—it's about becoming more. That is the power of living your *Must*.

QUICK START GUIDE

Set the Must Goal That Needs Your Attention Most Today

(And Revisit Your Goals After Experiencing Cutting-Edge Art and Science Next-Generation Goal Setting in the Following Pages)

Quick Start—At a Glance:

Set one Must Goal, break it into a micro-goal, build a key habit, and take your first step now. Momentum starts today.

If you're ready for action, the **Quick Start Guide** offers a clear, science-backed plan to move forward today. Return to deeper reflection and alignment whenever you choose.

Your Journey, Your Pace: Practical Growth Without Overwhelm

Use this Quick Start in whatever way serves you best—jump in now, or pair it with the deeper chapters whenever you're ready.

Here's how to begin Your Quick Start:

Step 1: Choose One Area of Immediate Focus

Pick one life domain where you most want to create change today.

Health and vitality

Relationships

Career achievement

Financial well-being

Personal growth and learning

Spirituality or inner peace

Community, Contribution, and Legacy

Ask yourself: "What area matters most to me right now?"

Step 2: Set Your Must Goal

Before you write your goal, take a moment to understand what makes a Must Goal unique within the Must Goals system:

A *Must Goal* is:

- A Calling, **Not a Comm**and:

  It emerges from your inner sense of meaning and freedom—not external pressure or obligation.

- **Rooted in Alignm**ent:

  It reflects harmony between your goal and your beliefs, values, personal narrative, and life direction.

- **An Extension of Ident**ity:

  Achieving it moves you closer to the person you are meant to become—it is not about chasing random outcomes, but about authentic self-expression.

- **Empowering and Inspiring:**
  Pursuing your Must Goal feels energizing and deeply motivating because it is anchored in the real you.

Every actionable step in Quick Start uses the I AM SMART TO ACT™ Goals Method—an identity-driven framework that ensures your goals arise from who you are, not just what you wish to achieve. By structuring your goals with I AM SMART TO ACT™, you'll create objectives that are specific, measurable, authentically aligned, and timed for real results. This approach moves you from simply writing goals to living them—starting with your very first action today.

Example I AM SMART TO ACT™ Must Goal:

"I am committed to my health and vitality. Aligned with my values, I will walk 8,000 steps at least five days a week for the next 30 days because maintaining my energy is essential to living my purpose and serving my family."

Use the I AM SMART TO ACT™ Goals Method to define your Must Goal:

- Alignment with your Identity (Must Mindset, Core Beliefs, Core Values, Enhanced Personal Narrative, Standards, and Purpose)
- Specific: What exactly do you want to achieve?
- Measurable: How will you track progress?
- Achievable: Is it realistic and within your control?
- Relevant: Why does this matter to you now?
- Time-bound: When will you complete it?

Example:

"Improve my health by walking 8,000 steps at least five days a week for the next 30 days."

Step 3: Identify Your *Must Micro-Goals*

A Must Micro-Goal is the smallest, most actionable step you can take today that directly moves you toward **your Must** Goal.

Micro-goals are not just ordinary tasks; they are designed to give you an immediate sense of progress and momentum, grounded in the science of behavioral psychology.

Each micro-goal is:

Identity-Driven:

It's intentionally chosen to reflect your Must Goal's deeper alignment with your beliefs, values, standards, and purpose—not random busy work but a meaningful step.

Manageable and Measurable:

A Must Micro-Goal is simple enough to complete right away, making success easy and sustainable. Science shows that small wins significantly boost motivation, reinforce positive self-talk, and help rewire your mindset for achievement through neuroplasticity.

Foundation for Building Habits:

Micro-goals break big ambitions into realistic daily actions, serving as building blocks for lasting routines, confidence, and habit formation. Each completed micro-goal makes the next step easier and more automatic, strengthening your commitment within what the book calls the Must Zone.

How to choose y*our Must Micro-***Goal:**

Ask yourself, "What is the next smallest step I can take right now that will move me closer to my Must Goal?"

Example:

If your Must Goal is, "Improve my health by walking 8,000 steps at least five days a week for the next 30 days,"

your Must Micro-Goal for today might be:

"Take a 15-minute walk at lunch today."

Focus on action, not perfection. Progress always begins with movement, however small.

The Courage to Begin and Take the First Step

Every great achievement, no matter how monumental, starts with the courage to take the very first step. Too often, perfectionism, uncertainty, or the sheer size of a dream becomes a barrier to action. But the truth is, forward motion always begins before clarity or confidence.

Having the courage to begin—no matter how small or imperfect that first action may be—initiates a chain reaction. Action generates feedback, which reduces fear, builds momentum, and provides real learning about what works. With each step, possibilities expand, and earlier excuses or fears lose their hold.

Author Michael Bungay Stanier describes *'Worthy Goals'* as those that are thrilling, important, and daunting—meaningful enough to energize you, matter to others, and stretch your comfort zone. This approach aligns closely with the Must Goals framework: choosing goals that are not only true to your values and identity but also spark growth and lasting impact as you take that essential first step (Michael Bungay Stanier, 2022).

"The hardest part of any important task is getting started on it in the first place. Once you actually begin work on a valuable task, you seem to be naturally motivated to continue." (Tracy, 2001)

Step 4: Create One Must Habit

A *Must Habit* is a simple, repeatable action you commit to performing daily or weekly, designed to make progress toward your Must Goal automatic and sustainable. What truly distinguishes a Must Habit is that it is consciously chosen to align with your foundational identity—as explored in depth throughout this book.

When you repeat a **Must Habit** consistently, you cast daily "votes" for your authentic self and reinforce the habits, patterns, and values that define your true identity.

Choose one daily or weekly habit to support your Must Goal.

Example Habits for Different Domains:

- Health: Drink a glass of water each morning.
- Career: Write your three most important tasks at the start of the workday.
- Relationships: Text or call a friend or loved one each evening.

Concrete Example:

Must Goal: Improve my health.

Micro-Goal: Walk 15 minutes at lunch every day this week.

Must Habit: Put on walking shoes as soon as you finish lunch.

Make it simple enough to be consistent—even on your busiest days.

Step 5: Embrace Courage, Tenacity, Perseverance, and Grit

Setting a goal is just the beginning; real transformation depends on your willingness to keep going, especially when things get hard. The journey toward your Must Goal will test your resolve, presenting obstacles, setbacks, and moments of doubt. This is where the principles of courage, tenacity, perseverance, and grit become essential.

- **Courage** means showing up every day for yourself, daring to act and persist even when the outcome is uncertain or your old story pushes back.
- **Tenacity** is your refusal to give up, your determination to show up and do the work because your Must Goal matters to you on the deepest level.
- **Perseverance** is steady, enduring effort—it is compassionate consistency, knowing growth comes not from perfection, but from pressing forward in the face of resistance.
- **Grit** is the sustained passion, discipline, and resilience to stay true to your authentic purpose over time.

The Must system teaches that these qualities are not just fleeting feelings, but extensions of your foundational identity. When you live from your Must—your most accurate values, standards, and beliefs—you draw endurance from within and become resilient in the face of setbacks. Each act of courage, each slight recovery after a failure, is evidence that you are living your authentic story and honoring your Must.

Affirmation:

"I will meet obstacles with courage. I will show up for my goal with tenacity. I will persist with grit—because I am honoring my Must and who I am meant to be."

Remember, your progress is not measured just by wins, but by the resilience and authenticity with which you show up every day. That is the real power of the Must path.

Step 6: Track and Celebrate Your Progress

Progress is built in small steps, measured not just by what you achieve, but by how consistently you honor your Must Goal and habits. Tracking is how you bring awareness to your journey and recognize the value of effort—especially when the path is difficult.

- **Record your actions:**

    Use a tracker, calendar, or notebook to log each instance of your Must Habits and Must Micro-Goals. Check off every completed action and make a note of the days when things don't go perfectly. Reflection is a form of self-compassion, not self-judgment.

- **Review weekly:**

    At the end of each week, ask: What worked? What needs adjusting? How do you feel about your progress so far?

    Weekly reviews provide a chance to recalibrate, celebrate small wins, and reconnect with your purpose.

- **Acknowledge small wins:**

    Each small success is evidence of your courage, tenacity, and alignment with your authentic self. Celebrating progress builds belief, confidence, and momentum, reinforcing your commitment to your Must Goal.

Optional: Accountability and Reflection

- Share your goal and habit journey with a trusted friend, mentor, or community.
- Take five minutes each week to write down insights, lessons learned, and areas you want to improve next.

Stay Accountable with MustGoals.com Resources

For even greater support and accountability, readers are encouraged to connect with the digital resources available at *MustGoals.com/Resources*. At this site, you'll find weekly check-in templates, practical worksheets, discussion forums, and access to a supportive community of Must Goals readers. Whether you're seeking accountability partners, templates for progress tracking, or a space to celebrate wins and troubleshoot challenges, these free resources give you flexible, ongoing guidance. Utilizing these tools as part of your weekly routine can reinforce your momentum and help you stay connected to your Must and to the broader journey of authentic, aligned goal setting.

Relationship Auditing: Mapping Your Support System

Achievement is never a solo act—your environment shapes your progress more than willpower alone. List every close influence—family, friends, colleagues, peers—and ask: Who inspires, encourages, and holds you to your highest standards ("nourishers")? Who saps your motivation or reinforces limiting beliefs ("toxins")? Regularly update this audit, intentionally invest more in those who elevate you, and set kind boundaries with those who drain you. Proactively managing your social architecture multiplies momentum and keeps your Must Goals on track.

Remember: You Can Deepen Later

This **Quick Start** is designed to help you act now and experience the motivation of real progress. Whenever you're ready, revisit the book's complete pathway to align your goals even more deeply with your beliefs, values, and purpose for long-term, holistic transformation.

STEPHEN RUE

Your journey can begin with just one step. Choose your *Must*, take action today, and witness the difference.

Turn the next page to access advanced transformational practices that will help you connect every goal with who you are truly meant to be.

"Dreams, wants, desires, and hopes are sparks—fleeting glimmers that ignite possibility. Left unattended, they drift into ash and regret. But when aligned with the truth of who we authentically are—and who we are capable of becoming—and poured into the crucible of clear intention and deliberate action, these sparks transform into true goals: ones that fuel lasting achievement and genuine personal transformation."

— Stephen Rue

PART ONE

EXPLORATION: FOUNDATIONS OF IDENTITY FOR AUTHENTIC GOALS

Exploration: Foundations for Authentic Goals

Before building a plan or pursuing bold ambitions, lasting success depends on knowing who you are beneath the surface. Most failed goals begin with "what do I want?" rather than "who am I, and what truly matters?" This book begins with the "who" because real goal-setting is about alignment—not just achievement.

Exploration is the start of this alignment. It means uncovering your inner architecture and connecting it to every goal you pursue. In this section, you will use six foundational elements to establish and perhaps redefine your identity, your **"I AM"**—your Must Mindset, Core Beliefs, Core Values, Personal Narrative, Standards, and Purpose—to shape goals that are both meaningful and sustainable.

When these six elements are clear and connected, your goals become natural extensions of identity and purpose—not random wishes or empty obligations.

Chapter 1: Must Mindset — Turning Intention into Identity

Your mindset creates the lens through which you approach every authentic goal. Every change starts in the mind. Here, you'll discover how your mental patterns shape every goal you set—and every commitment you keep. You'll learn how to align your thoughts and self-talk with your true self, build a resilient mindset that persists through setbacks, and turn "I should" into empowered Must Goals grounded in your core identity.

Chapter 2: Must Core Beliefs — Reprogramming the Hidden Rules

Your core beliefs drive your expectations and behavior, often below your own awareness. This chapter guides you in uncovering and updating beliefs that either sabotage or support your biggest goals. By reprogramming limiting thoughts and reinforcing new empowering beliefs—using proven science and real-life tools—you unlock potential and design goals that fit your true self.

Chapter 3: Must Core Values — Deciding What Matters Most

Your values are the criteria by which you choose and commit to any goal. Here, you'll identify your top values, translate them into daily actions, and use a Values Alignment Check to ensure your goals are authentic—so that what you chase is always meaningful.

Chapter 4: Must Personal Narrative — Rewriting Your Story of Possibility

The story you tell about yourself can limit or expand your goals. In this chapter, you'll learn to spot and rewrite narratives that keep you stuck, transforming hindsight into future-focused vision. The goal is to build a narrative in which possibility and growth are at the center, connecting every target you set to a greater sense of becoming.

Chapter 5: Must Standards — Defining Standards for Action

Standards convert intention into execution. This chapter helps you set high but realistic standards for key areas—work, health, relationships—so every goal you write is protected by your own rules for follow-through, not just fleeting motivation.

Chapter 6: Must Purpose — The Enduring Reason 'Why'

Purpose gives your goals emotional fuel and resilience. Here, you'll clarify your deepest why, connect it across all areas of your life, and ensure every goal is aligned with a source of meaning. When purpose is clear, motivation becomes second nature, and achievement becomes fulfillment.

Outcome of Exploration:

By the end of this section, you'll have constructed your personal *Must Alignment Map*—a living system that guides every goal you set. This map is both a compass and a filter, ensuring each new goal is both achievable and authentic. Exploration is the pause before power—now, you're ready to set goals that last, because they begin with your real identity.

CHAPTER 1

Must Potential: Awakening Your True Capacity

"When we are no longer able to change a situation, we are challenged to change ourselves."
—*Viktor E. Frankl*

From Pain to Purpose

It took years to understand that tragedy could become a teacher. My life has held both joy and deep pain. The darkest season came when my stepfather died by suicide when I was a child, forcing me to confront not only loss but also who I would choose to become in its aftermath.

After my biological father left and his presence faded, my stepfather, Rodney, entered our lives as a second chance at being loved. He was gentle, intelligent, and present. For a time, life felt like our own small Camelot—steady, affectionate, and whole. We believed he was here to stay.

Then, one summer day, he ended his life. My mother and nine-year-old sister found him. I was spared the scene but not the shock;

childhood ended in an instant. In the silence that followed, I made a private vow to be the "man of the house," swallowing my grief and trying to be strong for everyone else.

What shaped me most, though, was my mother's response. In her devastation, she made an internal decision: *this will not destroy us*. I remember seeing her on her hands and knees scrubbing the blood-soaked carpet. She looked up at me and said, "Honey, I've got this." In that moment, I witnessed what a Must looks like in real life—a fierce, unwavering commitment to protect her children, no matter the cost.

Those years taught me that when life collapses, the noise falls away and only the essentials remain—the people we will not abandon, the values we will not compromise, and the future we refuse to surrender. Our Musts become the how to our why—the lived commitments that carry us through pain and into purpose and later shape every Must Goal we choose.

We will all face seasons that cut life to the bone. The question is not whether suffering will come, but what we will do with it. Will it harden us, or will it clarify what we must stand for? Finding your Must in hardship is not about glorifying suffering—it is about refusing to waste it. When you name the few things you must honor and who you must become, you gain the clarity and courage to devote your energy to what truly matters.

As you move into this work, consider:

- What pain has most shaped who you are today?
- In that pain, what did you learn you can no longer ignore or postpone?
- What is one Must that became clear—something you know you must honor, no matter how hard it gets?

These questions are the bridge between your story and the goals you will set, helping you turn the Musts already present in your life into clear commitments, aligned goals, and courageous action.

Finding the Courage to Be Vulnerable

My journey has been a winding road of triumphs and hard introspection. Each step forward required me to confront fears, doubts, and the old stories I carried about my abilities. Law school became one of the defining seasons of my life. Under intense pressure, childhood insecurities whispered that I wasn't smart enough and that my past struggles proved I didn't belong.

Vulnerability felt dangerous. I didn't want anyone to see how afraid I was of failing, so I hid behind perfectionism and silence. But instead of collapsing under the weight of those doubts, I tried a simple experiment. Each morning, I spoke affirmations out loud—statements of capability, worth, and possibility. At first, the words felt hollow. But slowly, they became quiet counterweights to my inner critic.

As my mindset shifted, I took on challenges I once avoided: asking questions, seeking help, and volunteering for challenging assignments. Each small act of courage chipped away at the limiting beliefs I had carried for years.

Training for my first marathon became a physical mirror of that inner work. As someone who had once worn steel leg braces, running 26.2 miles felt unthinkable. But I approached training the same way I approached law school: one step at a time, committed to growth rather than perfection. Crossing the finish line, tears in my eyes, I realized I hadn't just run a race—I had rewritten the boundaries of my identity.

Through these experiences, vulnerability shifted from something to hide to something that made me stronger. Researcher Brené Brown reminds us that vulnerability is not weakness; it is the courage to show up when we cannot control the outcome. When I began sharing more of my story—my doubts, struggles, and growth—I noticed something powerful: people leaned in. Vulnerability created a connection, not judgment.

So I ask you: Where in your life are you being invited into the arena? What is one risk you have postponed because fear is guarding the gate? When you take that step—however small—you're not just pursuing a goal. You are practicing a new identity.

Embracing your Must requires courage. It means choosing authenticity over perfection and progress over protection. When you show up vulnerable and wholehearted, you don't weaken your journey, you deepen it.

The Circle of Life: A Holistic Approach

As you continue this journey of self-discovery and growth, it helps to have a clear framework for evaluating your life as a whole. The Circle of Life is that framework—a simple, visual tool that lets you see the major domains of your life at a glance and notice where you feel strong, strained, or neglected. Imagine a circle divided into segments, each representing a different area of life. Common segments include:

1. **Health and Vitality**
2. **Relationships**
3. **Career and Professional Achievement**
4. **Financial Well-Being**
5. **Personal Growth and Learning**
6. **Spirituality, Religion, and Inner Peace**
7. **Community and Legacy**

MUST GOALS

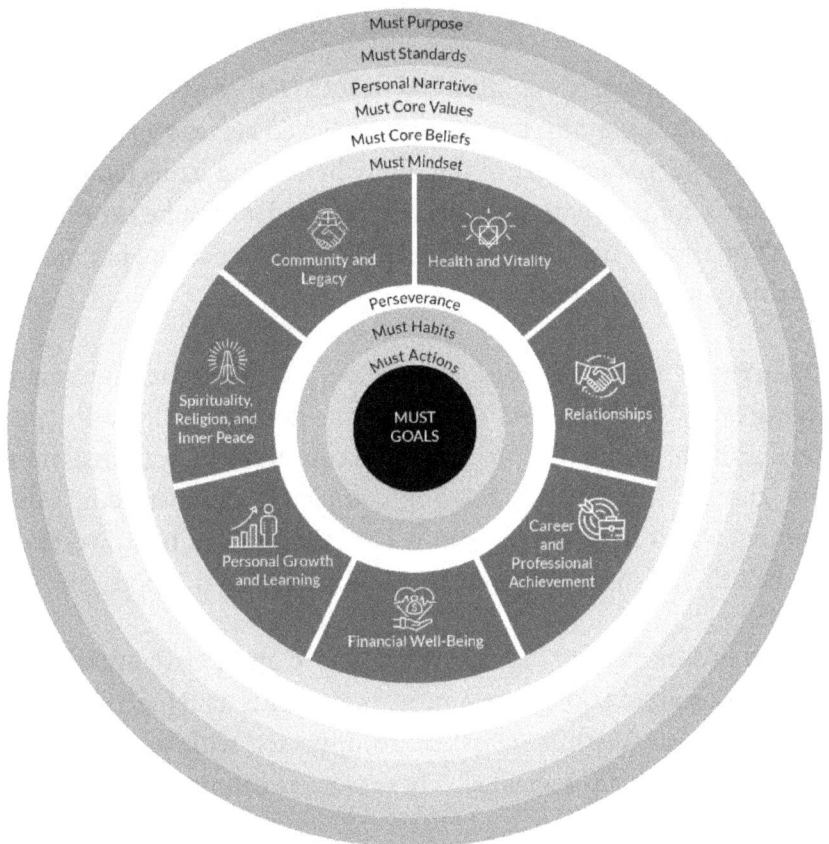

These elements function like the spokes of a wheel, each contributing to the smooth, balanced progression of your life. If one spoke is short or missing, the whole wheel wobbles. This idea, popularized in modern personal development by figures like Zig Ziglar and Paul J. Meyer, reminds us that real success is never one-dimensional.

One of my cherished memories from my own growth journey was meeting Zig Ziglar during his visit to New Orleans. He radiated authenticity and often said that you cannot truly call yourself successful in one area—like business—if another, like your home life, is in shambles. His message was simple: a great life requires attention across the whole wheel, not just one shiny segment.

The Circle of Life: Marcus's Story

Marcus was a talented engineer and devoted father who took pride in providing for his family. For years, he believed his career success was enough to prove he was thriving. But when a long-expected promotion didn't come, the disappointment hit harder than he expected. It wasn't just about the title—it revealed how little space he had left for anything outside of work.

At a friend's urging, Marcus completed a Circle of Life assessment. Seeing every life domain on a single page—health, relationships, personal growth, spirituality, finances, and community—was unsettling. His "career" segment was filled in completely. Almost every other segment was thin or nearly empty. His relationships had weakened. His health had slipped. His personal interests had disappeared.

Instead of sinking into regret, Marcus chose one area to nurture: his health. He started taking morning walks with his daughter. He signed up for a simple nutrition class. He reconnected with two friends he had unintentionally neglected. These weren't dramatic changes, but they were intentional ones.

Over time, something subtle shifted. As his health improved, so did his energy. His patience at home grew. His creativity at work resurfaced. His relationships strengthened. His sense of meaning expanded.

Marcus realized that fulfillment wasn't about excelling in one domain—it was about balancing the whole wheel. And sometimes, choosing to nurture even a single neglected area can create momentum that ripples into every other part of life.

Making the Circle Your Own

Success within the Circle of Life is about balanced growth across these areas, recognizing that each contributes to your overall sense of fulfillment. Excelling in one area does not erase profound neglect in another. What matters is a pattern of harmony and alignment with your values—not perfection, but progress.

The Circle of Life is not a fixed template. It is a living reflection of your unique journey. You may find that an additional area—creativity, adventure, environmental stewardship, or something else entirely—deserves its own segment because it feels essential to who you are. Honor that by adapting your circle to match your life, not someone else's ideal.

As psychologist Carl Jung observed, "The shoe that fits one person pinches another; there is no recipe for living that suits all cases." Your ideal circle will not look like anyone else's. When you honestly assess each area—career, relationships, health, growth, and beyond—you often uncover surprising truths: strengths that are less solid than they appeared, and hidden capacities waiting to be developed.

This process of self-assessment is meant to be both clarifying and empowering. It gives you a practical map for where to focus your Must Actions and future goals. The aim is not to perfect every slice at once, but to move intentionally toward greater harmony.

As you nurture the different aspects of your life, you cultivate a deeper resilience. You become better able to weather life's storms and emerge stronger, because your foundation is broader than any single success or setback.

Your Circle of Life – Do This Now

- Draw a simple circle and divide it into seven slices: health, relationships, career, finances, personal growth, spirituality, and community/legacy.
- Shade each slice from 0–10 based on how satisfied and supported you feel in that area today.

- Choose one domain with a low score that matters deeply to you right now and mark it with a star; this will be your first focus area as you move into the chapters ahead.

As you continue reading, keep your circle in view and notice how each practice and chapter can strengthen the domain you started first.

The Role of Fear

Fear is a universal force behind many of our self-imposed limitations. It shapes our thoughts, actions, and, ultimately, our destiny. We all grapple with it, but understanding its role can be transformative.

Fear of Failure

Fear of failure often whispers, *"What if you're not good enough?"* Many of us retreat before we even begin. But failure isn't proof of inadequacy—it's part of mastery. Each misstep is feedback, not a verdict. Shakespeare captured it well: *"Our doubts are traitors."* The real loss isn't in failing; it's in never attempting what could have changed us.

Fear of Success

Success can be just as intimidating. It asks, *"What will change if I truly grow?"* Because it stretches our identity, fear of success can keep us clinging to familiar limitations. Naming this fear is the first step toward moving beyond it.

Fear of Judgment

Fear of judgment tells us, *"People will think you're foolish or unworthy."* It silences our ideas and shrinks our goals. But as we mature, we learn that other people's opinions do not define our potential. Aristotle's reminder is timeless: we can entertain a thought—even criticism—without accepting it as truth.

Redefining the Role of Fear

Fear can be either a roadblock that keeps you small or a signal that you are standing at the edge of growth. The shift happens when you recognize fear for what it truly is: **information, not identity.**

- Fear of failure warns you there is something to learn.
- Fear of success warns you that life may expand.
- Fear of judgment warns you others may misunderstand—but their opinions cannot determine your destiny.

Every time you choose courage over avoidance, you reclaim a piece of your personal power.

Stepping Into the Arena

Jana never saw herself as brave. For most of her adult life, she stayed in the background—working hard, avoiding attention, and telling herself her voice wasn't needed. When she received a community service award for her volunteer work, the recognition shocked her, and the request to speak at the ceremony terrified her even more.

She almost declined. Public speaking felt impossible, but something whispered that this moment mattered. When the night came, her hands trembled as she walked to the podium. She acknowledged her fear, took a breath, and spoke from the heart about how small acts of kindness had changed her life and the lives of others.

She didn't deliver a polished speech—she delivered an honest one, and that honesty gave her a lasting sense of capability she never expected. From that night forward, Jana practiced speaking up—first in small ways, then in bigger ones. Each act became a step through the gate of fear and into the fullness of who she was becoming.

Her courage didn't erase anxiety; it simply meant she stopped letting fear decide. In choosing to step into the arena, Jana discovered a truth we all must face: growth begins with the willingness to show up, even when the outcome is uncertain.

Reflection

- Recall a time when you acted despite fear.
- What was the outcome, and how did it shift your sense of what is possible?

Every time you face your fears, you reclaim a piece of your personal power.

Fear as Fuel

Tony Robbins has noted that the quality of our lives is determined by how well we can navigate uncertainty. Instead of resisting fear, he encourages us to *"dance with it"*—to move with fear rather than let it dictate our limits.

Fear often feels like a locked gate. But that gate is usually self-created. The moment you act—speak up, take the risk, pursue the goal, the gate swings open and possibility expands.

Courage is not the absence of fear; it is the decision that something else matters more.

When you choose courage aligned with your Must—your values, identity, and purpose—fear becomes fuel. It clarifies what you stand for and reveals your path forward. This is the moment personal development stops being a concept and becomes a way of living.

CHAPTER 2

Must Mindset: The Mental Foundation of Authentic Goals

"The view you adopt for yourself profoundly affects the way you lead your life."
—Carol S. Dweck

Mindset is the lens through which you interpret your potential and shape your approach to growth. It guides your intentions, reactions, and the strategies you use to evolve. When your thinking aligns with your authentic values and beliefs, you define goals that truly matter and pursue them with clarity and commitment.

Must Goal-Setting Mindset

Mindset is the starting point for every meaningful goal. How you think about yourself shapes what you pursue, how you respond to challenge, and whether you persist when things get hard. When your mindset reflects your authentic self, clarity increases, fear shifts, and action becomes possible.

Brian Tracy notes that unsuccessful, unhappy people tend to dwell on what they do not want, while successful people deliberately focus on what they do want and how to move toward it. As you intentionally develop this mindset, hesitation gives way to decisive action.

Instead of merely writing targets, you cultivate the attitudes and values that power those targets. When your mindset is aligned with what truly matters to you, goals are no longer boxes to check; they become genuine steps toward lasting fulfillment and personal growth.

What You Will Learn in This Chapter

- The difference between Fixed, Growth, and Must Mindsets—and why mindset underpins all goal-setting
- How environmental and social influences shape the way you see your abilities and challenges
- Key steps and Must Habits to move from a Fixed Mindset to a Growth Mindset, and ultimately to a Must Mindset
- Practical strategies—reflection, reframing, and daily "must" mantras—to strengthen your mindset
- Simple self-checks and community feedback practices to track your progress and stay accountable

Quick Action

- Before writing your next goal, ask: "Is my mindset helping or hindering my progress right now?"
- Write a one-sentence declaration about the attitude you want to embody as you move forward:

The Science of Control: Locus of Control

Psychologists define locus of control as your belief about what most determines your life outcomes: your own actions (internal locus) or external forces such as luck, fate, or other people (external locus). Research consistently shows that people with a more internal locus of control are more likely to set ambitious goals, take proactive steps, persist through obstacles, and adapt to setbacks—key ingredients for authentic goal achievement.

If you often feel powerless or stuck, examine whether you see outcomes as something you influence or something that simply "happens" to you. As you shift toward seeing yourself as the primary agent of change, your motivation, sense of responsibility, and effectiveness in reaching your goals all increase.

The Power of Shifting Control

Maria, a mid-level manager, felt that politics and luck blocked her progress. In performance reviews, she focused on how others controlled outcomes and rarely asked what she could change. A mentor invited her to journal after setbacks with one question: What actions are in my control? Over a few weeks, Maria noticed that even in unfair situations, there were always micro-actions she could take—seeking feedback, building skills, strengthening relationships.

After another missed promotion, she wrote, If I cannot control the decision, I can control how I grow next. From then on, she invested her energy in the actions she could take. Over time, her confidence, performance, and opportunities rose, all rooted in a stronger internal locus of control.

Fixed and Growth Mindsets

Mindset shapes how you view your abilities, respond to obstacles, and approach achievement. It acts as an internal compass for personal development and goal-setting. Two core patterns form the starting point: the Fixed Mindset and the Growth Mindset.

Quick Visual: Side-by-Side Comparison

Aspect	Fixed Mindset	Growth Mindset
Belief About Ability	Intelligence/skills are innate and unchangeable	Intelligence/skills can be developed through effort and learning
Response to Setbacks	Gives up quickly; sees failure as weakness	Persists through setbacks; sees failure as feedback
Effort	Views effort as pointless	Sees effort as key to improvement

Practical Examples

- *Fixed Mindset:*

    Ava never applied for a promotion because she believed she was not "management material." When a peer was promoted, she felt threatened, and her self-doubt deepened.

- *Growth Mindset:*

    Jamal's first business failed, but instead of quitting, he studied what went wrong, adjusted his approach, and launched again. His willingness to learn from feedback turned a setback into future success.

Neuroscience research shows that your beliefs about mindset influence how your brain responds to challenge. Adopting a Growth Mindset increases motivation, openness to learning from mistakes, and long-term success in setting and pursuing goals.

Promotion vs. Prevention Goals: Choosing the Right Focus

Self-regulation research identifies two primary motivational systems for pursuing goals: promotion focus and prevention focus.

- **Promotion-focused goals** are driven by aspirations, growth, and gains. They energize creativity, innovation, and bold advancement.
- **Prevention-focused goals** are driven by responsibility, duty, and the desire to avoid losses or mistakes. They support safety, reliability, and error-free execution.

People naturally lean toward one style but can learn to flex between them. A promotion focus (using language like achieve, grow, discover) boosts engagement for entrepreneurial or creative aims. A prevention focus (using language like secure, avoid, fulfill) helps you perform better in process-critical, detail-heavy, or compliance-driven tasks.

Aligning your motivational focus with the situation—a concept known as regulatory fit—increases your sense that an activity "feels right," which boosts persistence and satisfaction with your goals.

Actionable Micro-Goal

This week, notice one moment when you hesitate to take on a challenge or shy away from feedback. Pause, then choose one small action you would take if you were operating from a Growth Mindset instead. Capture what you did and how it felt in your journal or share it with a trusted friend.

How Your Mindset Is Created

Mindset grows from a blend of internal beliefs and external influences. Family, teachers, peers, early praise, and feedback all shape your core beliefs about ability and intelligence.

- When effort and progress are recognized, a Growth Mindset becomes more likely.

- When praise centers only on being "naturally smart" or "talented," Fixed Mindset thinking can take root and discourage risk-taking and learning.

Science-Backed Takeaways

- Praising effort, strategy, and learning builds a flexible, resilient mindset.
- Praising only talent encourages a fixed view of ability.
- Growth-supportive environments and intentional mindset work can shift your patterns at any age.

Core beliefs accumulate over time from repeated feedback and cultural messages, but they are not permanent. Research indicates that anyone can cultivate more of a Growth Mindset through ongoing learning, reframing mistakes, and intentionally choosing relationships and environments that support effort and adaptability.

Quick Checklist

Who has influenced your beliefs about ability? List three names and one key belief each instilled in you.

- _____ — _____
- _____ — _____
- _____ — _____

Try This with a Friend

Ask a friend, "Who influenced the way you think about your abilities?" Compare stories about early praise, criticism, or turning points. Notice which beliefs you share, where you differ, and which old beliefs each of you might choose to update today.

Mindset, Environment, and Goal Setting

Mindset does not exist in a vacuum; it is reinforced every day by your feedback loops, relationships, and surroundings. Your environment can either expand or limit the goals you are willing to set.

- Environments that encourage experimentation and value learning make you more willing to try, risk, and persist.
- Environments that focus only on results or "natural talent" can push you toward perfectionism, safety, and avoidance.

When you intentionally choose environments, mentors, and communities that celebrate growth and perseverance, you reinforce a Growth Mindset that supports authentic, resilient goal achievement. Carol Dweck's research confirms that believing abilities can be developed with effort leads to greater resilience, achievement, and personal development over time.

Community Action Box

Share with a trusted peer or group:

- What environment—work, community, family, or personal routine—has most helped you develop a growth mindset?
- How does that setting influence your willingness to take on new goals or persist through setbacks?

To discover curated and trusted online groups—including official Must Goals spaces and partner communities—visit *MustGoals.com/Resources*.

Changing a Fixed Mindset

A fixed mindset is not permanent—science confirms it can shift through intentional practice, positive reinforcement, and self-awareness. This transformation starts by recognizing that abilities aren't set in stone; with effort and learning, you can systematically rewire your thinking.

If-Then Planning: Turn Intentions into Action

One of the most effective tools for bridging the gap between good intentions and real action is **if–then planning**, also called implementation intentions. Instead of vague resolutions like "I will eat healthier," you create specific plans in the format:

If X happens, then I will do Y.

For example:

- "If I start to procrastinate, then I'll set a timer for 10 minutes and just begin."
- "If I'm tempted to check my phone in the evening, then I'll put it in another room."

These plans work because they link your desired behavior to clear cues—time, place, or emotional state—automating your response. People who use if–then planning are far more likely to stick to good habits, overcome obstacles, and follow through even when motivation fades.

Do This Now: Mini-Challenges

Check each one off as you try it:

- **Hear and Reframe Your Limiting Thoughts**
  When you catch yourself thinking, "I can't do this," add "…yet."
    - Old: "I'm bad at presentations."
    - New: "I'm not great at presentations… yet, but I can get better."

- **Turn Feedback into** Fuel

  The next time you get constructive criticism, write down one way you might use it to improve—even if it's uncomfortable.

- **Celebrate Every Effort**

  Each time you persist or try something new, jot it in your "Win Tracker" at the end of the book. Little wins add up to massive change.

- **Flip a Setback**

  Reframe a recent failure as a learning opportunity.
    - Old: "I messed up that meeting—it proves I can't lead."
    - New: "I struggled in that meeting, so I know what skills to work on before next time."

These habits help reshape your brain's pathways through neuroplasticity. Every small, positive change builds mental resilience and fuels authentic goal setting, no matter your starting point.

Celebrate Micro-Wins:

Every time you reframe a limiting thought, add it to your Win Tracker. At the end of the month, look back—it's proof of your progress.

Rituals for Resilience: Savor, Reflect, and Be Grateful

To avoid burnout and maximize fulfillment, install simple positive psychology rituals.

Each week:

- Savor small victories: note them, share them with a trusted ally, and reflect not just on *what worked* but *what grew in you*.

- Practice gratitude: journal three specific things you're thankful for in your goal journey.
- Review one setback for hidden learning: What did it teach you? How did it clarify your Must?

These rituals build optimism, resilience, and a sense that your Must journey is not just effective but deeply rewarding.

From Growth Mindset to Must Mindset

A Must Mindset advances beyond Growth—it makes personal development a nonnegotiable daily priority. While a Growth Mindset believes you *can* get better with practice, a Must Mindset turns that belief into urgent, consistent action aligned with your core identity.

Key Differences

- **Growth Mindset:** Improvement is possible; effort matters; setbacks are instructive.
- **Must Mindset:** Improvement is required; growth is an essential, urgent priority; every goal aligns with your true self and is treated as mandatory.

In a Must Mindset, you don't simply hope to grow; you decide you *must* grow because your identity, calling, and purpose demand it.

Try This: Daily Action Challenge

- Write your own "must" mantra—an actionable, identity-based statement. For example:
  - "I must finish my book this year because my story matters."
  - "I must reach out to new clients daily because I am building my legacy."

- Each morning for one week, say your "must" mantra out loud to start your day with intention—before checking your phone or email.
- After a week, note any shifts in energy, motivation, or results.

Suggested Community Share

Post your "must" mantra in the group forum at MustGoals.com/Resources for feedback and inspiration. Reading others' mantras—and supporting their journeys—keeps you motivated and accountable as you move from intention to action

Chapter Takeaways: Must Mindset for Goal Setting

By the end of this chapter, you have done more than learn about mindset—you have begun to practice a Must Mindset. In the chapters ahead, you will align this mindset with your core beliefs, values, narrative, standards, and purpose so that every goal you set arises from who you truly are and who you are committed to becoming.

Must Mindset Takeaways

- Mindset fuels achievement: how you view your abilities and challenges shapes every goal.
- Mindsets evolve with intentional effort; you can move from Fixed to Growth to Must Mindset, unlocking deeper fulfillment.

Key strategies:

- Reframe limiting thoughts ("I can't do this—yet")
- Treat feedback as a tool
- Celebrate persistence and small wins
- See challenges and mistakes as opportunities

Goal-Setting Mindset Comparison Table

Mindset Type	Attitude Toward Challenge	Response to Failure	Approach to Effort	Goal Alignment
Fixed Mindset	Avoids, fears challenge	Withdraws, self-critical	Sees as risky or unnecessary	Weak; pursues external validation
Growth Mindset	Embraces, seeks challenge	Learns, persists	Sees as path to growth	Moderate; pursues self-improvement
Must Mindset	Acts urgently, daily	Adapts, learns, stays resilient	Effort is essential, ongoing	Strong; goals match core identity

Motivational Bookend

Circle your current mindset—Fixed, Growth, or Must. Then list three things you will do this month to level up (for example, tackle a challenge, invite constructive feedback, or write and use a "must" mantra):

1. _____
2. _____
3. _____

Social & Progress Actions

- Find an accountability buddy and complete this week's mini-challenge together.
- Share your monthly mindset shifts and "must" actions at MustGoals.com/Resources—download your printable micro-goal tracker, join conversation threads, and receive feedback from a supportive community.

Your mindset can be your greatest asset or your most significant barrier. Take one aligned step today—the momentum will build from there.

CHAPTER 3

Must Core Beliefs: Aligning Goals With Inner Truths

"For as he thinketh in his heart, so is he."
—*Proverbs 23 : 7*

"We become what we think about most of the time."
—*Earl Nightingale*

Goal Alignment with Your Core Beliefs

Core beliefs are the deeply held views you hold about yourself, others, and the world. Formed early in life and reinforced by experience, they act as your inner compass—guiding choices, shaping actions, and defining what you believe is possible. Some beliefs empower you; others quietly limit you, especially when negative, outdated, or unexamined.

Effective goal setting begins when you bring these beliefs into conscious awareness. When your goals align with supportive core beliefs, motivation and momentum rise, and your pursuits feel authentic and deeply satisfying. When goals and beliefs conflict, you are more likely to feel resistance, self-sabotage, or emptiness—even if you "succeed" on the outside.

Transformation and long-term fulfillment require honest reflection: intentionally examining and, when needed, reshaping your core beliefs so they support your highest aspirations. Beyond conscious intentions, subconscious goals and emotional states also influence achievement. Research shows that automatic, unconscious motives and scripts can drive behavior as powerfully as deliberate plans, and that interpreting a challenge as an opportunity rather than a threat improves motivation and performance. By bringing awareness to these hidden drivers—through journaling, mindfulness, and reframing—you can redirect energy toward more adaptive, empowered action.

Personal identity alignment is the foundation of meaningful, sustainable progress. When your beliefs, emotions, and goals match who you are and what matters most, achievement becomes both attainable and deeply resonant.

What You'll Learn in This Chapter

- Why early beliefs influence how you see yourself and what you believe is possible.
- Where core beliefs come from—and how to uncover hidden patterns
- Practical methods to evaluate, update, and align beliefs with your most important goals
- How to use the Must Circle of Life for holistic goal alignment
- Steps to replace limiting beliefs with empowering Must Core Beliefs—for lasting personal growth

Origins of Our Core Beliefs

Reflection

What is an early message you remember hearing about your abilities, worth, or what is possible for you?

STEPHEN RUE

Rewriting My Story: From Limitation to Possibility

As a child, I wore steel leg braces that made me feel different from the kids around me. The comments I heard—some kind, some careless—carried an unspoken message: be careful, do not expect too much, you may never move like everyone else. Those words sank in as early beliefs about my capabilities and quietly narrowed what I thought was possible.

For years, any new challenge triggered that inner whisper: *Not for you. Too hard. Play it safe.* Because it felt like the truth, I did not question it. That is how core beliefs operate. Slowly, small wins—taking off the braces, finishing school events, receiving encouraging feedback—began to crack the old narrative. Each positive experience showed that those limiting beliefs were not facts, just echoes from childhood.

Through journaling, reflection, and choosing goals that stretched me bit by bit, a new conviction took root: *I am not defined by what others once expected of me.* That belief became the foundation for every significant achievement that followed. Once I knew beliefs could be rewritten, I understood my future could be rewritten too.

Everyone carries stories formed long before they knew how to test them. Some beliefs empower; others quietly confine. Transformation begins when you bring these beliefs into the light and ask: *Is this truly mine? Does this still serve the person I am becoming?* When the answer is no, you are free to choose a better one.

Core beliefs tend to develop early as you make sense of your environment, relationships, and key experiences. Messages from caregivers, teachers, peers, and media strongly shape these convictions—often before you have the maturity to evaluate them. Significant events, both uplifting and painful, leave lasting imprints on beliefs about success, self-worth, safety, and possibility.

Because many beliefs form before conscious self-reflection, they can persist unnoticed in adulthood, guiding choices even when they no longer fit your current reality. The key to transformation is awareness: by identifying the origins and patterns of your core beliefs, you gain the power to challenge and rewrite those that no longer serve your goals or your authentic self. With intention, self-compassion, and steady effort, anyone can cultivate new, more supportive beliefs and create a stronger foundation for growth and change.

How Core Beliefs Form

- Core beliefs often take shape in childhood as you absorb your environment: family, friends, culture, and media.
- Messages from caregivers, teachers, and significant life events—both positive and negative—leave lasting marks on what you believe about success, self-worth, safety, and potential.
- Many beliefs form before you can critically examine them, so they may not reflect your current values or present circumstances.

Action Step: Pattern Spotter

- Think back to an important moment or message from your childhood or adolescence. What belief did you form from that experience?
- Write down one way this belief might still affect your choices or goals today.

Why This Works

Studies show that early, unexamined beliefs function like invisible scripts, guiding adult behavior and reactions until they are consciously reflected on and updated.

Moving Forward

Awareness is the first step to change. By spotting the origins and patterns of your core beliefs, you gain power to revise those that limit you and reinforce those that elevate your goals, relationships, and quality of life.

How Do We Identify Our Core Beliefs?

Reflection

When you face stress, conflict, or strong emotion, what is the first story you tell yourself—about what is happening or about yourself?

To uncover core beliefs, begin by observing your thoughts, emotions, and automatic reactions to everyday experiences. Strong or recurring responses—especially under stress or setback—often reveal underlying beliefs about yourself, others, or the world.

Step-by-Step Guide

1. **Observe Automatic Thoughts**

   Pay attention to your spontaneous reactions in moments of tension or challenge. Repeated themes, sensitive "triggers," and strong emotional spikes often point to hidden beliefs.

   - Tip: Keep a brief journal of your self-talk during these times to reveal repeating patterns.

2. **Ask Reflective Questions**

   Explore your reactions with questions like:
   - "What does this thought or feeling say about me?"
   - "Why is this important to me?"
   - "What automatic 'rule' or assumption am I following here?"

3. **Apply the Downward Arrow Technique**

   Start with a persistent thought (for example, "I'll never be good at this"). Ask yourself:
   - "If this were true, what would it mean about me?"
   - "If that is true, why is it so bad? What does it say about my worth, ability, or safety?"

     Repeat until you reach a fundamental belief, often an absolute statement about yourself or the world.

After identifying core beliefs, evaluate their evidence and usefulness. With openness and self-compassion, you can challenge limiting ideas and replace them with beliefs that support your growth and goals. Examining where beliefs originated, questioning their accuracy, and intentionally updating them leads to more authentic living and better-aligned goals.

Mini-Exercise: Laddering Example

Write down a recent upsetting thought. Ask:

- "If this were true, why would it matter?"
- "What would that mean about me?"
- Continue until you uncover a core conviction, such as "I am not good enough" or "The world is not safe."

Compassionate Challenge

Once you discover a belief, meet it with empathy:

- "Is this belief serving me—or holding me back?"
- "Is it based on facts, or on a pattern from my past?"
- "What new belief could I experiment with that would better support my growth?"

Why This Works

Uncovering core beliefs gives you the power to update your self-definitions and personal story. This opens space for new actions and more authentic goal alignment.

Next Steps

Now that you have tools for identifying core beliefs, the next move is to evaluate them using evidence and experiments, then reshape them to fuel your progress.

Considering Evidence

Challenge

Is your belief based on real experience and evidence—or on old assumptions?

To align your goals with reality and foster authentic growth, commit to regularly evaluating your core beliefs using both your life experience and feedback from others. Notice when you cling to beliefs that persist despite clear evidence to the contrary; these are strong candidates for intentional change.

How to Evaluate Your Core Beliefs

1. Compare Belief to Experience

    Ask:
    - "What facts or feedback from my life genuinely support this belief?"
    - "What examples or comments actually contradict it?"

    Write both supporting and opposing evidence side by side. Even small examples count.

2. **Seek Disconfirming Evidence**

   Actively look for data that challenges long-held, negative beliefs.

   - Notice compliments, accomplishments, or positive moments you might otherwise dismiss.
   - Pay attention when new information feels awkward or surprising.

3. **Test with Experiments**

   Choose one belief you would like to challenge.

   - For one week, act "as if" a more empowering belief were true (for example, instead of "I'm always awkward in meetings," try "I can contribute something valuable today").
   - Observe outcomes: How do people respond? How do you feel?

Action Box: Rewriting Old Beliefs

Pick one stubborn belief that may no longer serve you.

- What is the strongest evidence against it?
- What would you try if you did not hold that belief anymore?

Compassionate Reminder

Be gentle with yourself. Shifting lifelong beliefs takes patience and practice. Consider sharing your reflections with a trusted friend, coach, or the Must Goals community for added support.

Why This Works

Testing beliefs through evidence and micro-experiments makes change tangible and sustainable. New experiences can weaken old, unhelpful convictions and open doors to more authentic growth.

Approach this process with patience and self-compassion. Every time you question, test, and refine a core belief, you increase self-awareness and strengthen your capacity for value-aligned achievement.

Rewriting My Money Script

At a friend's urging, Marcus completed a Circle of Life assessment, shading segments for health, relationships, growth, spirituality, finances, and community. For the first time, he could see obvious gaps across his life. Instead of feeling defeated, Marcus chose one weak domain—his personal health—to nurture.

He scheduled morning walks with his daughter and enrolled in a simple nutrition class. The changes were gradual, but as he watched each segment slowly fill out, he noticed greater fulfillment not just in his health but also in his work and relationships. Success became less about chasing one goal and more about balancing the wheel. Marcus discovered that growth in one neglected area could unlock energy and resilience in every other domain

Reflection

Think about a common belief or "script" you've carried about money or another area of your life (such as health, relationships, or learning).

- Where do you think this belief came from—family, culture, early experiences, or repeated setbacks?
- If you were to write a new belief to support your growth and goals, what would it be?

The *Must Circle of Life*

Earlier in this book, you were introduced to the Must Circle of Life—a simple visual that shows seven key domains such as health, relationships, career, finances, personal growth, spirituality, and community. In this chapter, the focus is on how your core beliefs either support or

MUST GOALS

strain those domains, and how updating your beliefs can bring the whole circle into better alignment.

You can see where your beliefs support growth and where they may need adjustment by viewing each domain as part of a single whole. This holistic lens empowers you to set more integrated, authentic goals that resonate with your deepest values.

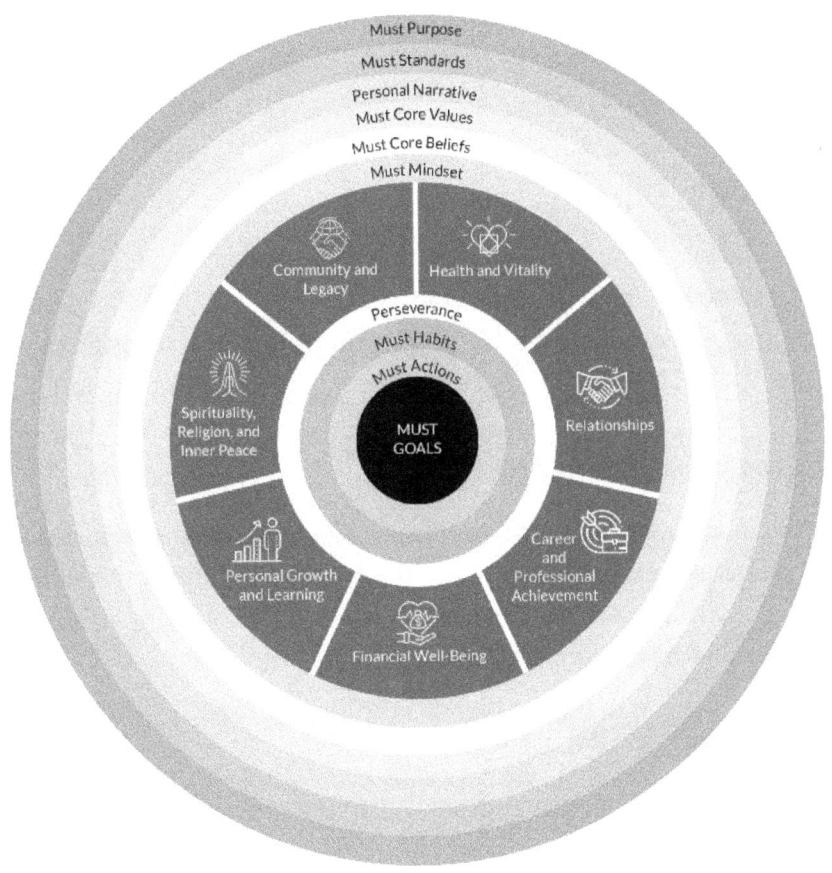

Core Beliefs, Goal-Setting, and the Circle of Life

Core beliefs shape every domain:

Health and Vitality

Positive health beliefs foster actions such as informed nutrition, regular exercise, and proactive self-care. Limiting beliefs may reduce motivation and resilience. Align health goals with empowering beliefs for lifelong well-being.

Relationships

Beliefs about self-worth and love affect how you connect, trust, and open up to others. Affirming your value and cultivating acceptance encourages deeper, more fulfilling connections. Align relationship goals with beliefs rooted in trust, respect, and self-compassion.

Career Development

Belief in your capability and resilience fuels ambition and persistence. Negative assumptions can hold you back or cause dissatisfaction. Regularly examine career beliefs to ensure professional goals reflect your strengths and genuine aspirations.

Financial Well-being

Beliefs about abundance and possibility influence financial actions, opportunities, and self-confidence. Challenge scarcity narratives to unlock growth and pursue financial goals from a place of empowerment.

Personal Growth and Learning

Beliefs about your ability to learn and change govern your willingness to embrace new skills and experiences. Choose beliefs that nurture curiosity and resilience, and keep your growth goals aligned with your deeper values.

Spirituality, Religion, and Inner Peace

Spiritual beliefs guide you through challenges and help you find meaning and connection. Align spiritual goals with compassionate beliefs for personal peace and broader purpose.

Community and Legacy

Beliefs about the value of community, service, and impact shape the legacy you create. Acting from core values such as compassion and integrity strengthens both your life and the lives of others. Reflect on your desired legacy to inspire daily choices that foster connection, contribution, and resilience.

Continually refining and living by your most authentic beliefs enables balanced goal alignment and holistic progress—leading to fulfillment, positive impact, and enduring growth.

Limiting Beliefs

> *"The only limits that exist are the ones you place on yourself."*
> —Les Brown

What Are Limiting Beliefs?

Limiting beliefs are deep, often unconscious convictions that define what you think is possible for you. They frequently develop from negative experiences, cultural expectations, or repeated setbacks and become mental "fences" that keep you from growing, taking risks, or pursuing your biggest goals.

These beliefs often sound like:

- "I'm not creative."
- "I don't deserve success."
- "I'm too old/young."
- "I'll never be good at this."
- "People like me never get ahead."
- "That's not for someone with my background."

Why Do They Matter?

When left unchallenged, limiting beliefs become invisible walls that shape your daily choices and routines. They can:

- Hold you back from trying new experiences.
- Lead to self-sabotage or procrastination.
- Trigger anxiety or a sense of "stuckness."
- Cause you to shrink your dreams to fit your doubts rather than expand your mindset to fit your potential.

Break This Cycle: Step-by-Step

1. **Spot the Limiting Story:**

   When you catch yourself hesitating, discounting your abilities, or feeling undeserving, pause and write down the automatic thought.

   - Example: "I'm just not good with people."

2. **Question the Evidence:**

   Challenge the belief:
   - "Do I have real proof that this is always true? When has the opposite happened?"
   - "Is this my belief, or someone else's old opinion?"

3. **Replace with Empowering Language:**

   Flip the narrative:
   - Instead of "I can't do this," try "I'm learning to do this" or "I can get better with practice."

4. **Small Experiments:**

   Take tiny actions that directly oppose your old belief.
   - If you believe "I'm not creative," doodle, brainstorm, or try a new hobby for ten minutes.
   - Celebrate even the smallest success—every action helps rewrite your mental script.

5. **Surround Yourself with Encouragement:**

   Engage with people, books, or communities that reinforce growth and possibility.
   - Share your challenge in the Must Goals forum or with a positive friend.

Learned helplessness is a related pattern: after repeated negative experiences, you may feel unable to change even when new opportunities appear. Overcoming it involves recognizing these self-imposed limits, challenging them with supportive self-talk, and building small habits that restore your sense of agency

Learned Helplessness Check:

Watch for urges to give up quickly or thoughts such as "This is just how I am." Use a small, new action to challenge that story and then acknowledge even tiny wins.

Surround yourself with positive influences and growth-aligned feedback. Progress takes patience and consistent effort, but replacing limiting beliefs with empowering ones unlocks your potential and aligns your mindset with authentic achievement.

Overcoming Limiting Beliefs and Cultural Myths

Many deep limiting beliefs come not from personal experience but from cultural myths and social conditioning. Author Simon Squibb highlights narratives around wealth, relentless work, and fear of failure that can push people toward goals that feel empty rather than meaningful. Questions like "Whose story am I living?" and "Which beliefs actually belong to me?" help expose these borrowed scripts.

To shift them, experiment with alternative beliefs—such as defining wealth beyond money or dedicating a day to "minimum effort, maximum joy"—and gather real-world evidence that counters old cultural stories. Reframing failure as a necessary part of growth, not a verdict on your worth, further loosens the grip of these myths.

Weekly exercise:

Write down one cultural or limiting belief. Intentionally act in a way that contradicts it, then record what happened and how you felt. Over time, this practice builds the clarity and confidence to pursue only those goals that truly resonate with your values, not just external expectations.

Defining and Embracing Your Must Core Beliefs

At the summit of self-development is the intentional creation of Must Core Beliefs—essential convictions you consciously choose and cultivate to drive transformation, resilience, and purpose. While many core beliefs are inherited or passive, Must Core Beliefs are the firm principles you decide to hold, regardless of circumstances or history.

Unlike unconscious beliefs, Must Core Beliefs are built through deliberate affirmation and practice. They empower you to move beyond current limitations and serve as internal standards for who you must become to reach your potential

Examples of *Must Core Beliefs*:

Must Belief	What It Looks Like in Action
Self-Love and Love for Others	Treating yourself and others with respect, even in conflict
Self-Sufficiency	Trusting you are enough as you are, while continuing to grow
Competence and Capability	Tackling new challenges and trusting that you can adapt
Embracing Imperfection	Learning from mistakes and sharing lessons openly
Positive Worldview	Looking for opportunity, hope, and solutions in setbacks
Significance	Believing your daily choices can meaningfully impact the world

Experts in personal growth and psychology agree that intentionally adopting such beliefs tends to increase resilience, optimism, fulfillment, and constructive action. Developing Must Core Beliefs requires daily choice—especially when old patterns or setbacks appear. The goal is not to deny reality but to build a mental framework that meets reality with courage and clarity.

How to Build and Strengthen Must Core Beliefs

1. **Clarify:**

   List 1–2 beliefs you already live, and 1–2 you want to strengthen.

2. **Affirm:**

   Write a brief, personal affirmation for each Must belief (example: "Every day, I am worthy of kindness and growth").

3. **Practice:**

   Start each morning and end each evening by rereading or speaking your chosen belief.

4. **Act:**

   Throughout your week, look for choices and moments that embody your Must beliefs, especially when doubt creeps in.

5. **Reflect:**

   Use a journal or group support to track the difference in attitude, motivation, or results as you reinforce your chosen beliefs.

Self-Reflections

- Which Must beliefs already feel natural to me—and where do I still need support?
- How might my goals, relationships, or self-image change if I lived these beliefs every day?
- Who can support and encourage me as I choose and practice these new standards?

Commit to nurturing these foundational beliefs each day. The journey is about persistent progress, not perfection—each step brings you closer to your greatest self.

Chapter Takeaways: Must Core Beliefs and The Must Circle of Life

- **Must Core Beliefs are essential:** More than just inherited or automatic convictions, Must Core Beliefs are deliberately chosen, nonnegotiable principles—forming the inner core of your personal growth and transformation. They shift self-perception from passive acceptance to empowered intention, shaping every thought and action.

- **The Must Circle of Life integrates belief and action:** Visualized as a layered chart, the Must Mindset forms the center, surrounded by Must Core Beliefs, which then radiate out to the seven critical life domains: health, relationships, career, finances, personal growth, spirituality, and community. This structure clarifies how intentional beliefs drive authentic, sustainable outcomes in every area of life.

- **Alignment is power:** Goals set on the foundation of Must Core Beliefs are directly aligned with who you must become to thrive. This alignment supercharges motivation, direction, and fulfillment—making goal pursuit both meaningful and resilient in the face of setbacks.

- **Lasting transformation requires reflection and choice:** Examining and updating your beliefs isn't just a one-time event, but an ongoing practice. You lay the groundwork for steady progress and adaptation across all life domains by consciously embracing Must Core Beliefs like self-love, capability, resilience, and significance.

- **The journey is layered:** With each step—establishing the Must Mindset, then Must Core Beliefs, then domain-aligned goals—you build outward, ensuring every level supports lasting personal achievement.

Foundations Integration Chart

Foundations of *Must Mindset* and *Must Core Beliefs* Overlaid on the *Must Circle of Life*:

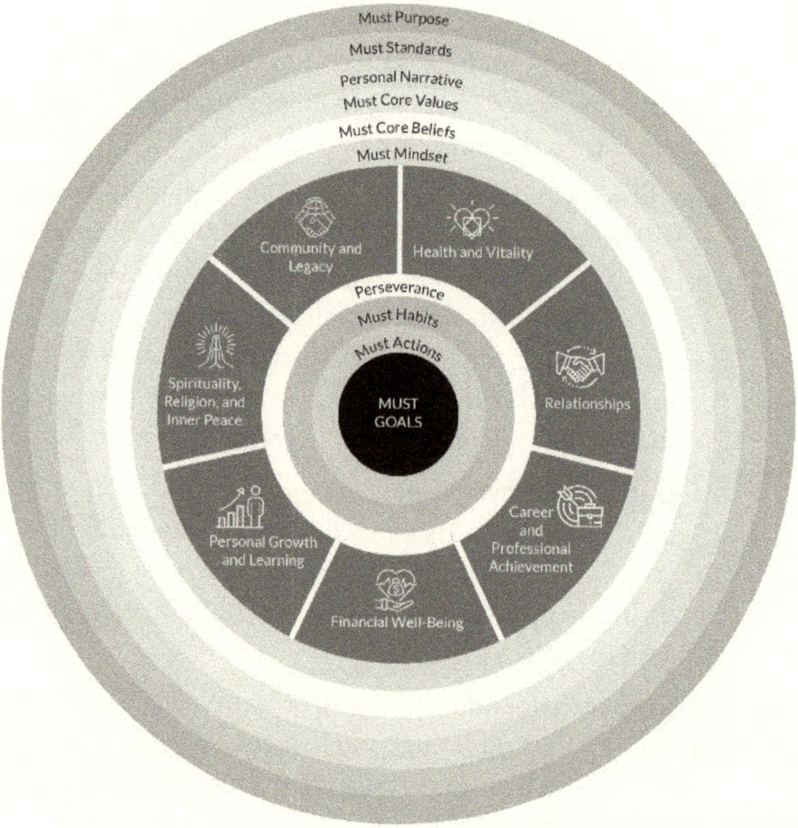

- **Inner Rings/Core**: Implementation of Must Goal-Setting, aligned actions, Must Habits, and perseverance, tenacity, and grit—the unwavering commitment to growth and action.
- **Middle Area: (pie):** The seven domains of the Must Circle of Life, where aligned goals are set and lived each day.

- **Outer Rings:** Exploration of identity—Must Mindset, Must Core Beliefs, Must Core Values, Personal Narrative, Must Standards, and Must Purpose.

Final Motivation:

As you continue through this book and your life, remember that the most significant transformation is built from the inside out.

CHAPTER 4

Must Core Values: Aligning Goals with What Matters Most

"Values are like fingerprints. Nobody's are the same, but you leave them all over everything you do."
—Elvis Presley

What You'll Learn in This Chapter

- What core values are and why they shape every major achievement
- How identifying your authentic values leads to fulfillment (not just external success)
- Key questions to clarify your actual values and move beyond "shoulds" and social pressures

Must Core Values

As we begin this part of the journey, expectations are often shaped by social norms: climb the corporate ladder, earn prestige, and accumulate wealth. These pressures can grow from a need to prove ourselves—to be capable, worthy, and successful despite early challenges. Yet in quieter moments, away from external demands, deeper truths emerge and long-hidden layers of self-come into view.

What is a Core Value?

A core value is more than an ideal; it is a foundational principle that anchors your identity and guides your choices, large and small. It acts as a quiet compass, shaping who you are and who you aspire to become. Core values show up most clearly in moments of adversity and decision, steadily orienting you toward what is most meaningful and authentic.

Society may nudge you toward familiar measures of success—status, titles, and constant achievement. Beneath that noise, however, your deeper priorities reveal what truly matters as you grow. Clarifying these values is essential for setting goals that feel both authentic and sustainable.

Living Out of Alignment, Rediscovering True Values

For much of my early adulthood and well into my professional life, my internal compass pointed toward achievement, status, and doing what I thought was expected. My days were packed with striving and "shoulds"—work harder, achieve more, win recognition, and keep up appearances. Outwardly, this path brought professional rewards; inwardly, it created a growing emptiness.

A turning point came after a series of losses and setbacks—a family tragedy, a health scare, and a deep sense of disconnection from my true self. In the quiet that followed, I realized how long I had been living by values handed to me by society, upbringing, and circumstance. I was pursuing goals that looked admirable from the outside but did not nourish my soul or honor the person I longed to become.

Through journaling, I finally admitted that values like service, authenticity, and love felt more real and urgent than success or outside approval. Naming these actual values was only the first step; the real work was living them—changing habits and releasing the need to please others constantly.

As I gradually aligned my goals with these values, everything shifted. Work gained meaning, relationships deepened, and even my health improved as my choices came from self-respect instead of obligation. Living by actual values is not always comfortable, but it is the only way to build a life that genuinely feels like your own

Reflective

- Recall a season when you were living by "shoulds" or others' expectations. What value did you need to reclaim or rediscover?
- How did your experience or sense of self-confidence change once you started honoring that value in your daily actions or goals?
- Where in your life right now do you need to realign a choice or goal with your core values?

Roy E. Disney put it simply: "It's not hard to make decisions when you know what your values are." As you read this chapter, ask yourself:

- Which principles truly guide my daily choices?
- What values do I cherish most—and want to leave as my legacy?

Try This Now:

Briefly list three values you admire in those you respect most. Are they reflected in how you approach your own life and goals?

1. _____
2. _____
3. _____

Differentiating Core Beliefs and Core Values

Core Beliefs:

- Deeply rooted convictions you hold about yourself, others, and the world
- Formed primarily in childhood and shaped by early experiences, beliefs act as invisible lenses—coloring your perceptions, emotions, and responses.
- When empowering, they fuel growth and resilience; when limiting, they quietly reinforce fear or self-doubt, often beneath conscious awareness.

Core Values:

- Intentionally chosen guiding principles that reflect your highest ideals and commitments
- Your "moral compass," shaping daily choices, relationships, and standards for what truly matters in life and work

Key Distinction:

Core beliefs shape how you see the world; core values guide how you choose to act within it.

How They Interact:

- Beliefs influence which values you embrace (e.g., believing the world is dangerous may elevate security as a value).
- Values can reinforce or reshape beliefs over time (e.g., committing to honesty can support the belief "I am trustworthy").
- Both evolve with reflection and experience, especially when you make conscious choices aligned with your authentic self.

Why This Matters:

- Understanding and revisiting your beliefs and values is vital to real growth and fulfillment—they are the "nucleus" of purposeful living.
- Authentic self-discovery means claiming values and beliefs that are truly yours—not simply inherited or borrowed from others.
- As you evolve, so too will your values and beliefs, ensuring your goals stay personally meaningful and fully aligned with who you are becoming.

Values and beliefs form a dynamic system: beliefs shape perception, while values shape response. Beliefs influence which values you prioritize, and lived values can, over time, support and strengthen healthier beliefs. As you continue this journey, returning regularly to both your beliefs and your values gives your choices direction, authenticity, and resilience.

Values Change as You Grow

- Core values are not fixed; they adapt and deepen with life's seasons, experiences, and new perspectives.
- Discovering and refining your actual values is a foundation for authentic growth and self-actualization.

The Science

Neuroscientific research indicates that reflecting on personal values activates brain regions tied to self-reflection and decision-making. Living by well-defined values is linked with greater satisfaction, resilience, and well-being, helping you persist through challenges and continue growing even when the path is difficult.

Radical Authenticity and Dream Discovery

Aligning goals with values and core beliefs is foundational, but recent thought leadership invites going further—engaging in radical self-questioning to discover which dreams are truly yours rather than adopted from family, culture, or convention. Simon Squibb's "Dream Declaration," for example, encourages probing questions such as:

- What would I choose if no one were watching or judging?
- What excites me for its own sake, beyond others' approval?
- What themes keep returning in my daydreams and moments of hope?

You bring inherited beliefs and motives into conscious review by journaling honest answers and asking what you would try if external approval or tradition were irrelevant. Weekly radical self-reflection helps surface not just what you want, but what you are uniquely moved to pursue, making space for goals that feel deeply fulfilling and sustainable over time.

How to Use the *Must Circle of Life*

To assess your core values in a balanced and actionable way:

1. **Select Your Core Values:**

    From a provided list for each of the seven Circle of Life domains, pick three that resonate most with you and best represent your guiding principles.

2. **Add Personal Values:**

    Customize your selection. If a value isn't listed but feels central, add it—ensuring every domain is truly personal and meaningful.

3. **Prioritize Your Values:**

   Order your values from most to least vital in each area. This helps clarify how each influences your daily decisions and larger life goals.

4. **Reflect on Your Choices:**

   Consider why these values matter—how they affect behavior, ambition, and fulfillment in every part of your life.

You gain clarity and balance by examining and prioritizing values within each segment of the *Must Circle of Life*, making your actions truly reflect what matters most. This practical commitment shapes a life that is vibrant, resilient, and deeply fulfilling.

Try This Now

Think of a recent decision you made. Ask, "What value was underneath that choice?" Write it down. Repeat with a few more decisions and notice which values keep showing up.

A New Lens: Megan's Realignment

Megan entered her thirties, committed to climbing the corporate ladder. Promotions and accolades followed, yet she felt increasingly depleted and restless. A leadership program invited her to complete a "values inventory," and she discovered her true core values were creativity, collaboration, and adventure—qualities her role left little room to express.

With support, Megan began making small changes at work and home. Tentative adjustments grew into realignment as her daily life began to match what mattered most inside. Her story shows how intentional value discovery can transform restlessness into genuine fulfillment.

Reflection

Reflect on a time when outward achievement or routine did not match your inner sense of what mattered.

- Which value did you realize was missing?
- What is one small shift you could make this week to better align your goals or daily actions with a value that brings you alive?
- Who could support or encourage you as you experiment with this new alignment?

Many happiness experts, including Arthur Brooks and Oprah Winfrey, highlight four pillars that consistently support lasting well-being: faith or spirituality, family, friendship, and meaningful work. For each Must Goal and domain, pause and ask:

- "How does this goal support or strengthen my faith/spirituality, loved ones, friendships, or purposeful work?"

Take a moment to reflect or journal—using a simple checklist or priority statement—about how your goals nurture these foundational pillars. Investing in them often multiplies fulfillment and strengthens your outcomes, whatever your ambitions.

Health and Vitality

Health and vitality are about living with resilience, energy, and balance—not merely the absence of illness. When you ground your wellness practices in your true values, you tap deeper into purpose and longer-lasting motivation for self-care, moderation, and mental clarity.

Core Health Values May Include

Well-being, vitality, resilience, self-care, balance, fitness, nutrition, mindfulness, rest, prevention, mental clarity, stress management, longevity, self-discipline, and empowerment.

Reflection

- Which health value speaks most strongly to you right now?
- How well do your current routines actually reflect this value?
- Why Values-Driven Health Works

Living by your health values not only boosts energy and wellness; it also creates a reinforcing loop. When your habits reflect your principles, you are more likely to persist through setbacks and experience genuine satisfaction. Philosophical traditions and modern science alike suggest that practices rooted in balance and deliberate choice—rather than pressure or trends—are the ones that sustain long-term well-being.

Action Step: Put Your Values Into Practice

- Build one new routine this week that reflects your top health value (for example, "Rest": a set bedtime; "Resilience": a recovery walk after difficulties).
- Check in weekly: Is this habit still aligned with your values? Adjust as needed.

Tip

Minor, values-driven adjustments—honoring rest, choosing balanced meals, including joyful movement—compound over time into lifelong wellness.

Relationships

Healthy relationships are built and sustained by lived core values such as love, trust, and respect. These values act as the "glue" that creates safety, connection, and meaning in each interaction.

Foundational Values

- Love: Deep care and authentic bonds
- Trust: Reliability and safety built over time
- Respect: Honoring boundaries and celebrating differences

Other powerful relationship values include communication, empathy, kindness, loyalty, forgiveness, commitment, and support. When intentionally cultivated, these values strengthen the foundation for meaningful bonds in romantic, family, and friendship contexts.

The Win–Win Mindset—Relationships and Mutual Success

Stephen Covey, in The 7 Habits of Highly Effective People, describes a "Win-Win" mindset as the belief that lasting success comes when both parties benefit and help each other grow. In high-trust relationships, this means addressing conflict with honesty, seeking creative solutions that honor both sets of needs, and resisting the urge to "win" by having others lose.

Key Practices

- In any conflict, ask: "What outcome would truly benefit both of us—not just me?"
- Listen first for understanding, aiming to grasp the other person's real needs before asserting your own.

- Use shared values as a guide to find solutions that enhance, rather than erode, mutual respect and trust.
- In negotiations, look for creative options that expand possibilities instead of zero-sum trade-offs.

Adopting a Win–Win approach is not naive; it forms the backbone of resilient relationships at work, in families, and in communities. When people see you striving for mutual benefit, you strengthen core relationship values, elevate your leadership, and generate support for your Must Goals.

Reflection

Which core value do you want to experience more deeply in one key relationship right now? What would it look like in action this week?

Actionable Practices

- Practice active listening and empathy—show you truly hear and understand, not just react.
- Intentionally schedule quality time and give undivided attention to those you value.
- Share your core values—explain what matters most to you and invite others to share theirs.

Try This Now:

Choose one value (such as kindness, respect, or patience) and make it your theme for the week. Track one small moment each day when you put that value into practice

Why This Works:

Alignment on relationship values increases trust, satisfaction, and the ability to work through challenges—all of which are essential for lasting connection and fulfillment.

Career and Professional Achievement

Meaningful work begins when your career goals and daily actions reflect what matters most to you—not just what others label "success." Aligning your core career values makes your professional journey more purposeful, sustainable, and personally rewarding.

Career values might include growth (commitment to learning and skill-building), achievement (pursuing meaningful milestones), integrity (honesty and ethical conduct), innovation (creativity and fresh problem-solving), collaboration (teamwork and mutual success), and responsibility (accountability for your contributions). Other important values are leadership, adaptability, work–life balance, and mentorship—supporting others' growth and building a thriving professional community.

Reflection

- Which core value do you want to express more in your work this month?
- Do your current goals truly honor that value?

Actionable Practices

- Review your daily work actions—do they support your top values? If not, adjust priorities or routines.
- Make your values visible: share them with colleagues or a mentor and seek assignments that reflect those values.
- Use regular check-ins to revise your goals, so they keep pace with your evolving values and ambitions.

Try This Now:

Take a value—like integrity or creativity—and choose one small action this week that puts it at the forefront of your workday.

Why This Works:

When your career aligns with your core values, motivation, job satisfaction, and resilience increase, even in demanding environments. Persistent misalignment, by contrast, is a common source of burnout and stress.

Financial Well-Being

Financial well-being means having the clarity, security, and freedom to make intentional choices that support the life you truly want. Aligning your money habits with values such as security (building a stable foundation and safety net), abundance (seeking opportunity rather than scarcity), and financial freedom (gaining independence to pursue your passions) gives each financial decision added meaning and motivation.

Other important values in this domain include responsibility (wise stewardship of resources), planning (thoughtful preparation), generosity (sharing with others), and investment (growing assets for the future). Discipline reflects self-control, and clarity is knowing your real financial situation.

> *"Money is not the most important thing in life, but it is reasonably close to oxygen."*
> —Zig Ziglar

Reflection

What is one financial value you want to live by more intentionally this year? How might your daily choices reflect that value?

Actionable Practices

- Set up automatic savings or charitable contributions guided by your values (e.g., responsibility, generosity).

- Use digital or notebook trackers to check if your spending and investing reflect your priorities.
- Schedule regular financial check-ins to ensure you remain aligned with your top values.

Try This Now:

Choose a value such as planning or generosity and list one small, specific financial behavior to practice this week.

Why This Works:

Living your financial values increases motivation to maintain healthy habits and infuses everyday economic choices with meaning, supporting both stability and long-term growth.

Personal Growth and Learning

Personal growth is fueled by values such as authenticity (being true to yourself), self-discovery (exploring your strengths and potential), curiosity (desiring new knowledge), and courage (welcoming challenge and uncertainty). Resilience helps you bounce back from setbacks, and a growth mindset encourages learning from every experience.

Self-awareness means knowing your strengths and weaknesses; empowerment is about taking initiative; and vision guides you in setting meaningful goals. Adaptability and mindfulness keep you nimble in a changing world, while self-compassion fuels perseverance during difficult seasons.

Reflection

Which single growth value do you most need to prioritize in your next season of change, and how will it look in action?

Actionable Practices

- Build a daily or weekly habit around a chosen growth value—for example, journaling to deepen self-awareness or learning a new skill each month.
- Seek feedback and regularly reflect on both successes and missteps.
- Set one stretch goal that moves you beyond your comfort zone into active practice of your growth values.

Try This Now

Pick a value such as authenticity or resilience and write one sentence about what it means to you. Each day this week, take one concrete action that aligns with this value.

Why This Works

Embedding values into growth habits makes your learning more intentional, satisfying, and lasting—and ensures your goals are uniquely yours, not borrowed from others.

Spirituality, Religion, and Inner Peace

Spirituality, religion, and the quest for inner peace give life deeper meaning, anchoring you to purpose, wisdom, and tranquility—whether through organized faith, personal practice, or a connection with nature. When you identify and live by your spiritual values, you build resilience, clarity, and compassion that flow into every area of your life.

Core values in this domain include faith (trust in a higher power or principle), compassion (kindness beyond yourself), purpose (finding meaning in each day), gratitude (recognizing daily blessings), forgiveness (releasing anger and healing), and mindfulness (staying present). Integrity means living consistently with your highest ideals;

humility is openness to learning; harmony seeks balance; and service is choosing to help others.

Reflection

Which spiritual or inner value do you want to nurture more deeply, and how would it show up in your everyday life?

Actionable Practices

- Establish a daily spiritual or reflective ritual (such as prayer, meditation, a nature walk, or a gratitude list).
- Join a community or group that supports and reinforces your chosen values.
- Ask, "How can this principle guide my decisions today, especially in moments of stress or conflict?"

Try This Now

Choose a value like compassion, faith, or harmony and find one small way to express it each day this week.

Why This Works

Spiritual practices and values have been shown to promote well-being, resilience, and a sense of interconnectedness, supporting both personal growth and deep life satisfaction.

Community and Legacy: Living Your Values Through Goal Setting

As you connect each value domain—health, relationships, career, finances, personal growth, spirituality, and contribution—to your goals, you are not just making a checklist. You are actively shaping your "I AM" identity for lasting impact. Your chosen values become the foundation for who you become and the legacy you leave through your goals.

Community and legacy focus on making your life matter beyond yourself. Values like service (meaningful action to help others), legacy (intentional contribution with enduring influence), and compassion (deep empathy for others' well-being) call you to show up for causes and people beyond your immediate world.

Generosity means offering your time, skills, or resources, while responsibility and integrity ensure your actions are rooted in honesty and ownership.

If you want to empower and uplift others, prioritize values such as mentorship (supporting growth and passing on knowledge), advocacy (standing up for fairness), or impact (measuring change in the lives you touch). If inspiring and collaborating energize you, values like leadership, inspiration, and collaboration will naturally shape your daily actions and long-term goals.

Integration Reminder

Every value you select is reflected not only in what you do but also in who you are becoming—your "I AM." Goal setting is the mechanism through which your chosen values are lived out and multiplied in your life and community over time.

Reflection

Which value do you most want your community or loved ones to remember about you? How could today's choices become tomorrow's legacy?

Actionable Practices

- Volunteer, mentor, or engage in advocacy tied to your core values—make contribution a regular part of your life, not a once-a-year event.

- Regularly review your goals: Are they building both your life and the lives of others in line with your top values?
- Share your intentions and progress to encourage and inspire those around you—community values grow through visible, shared action.

Try This Now

Choose a value such as service or empowerment and identify one small action you could take this week to benefit someone other than yourself.

Why This Matters

Legacy is not about titles or wealth; it is about the ripple effect created by living your values each day. Goal setting becomes truly meaningful when it is anchored in the principles that define your "I AM," ensuring that what you achieve and who you become are aligned for the good of both you and the world around you.

Must Core Values

Must Core Values are your most essential guiding principles—personally chosen to shape your identity, drive your behavior, and guide your decisions across every area of life. They are the values that matter so deeply that you refuse to compromise them, even under pressure or challenge.

As you move through the Must Circle of Life, you will select three Must Core Values in each of the seven key life domains: health, relationships, career, finances, personal growth, spirituality, and community. These chosen values play two critical roles:

- As your irreplaceable values, they form the foundation of your sense of self, influencing every meaningful choice and how you show up in the world.

- As your personal key search terms, they act as anchor points and identity "keywords" you will use while crafting the inward-focused, authentic goals in the chapters ahead—ensuring your I AM identity and ambitions express your true self at every step.

This focused selection process brings both clarity and alignment. Limiting yourself to three values per domain helps you zero in on what is truly vital without denying the importance of your other convictions. Your Must Core Values bridge who you are now with who you choose to become, providing context for every major and minor goal you set.

Putting your Must Core Values into action creates a ripple effect: when you align daily behavior with these foundational principles, you experience deeper fulfillment and often inspire growth in those around you. Their power is not only in driving individual success but also in sparking collective, positive change.

Pause as you continue: Which values, in every domain, are absolutely necessary for the person you wish to be? Choose them as your daily touchstones and "keywords" for building your I AM identity.

And always remember, in the words of Oscar Wilde: "Be yourself; everyone else is already taken."

Chapter Recap: Foundations of Authentic Value-Based Goal Alignment

In this chapter, you built a foundation for genuine fulfillment by aligning your Must Core Values with every major goal. Using the Must Circle of Life, you explored seven domains—Health & Vitality, Relationships, Career, Financial Well-Being, Personal Growth, Spirituality, and Community & Legacy—to identify the three most essential Must values in each area. These carefully chosen values are not just ideals; they are your personal "keywords," shaping your I AM identity and providing clarity for every future goal you craft.

Why Alignment Matters

When you root your goals in Must Core Values—such as well-being, love, growth, integrity, and resilience—you harness the motivational power of what is truly meaningful to you. To illustrate how these values come together, meet "Must"ang Sally.

Introducing Our Avatar: *"Must"ang Sally*

"Must"ang Sally is a representative avatar who models the value-selection process you have just completed. For each of the seven domains, Sally identified her top three Must Core Values, not ignoring other values, but focusing her energy for clarity and powerful alignment.

"Must"ang Sally's Must Core Values

Domain	Top Value 1	Top Value 2	Top Value 3
Health & Vitality	Well-Being	Balance	Resilience
Relationships	Love	Trust	Respect
Career	Growth	Integrity	Achievement
Financial Well-Being	Security	Responsibility	Financial Freedom
Personal Growth	Authenticity	Learning	Growth Mindset
Spirituality	Inner Peace	Compassion	Purpose
Community & Legacy	Service	Legacy	Generosity

Actual goal setting is not about chasing other people's benchmarks; it is about anchoring every intention in what matters most to you personally. You define the "personal key search terms" that guide your identity, decisions, and next-level achievements by clarifying your Must Core Values.

How to Use Your Must Core Values

- **Pick Your Three:** In each domain, listen to your intuition and choose three values that resonate most deeply.
- **Focus Your Energy:** Let these values act as your "keywords" whenever you set, revise, or reflect on your goals.
- **Align Your Actions:** As you build your dreams and daily plans, check that your core values support each one. This ensures every achievement represents both progress and authenticity.

Danielle LaPorte's Desire Map deepens this foundation by encouraging you to begin each goal-setting journey with your core desired feelings—states like calm, creative, courageous, or connected. Write three to five feelings you most want to experience and use them as a touchstone each time you set or review goals by asking, "Does this move me closer to my core desired feelings?" This approach helps ensure that every Must Goal supports not only your values and identity but also your emotional well-being and fulfillment, which drive genuine transformation and happiness.

Building from Must Mindset, Must Core Beliefs, and now Must Core Values, you have created a resilient, unified framework for transformative goal-setting. Each choice—no matter how small—adds up, shaping both your personal journey and your broader legacy in the world.

The Must Circle of Life: Visual Framework

In the visual framework of the *Must Circle of Life*, the heart of the circle features the Must Mindset, then expands outward to Must Core Beliefs and Must Core Values. The specific values in each area form the foundation for aligned goal setting and flourishing across all dimensions of your life.

This unified foundation will become your compass as you move into the next phase, where you will methodically, artfully, and scientifically craft meaningful goals for every area of your life. The process ensures your goals are not only well designed, but genuinely aligned with your best self and your Must for life

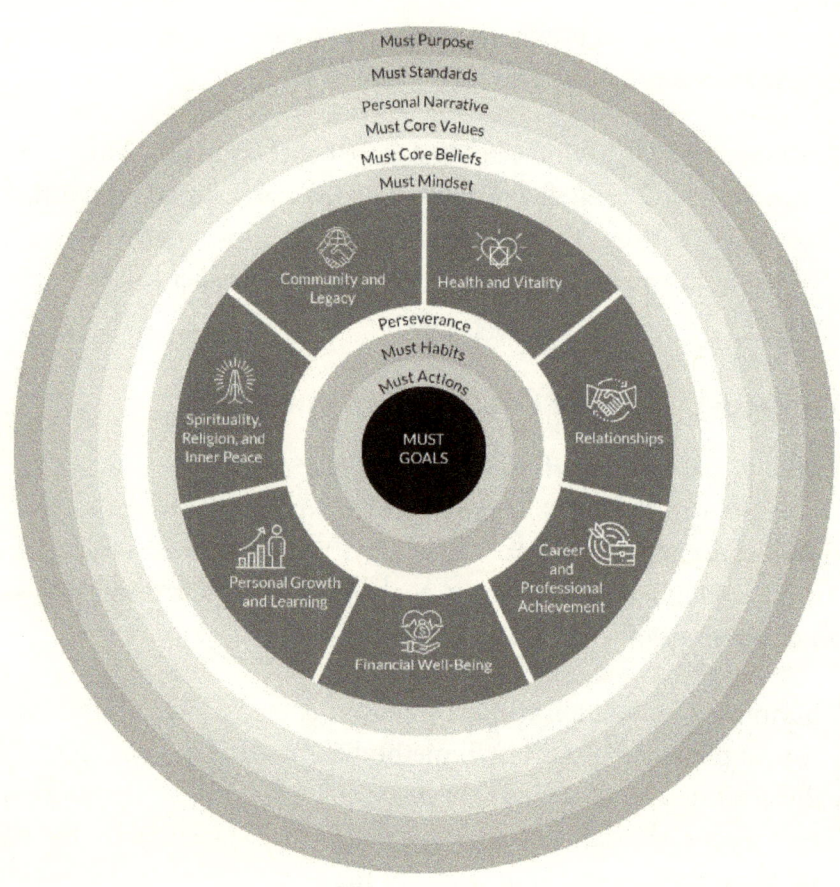

CHAPTER 5

Must Personal Narrative: Shaping Your Story for Authentic Goals

"The first step that leads to our identity in life is usually not 'I know who I am,' but rather 'I know who I'm not.'"
—Matthew McConaughey

"The stories we tell ourselves shape our lives and our world."
—Unknown

Integrating Narrative and Goal Setting

Every goal in the Must Framework is more than a task; it is a statement about who you are and who you are becoming. Your I AM SMART TO ACT goals remain the structure, but now the focus shifts to the story underneath them—the narrative that says, "This is who I am" and "This is where my life is going."

Reflection

How does your current personal narrative support—or quietly undermine—your goals? What story about yourself do your goals currently affirm?

What Is a Must Personal Narrative?

At the heart of real transformation is not just what you want, but the story you believe about who you are and what you are becoming. A Must Personal Narrative is an intentionally crafted, ever-evolving story—rooted in your Must Mindset, Core Beliefs, and Core Values—that connects your life experiences with your highest aspirations and daily decisions.

Pioneering psychologist Dan McAdams notes that we are all storytellers and that the life stories we create and live provide us with a meaningful way to understand who we are. His research shows that consciously shaping your personal story can foster resilience, purpose, and sustained motivation for growth and achievement.

A Must Personal Narrative is not passive. It is rewritten as you clarify what you stand for, what you are learning, and how you envision your evolution. This narrative becomes an internal compass for each new goal you set, especially when paired with your I AM SMART TO ACT process.

Journal:

What elements of your current story (identity, habits, beliefs) feel outdated or limiting? What would a "next chapter" sound like if you wrote it from the perspective of growth and possibility?

A Must Personal Narrative is never passive. It is consciously rewritten as you clarify what you stand for, what you're learning, and how you envision your personal evolution. This narrative becomes the internal compass steering each new goal you set—especially when you use your I AM SMART TO ACT process to make your narratives actionable, specific, and future-driven.

Try This Now:

Write a single sentence beginning "I am..." that captures the direction you most want your new story—and your next main goal—to reflect.

_____

_____

_____

The Art and Science of Your Story

Your personal narrative is not just a biography of your past. It is a living, forward-looking account that links your values, beliefs, and experiences into a sense of direction. When intentionally shaped, this story becomes a guide for your decisions and a source of energy for your goals.

Scientific studies in narrative psychology show that rewriting your story to emphasize autonomy, meaning, and growth strengthens resilience and persistence, even when obstacles appear. Your story is more than memory; it is a powerful tool for aligning choices, ambitions, and daily actions with your Must Core Beliefs, Values, and Mindset.

Reflection

Is your story one of limitation or possibility? Does it echo resilience or victimhood? Is it driven more by fear or by courage?

Try This Now

- Write a short paragraph that starts, "I am becoming..."

- List three shifts you would make to your inner narrative to align it more closely with your highest aspirations.

You remain the architect of your story. You unlock new levels of possibility, persistence, and fulfillment by challenging outdated scripts and reinforcing empowering self-talk.

How Your Narrative Forms

From early childhood, your internal story takes shape through upbringing, culture, and repeated experiences. Conversations, feedback, and important moments become the raw material for how you explain who you are and what your life means.

Core beliefs influence how you interpret events; Must Core Beliefs anchor you in conscious, empowering truths. Core values guide daily choices; Must Core Values ensure those choices reflect your deepest priorities. Your narrative weaves these elements together into a coherent identity—your "I am" and "I am becoming" statements.

By revisiting and reshaping this story as a Must Personal Narrative, you create a more truthful, hopeful, and resilient account of your life—one that fuels purposeful development and clearer direction.

From Underdog to Author: David's Story Rewrite

David always described himself as the underdog. Growing up with learning challenges and a critical parent, his inner script was, "I'm the one who has to work twice as hard just to keep up." For a while, that story fueled determination; over time, it became a burden. Every setback felt like proof that he was meant to struggle and survive, but never truly thrive.

Working with a coach, David was asked to write his life story—not just the hard parts, but moments of cleverness, perseverance, and joy.

On paper, a different pattern emerged. He saw that he was more than "behind." He was resourceful, creative, and resilient.

From there, David began telling a new story: "I am resilient, creative, and resourceful." Failing an exam became a prompt to design a better study system. A stalled promotion became a signal to pivot toward work better suited to his strengths. His goals changed from "just getting through" to statements of growth and contribution.

Looking back, David says his facts did not change—his history remained the same. What changed was the story he chose to tell about those facts. By consciously rewriting his narrative, he shifted from an identity of survival to an identity of adaptability and fulfillment, opening the door to goals that once felt out of reach, including ultimately becoming an author himself.

Reflection

- What label or story—"underdog," "outsider," "not a leader"—has been quietly shaping your decisions?
- If you wrote your life as a strengths-based story, what headline would you give it now?
- What is one goal or action you would pursue differently if you truly believed that new story?

The real power of narrative lies in agency: you can choose to tell a story of strength, redemption, and growth. Intentional storytelling, aligned with positive psychology, fosters meaning, hope, and empowered self-leadership.

The Influence of Language and Self-Talk

The language you use with yourself—your self-talk—profoundly shapes your personal narrative and either powers or paralyzes your progress toward meaningful goals. Inner dialogue, repeated daily, acts as both a mirror of your beliefs and a lever for change: positive self-talk fosters stories of resilience and capability, while negative self-talk cements patterns of self-doubt and defeat.

For example, repeating "I am always failing" entrenches a narrative of powerlessness, while reframing it as "I am learning and growing from my experiences" cultivates a growth-centered mindset essential for sustained achievement.

Contemporary psychology highlights the power of self-compassionate language for building a healthy self-image and reducing harsh self-criticism. Dr. Kristin Neff's research identifies three pillars:

- **Mindfulness:** Noticing how you speak to yourself, especially under stress.
- **Common humanity:** Recognizing that setbacks are universal.
- **Self-kindness**: Choosing encouraging words, especially in difficulty.

Supportive self-talk does more than improve your mood; it fuels motivation, focuses your attention on actionable possibilities, and builds a bias toward success, helping you remain committed even through setbacks.

Journal: Self-Talk Reflection

- Write several phrases you frequently use to describe yourself—especially under pressure.
- Are these statements empowering and growth-oriented, or do they reflect doubt and limitation?
- What might change in your future story and results if you intentionally replaced self-criticism with language that builds capability?

By cultivating compassionate, positive self-talk, you continuously transform your personal narrative into one that supports authenticity, resilience, and lasting progress.

The Must Book Guided Journal and online resources offer practical exercises for deepening this transformation. Visit MustGoals.com/Resources.

The Power of Focus

Where you focus your attention each day shapes not only your inner experience but the arc of your story. Positive psychology research shows that directing attention to strengths, achievements, and gratitude substantially boosts competence, optimism, and motivation—key drivers of progress and goal fulfillment.

Tony Robbins' insight, "Where focus goes, energy flows," is supported by research: what you habitually focus on—growth or limitation—steadily expands in your life, influencing both, your outlook and your outcomes.

- Focusing on skills, victories, and lessons learned seeds a narrative of capability and resourcefulness, attracting supportive relationships and positive feedback loops.
- Fixating on shortcomings, failures, or setbacks reinforces a story of inadequacy, making it harder to break negative patterns or pursue ambitious goals.

Strengths-based interventions—intentionally identifying and using personal strengths—have been shown to increase happiness, meaning, and psychological well-being for months after application. Your repeated focus is one of the most powerful ways to shape a Must Personal Narrative built on authenticity and growth.

Journal: Redirecting Focus for Empowerment

- Reflect on a recent challenge. Where did you direct your focus—obstacles or solutions, setbacks or strengths?
- How did that focus impact the story you tell yourself about your capabilities and future?
- Describe how deliberately shifting attention toward strengths, even in small ways, could reshape your narrative into one of confidence, resilience, and progress.

An intentional, strengths-based focus, practiced consistently, makes your narrative more flexible, hopeful, and conducive to lasting goal attainment.

The Impact of Physiology

How you carry yourself—your posture, presence, and body language—also shapes your internal narrative and confidence in pursuing goals. Amy Cuddy's work on "power posing" suggests that adopting expanded, confident stances can increase feelings of self-assurance and readiness to act.

Practicing an open, upright posture is linked to greater feelings of confidence and assertiveness. While physiological findings are mixed, meta-analyses consistently show that power poses make people feel and act more confident and better prepared to face challenges. Your body cues do not just signal confidence to others; they help retrain your self-perception, reinforcing a narrative of strength, capability, and "I can do hard things."

This creates a feedback loop: small, daily choices in how you stand and move both reflect and actively construct an empowered Must Personal Narrative. Carrying yourself with openness and presence influences your mood and motivation, making it easier to approach stretch goals with courage and resilience.

MUST GOALS

Journal: Body Language for Empowerment

- Reflect on how you usually carry yourself when facing a challenging task.
- Experiment with a two-minute "power pose" (open, upright, expansive posture) before your next important goal-setting moment or conversation.
- Notice any shift in your thoughts, confidence, or actions. Does it make your "I am" narrative feel more real and reachable?

By intentionally practicing strong, expansive posture—standing tall, dropping your shoulders, and looking ahead—you change not only how others see you, but how you see yourself, supporting any transformation in your self-story and goal pursuit

Standing Taller: Changing My Self-Story in Real Time

Years into my professional life, I often appeared confident in court, yet inside, I still carried an old story: I was the "kid with the pigeon-toed feet," an outsider trying to prove I belonged. Before a crucial presentation, I caught my reflection—hunched shoulders, tentative posture—mirroring those quiet doubts.

Instead of rehearsing another talking point, I took a moment to stand tall, expand my arms, and anchor into a new truth: "I am prepared. I am meant to contribute here." That simple act of claiming my space and updating my physical and mental story shifted my mood, my delivery, and the respect I felt for myself.

Practicing physical and inner strength as a daily ritual slowly rewrote my "I am" statement from "I am an outsider trying to prove I belong" to "I am confident, capable, and fully here." It is not a one-time switch, but an evolving habit that has transformed how I approach both public moments and everyday challenges.

Reflection

Think of a time when your posture, presence, or "I am" story under pressure echoed old doubts instead of emerging strengths.

- What small physical or mindset shift could you try next time?
- How might claiming a new "I am" narrative shape your next challenge, relationship, or opportunity?

Identity and the Roles We Adopt: The Power of "I Am"

Identity is not a fixed label, but a dynamic process shaped by the many roles you occupy: student, parent, leader, friend, professional, athlete, caregiver, and more. These roles serve as deep frameworks for how you see yourself and for organizing your aspirations, choices, and responses to the world.

Every "I am" statement you declare, whether conscious or not, crystallizes part of your identity and subtly directs your behavior. "I am a creator," "I am resilient," or "I am stuck" are not just descriptions; they reinforce self-stories that influence which goals you pursue, how you respond to setbacks, and how you interpret your journey.

Research and wisdom traditions agree: periodically reflecting on and updating your "I am" statements is central to a flexible, empowered identity. Embracing positive, growth-oriented identities—"I am creative," "I am learning," "I am a helper"—is strongly linked to motivation, psychological well-being, and the ability to rebound from adversity. The more willing you are to revise and expand your "I am" narrative, the more likely you are to experience meaningful success and fulfillment.

Just as the janitor at NASA reframed his work as "helping put a man on the moon," aligning your sense of self with a larger mission gives daily actions fresh purpose and energy. The right "I am" statements do more than describe who you are now; they chart the future you are choosing to build.

Reflections

- List three "I am" statements that reflect both your current roles and the person you aspire to become.
- How might updating these statements reshape your confidence and the goals that matter most to you?

Your identity is not a static fact, but an ever-evolving resource for intentional living.

Expanding and Redefining Our Roles: Rewriting Your Narrative

> *"You are the author of your own life story. You have the power to create a narrative that reflects your true self."*
>
> —Unknown

Lasting fulfillment requires not just setting goals, but continuously refining the story you tell about who you are and who you are becoming. Narrative psychologists and neuroscientists show that identity is dynamically constructed and reconstructed through the stories and beliefs you rehearse each day. McAdams' narrative identity theory describes this as an ongoing process of weaving past, present, and future into a self-authored story that gives purpose and direction.

Neuroplasticity sits at the heart of this transformation. Each time you update an "I am" statement, act in a new way, or visualize yourself thriving in a chosen role, you reinforce neural pathways that strengthen your emerging story. Holding tightly to rigid, outdated identities makes change far harder, whereas flexible, positive, coherent narratives are linked with greater resilience, adaptability, and motivation.

Redemptive storytelling—finding meaning, agency, and growth even in setbacks—emerges as a key factor in well-being and sustained progress. Social neuroscience further shows that supportive communities, mentors, and affirming environments amplify your efforts to update your story by providing validation and encouragement.

Action

- List one outdated or limiting role you would like to outgrow (for example, "I am always the outsider," "I am not creative").
- Replace it with a new, empowering "I am" declaration that better aligns with your Must vision and values.
- Share this new story with someone you trust or write it as a public commitment in your journal.

Every new chapter—mindset, belief, value, chosen role—adds to your living narrative. You possess both the biological capacity and the conscious agency to rewrite it. You unlock more freedom, fulfillment, and the power to set and accomplish your most meaningful goals by intentionally revising your beliefs and roles.

Addressing and Reframing Learned Helplessness

Learned helplessness is a pattern in which repeated experiences of uncontrollable setbacks lead you to believe that nothing you do will change your situation—producing passivity, low motivation, and a sense of defeat even when opportunities exist. It has been linked with challenges such as depression, disengagement, and chronic stress.

To overcome learned helplessness, you must disrupt old stories of powerlessness. One effective strategy is to craft new, empowering self-stories and pair them with small, identity-based actions—visible moments of control and progress. Each concrete "win," no matter how small, becomes evidence that you can alter your situation, breaking the psychological cycle and building hope and self-efficacy over time.

Reframing Your Narrative: From Limiting Beliefs to Empowered Identity

- Reflect: List roles, labels, or core beliefs that feel limiting.
- Challenge: For each, gather evidence that contradicts it and restate your story as a positive, growth-focused affirmation.
- Example: Shift "I am not good enough" to "I am learning, growing, and capable." Replace "I am just a parent" with "I am nurturing and creative."

For added impact, you might destroy the written version of your old, restrictive narrative, then keep your new affirmations visible as daily reminders. Neuroscience confirms that repeated, intentional practices—affirmations, journaling, visualization—support changes in mindset and emotional resilience by forging more adaptive neural pathways.

Remember: learned helplessness and limiting beliefs can be reversed. Through small actions, new self-stories, and consciously chosen identities, you build the motivation and confidence to pursue even your boldest goals.

Declaring and Visualizing Your New Story

Positive "I am" statements move your new narrative from theory into lived reality. When you affirm, for example, "I am resilient and capable of overcoming challenges," "I am a positive force in my community," or "I am growing and creating a life of meaning," you anchor your story in possibility and strength, guiding choices and behaviors across every domain.

Your empowered narrative is a living document, that evolves as you gain insight, experience, and achievement. Carry these affirmations forward as touchstones. Let them guide the actions you take, the relationships you invest in, and the goals you set.

Narrative Coherence and Goal Commitment

Research shows that the more logically connected and coherent your life story feels, the more committed you become to meaningful, long-term goals. Narrative coherence means making sense of setbacks and triumphs, seeing a thread of resourcefulness, growth, and purpose in your journey. When difficulties are reframed as sources of learning and agency, motivation deepens, and goal pursuit strengthens.

People who build coherent, integrated narratives are more likely to set ambitious goals, persevere through obstacles, and experience greater stability and life satisfaction. Your Must Personal Narrative should link the key chapters of your life so each goal becomes a logical, empowered next step rather than an isolated attempt.

Visualization Exercise

- Write your top three new "I am" statements.
- Close your eyes and picture yourself acting from each one in a real situation.
- Notice how this visualization feels, then choose one tangible action today that expresses your new story.

By organizing your life into a coherent, growth-focused narrative—and declaring your intentions—you reinforce both motivation and clarity, ensuring your goals are integrated expressions of who you are and who you are becoming.

The Dynamic Interplay Between Goals and Narrative Identity

Emerging research in narrative psychology reveals a powerful feedback loop between your narrative identity—the story you tell about yourself—and the goals you pursue. When your goals align with your self-authored story, growing from your authentic values, vision, and "I am" statements, each step toward those goals strengthens your sense of agency, coherence, and authenticity.

As you accomplish meaningful goals, your inner narrative becomes more positive, dynamic, and resilient, which in turn makes you more likely to set and sustain ambitious, self-congruent goals in the future. As your story evolves through reflection, learning, and new experiences, your definition of "success" naturally shifts, keeping your goals current and deeply motivating.

Key Practices

- Revisit your mindset, beliefs, values, identity statements, and vision regularly—especially at major milestones, setbacks, or life transitions.
- Use journaling to connect current goals with past turning points and future aspirations.
- Let each accomplishment feed back into your narrative as fresh evidence of capability and growth.

This cycle of narrative and goal evolution helps explain why people with coherent, self-authored life stories enjoy greater psychological well-being, stability, and long-term fulfillment, even as they continue to stretch toward their next Must.

Chapter Recap: Aligning Goal Setting with Your Enhanced Personal Narrative

- Your personal narrative shapes how you set, pursue, and ultimately achieve meaningful goals. By examining and intentionally rewriting your inner story, you align your deepest self with your daily actions, unlocking lasting motivation and resilience.

- Neuroplasticity research indicates that reframing limiting "I am" statements into empowering affirmations can strengthen new neural pathways, supporting ongoing growth, adaptability, and higher personal achievement.

- Roles and identities are not fixed; they are flexible lenses you can revise and expand as you respond to new aspirations and challenges. Embracing a diversity of positive identities fosters greater creativity, flexibility, and sustainable fulfillment over time.

- The people and environments around you significantly influence your ability to revise your narrative and stay committed to what matters most. Seeking supportive communities and mentors can reinforce and accelerate your new story.

- Consistently using reflection, journaling, visualization, and daily affirmations helps embed your revised narrative. As you connect your story with your aspirations, your goals shift from distant ideas into tangible, attainable realities.

- The stronger and more coherent your narrative—and the more closely it aligns with your Must Goals—the greater your clarity, motivation, and results, allowing each chapter of your life to become an authentic step toward lasting achievement

Your "Personal Story" ransformation Map

Here is a structured, research-backed "**Transformation Map**." You can use it to systematically update your identity and narrative. It helps you to visualize and sustain your narrative transformation (You can find further resources on this at *MustGoals.com/Resources*)

Left column: Write *limiting "I am" statements* that have held you back.

Center column: *Gather evidence, contradictions, or positive experiences that dispute the old story.*

Right column: *Declare your new, empowered "I am" statements* and connect them to the new roles and goals you wish to embody.

First, you are provided with a *sample map*, then you have your own to complete.

Sample Personal Story Transformation Map

Limiting "I am" Statement	Contradictory Evidence / Positive Experiences	New Empowered "I am" Statement (Tied to Desired Roles/Goals)
I am not creative	I came up with a unique solution at work last month	I am a creative problem-solver and visionary leader
I am always overwhelmed	I successfully managed a crisis and met my deadlines	I am resourceful and able to stay calm under pressure
I am just a helper, not a leader	I organized a community event that inspired others	I am an inspiring leader and positive force in my community
I am not disciplined	I've kept up with daily journaling for three weeks	I am consistent and committed to my goals

Personal Story Transformation Map

Create your own three-column map and revisit it regularly as your story evolves.

As you move forward, let this map be a living tool—revisited and refined as you pursue ever-greater alignment between your narrative and your most meaningful goals. Every step you take to rewrite your story is an investment in the future you are determined to create.

Limiting "I am" statements	Evidence/Contradiction/ Positive Experiences	Empowered "I am" statements and new roles/goals

The Evolving Must Circle of Life
Further Integration of the Foundations of Your "I AM" Authentic Self

The evolving *Must Circle of Life* represents the deep integration of your foundational elements—**Must mindset, core beliefs, values, and your evolving personal narrative**—at the very heart of your journey. This wheel is not just a visual; it's a living map that demonstrates how the authentic "I AM" self-radiates outward to support alignment, purpose, and meaningful achievement in every area of your life.

Each domain—whether health, relationships, career, personal growth, spirituality, or community—is distinct yet interconnected, orbiting your most authentic self. As you deepen each element, the Must Circle supports continuous reflection and recalibration, ensuring that all your goals and actions are anchored in your authentic identity—not scattered or disconnected.

Key integration practices:

- Periodically review your core beliefs, values, and personal narrative; revisit your "**I AM**" statements as life evolves.
- Use your *Must Circle of Life* as a roadmap to spot strengths, identify areas for growth, and address imbalances while preserving your alignment with what matters most.
- Visualize your ongoing development as dynamic—a Wheel of Life that grows in both balance and depth as new insights and aspirations emerge.

With each turn of intentional growth, the *Must Circle of Life* helps you ensure the goals you set and the actions you take are always grounded in your truest identity—propelling you toward a flourishing, purpose-aligned life.

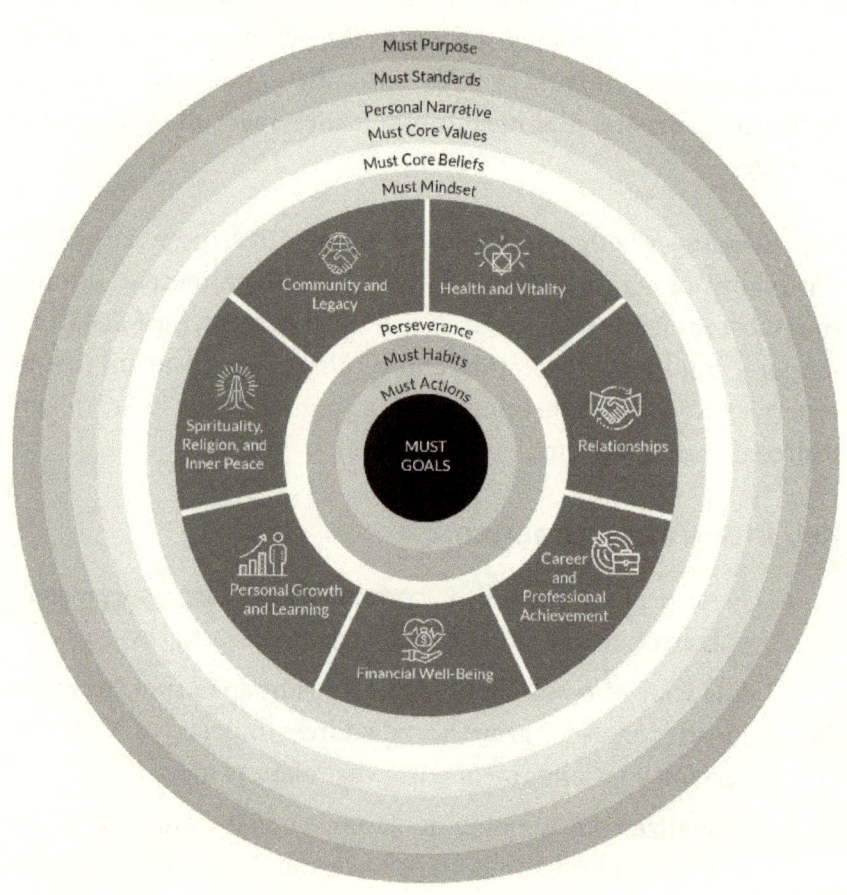

CHAPTER 6

Must Standards: Elevating Your Benchmarks for Authentic Success

"The quality of a person's life is in direct proportion to their commitment to excellence, regardless of their chosen field of endeavor."
—Vince Lombardi

The Role of Standards in Goal Setting

Must Standards sit at the heart of goal achievement. They turn intentions into reality by creating clear, nonnegotiable expectations for what you accept in every important domain—career, relationships, health, finances, personal growth, spirituality, and community. You anchor your goals in your deepest values and give structure to the identity you are actively creating by defining your standards.

Unlike static rules, Must Standards are living boundaries that transform daily choices into consistent progress. They create integrity between your values and actions, shifting you from reactive living to a purposeful path toward excellence and fulfillment.

Reflecting on Your Standards

- Raising your standards is a conscious choice that changes your trajectory and the outcomes you experience.
- Reflect on where you have elevated your standards—health, family, learning, work ethic—and how that affected your results.
- Which areas are still guided more by comfort or old habits than by the person you want to become?

Recognizing where higher standards have already driven better results reveals new opportunities to challenge yourself and set more meaningful benchmarks.

Must Standards in Daily Life

To create lasting change, Must Standards must move beyond theory into daily practice:

- Concrete consistency: Apply your standards in real decisions—at home, at work, and in relationships—and use them as the minimum acceptable level for your behavior.
- Self-audit: Schedule regular reviews and ask, "Are my actions matching my Must Standards? What needs adjustment?"
- Decision compass: Let standards guide you when choices are unclear, ensuring each outcome supports your core identity and long-term vision.

Reflect

- Are your current standards helping you rise, or causing you to settle?
- What are you willing to release or reinforce for a life of authentic achievement?

> "We are all self-made, but only the successful will admit it."
> —Earl Nightingale

When you fully own and actively update your standards, your goals shift from abstract wishes to authentic, identity-driven outcomes, building a legacy of excellence in every sphere of life.

Aligning Must Standards with I AM SMART TO ACT

To ensure lasting change, Must Standards must become living benchmarks inside your I AM SMART TO ACT goals. Before you set or review any goal, ask, "Does this reflect my Must Standards?"

How to Align Must Standards with I AM SMART TO ACT

- **Integration with identity**: Use your standards as a filter at the start of any planning. Look at each existing goal and ask whether it honors the way you insist on thinking, behaving, and showing up. If a goal conflicts with your standards, refine it, replace it, or remove it.
- **Concrete consistency:** When you choose a goal, connect it explicitly to a Must Standard (for example, "I am a compassionate leader; this week I will…"). Let standards calibrate the specificity, achievability, and relevance of each goal.
- **Regular self-audit**: At weekly or monthly checkpoints, review your I AM SMART TO ACT actions and outcomes against your declared standards. Where are you aligned? Where do your behaviors need to be raised to match your "I am" identity?
- **Decision compass:** When new opportunities arise, consult your Must Standards as a nonnegotiable test of whether a goal or action is worthy of your next I AM SMART TO ACT commitment.

Must Standards are nonnegotiable. If your current standards do not stretch you, design goals that pull you—and those standards—higher.

> *"Any time you sincerely want to make a change, the first thing you must do is to raise your standards."*
> —Tony Robbins

In Practice

- As you craft each I AM SMART TO ACT goal, ask: "How does this goal embody my highest Must Standard?" Make each element—Identity, Alignment, Meaning, Specificity, Measurability, Achievability, Relevance, and Time-bound—pass the test of your declared standards.
- Use Must Standards as a daily filter. If a new behavior, relationship, or opportunity does not respect your commitments, choose differently.

Your trajectory is set less by what you hope for and more by the standards you are willing to enforce through your goals and actions.

The Importance of Standards

Standards are the outward expression of your self-worth and identity. High standards move you beyond mediocrity, fueling integrity, fulfillment, and purpose, while low standards keep you stuck in dissatisfaction and unfulfilled potential.

As Les Brown asserts, *"You don't get in life what you want; you get in life what you are."* The I AM SMART TO ACT model ensures you consistently get what you are committed to becoming by linking every goal to the standards of your authentic self.

Scientific work on the "Pygmalion effect" shows that holding high expectations—even for yourself—encourages you and those around you to rise and excel. Set your commitments high, and your reality is more likely to rise to meet them.

Key Principles for High Standards

Research across business, sports, relationships, and personal development suggests that high standards are achieved by design, not by accident. Effective standards elevate performance while supporting motivation, resilience, and well-being.

1. **Ambition with attainability**

    Set standards that stretch you yet remain realistic, given your current capabilities and resources. The aim is inspiration, not chronic overwhelm.

2. **Communication and clarity**

    Define your standards clearly—on paper and, when relevant, in conversation. Reinforce them consistently to align your actions (and, if applicable, your team's actions) with what you truly expect.

3. **Support and structure**

    High standards require matching support: resources, feedback, and encouragement. Pair challenge with tools, training, and healthy routines.

4. **Continuous assessment and flexibility**

    Regularly evaluate results and the relevance of your standards. Adjust and raise the bar gradually as growth occurs and circumstances shift.

5. **Personalization and context**

    Tailor standards to your unique goals, values, and environment. Avoid one-size-fits-all norms; what stretches and inspires you may differ from cultural expectations.

Sustainable high standards, implemented thoughtfully and paired with support, drive innovation, resilience, and steady progress toward your most meaningful goals.

Examining Standards with the Must Circle of Life

> *"To be yourself in a world that is constantly trying to make you something else is the greatest accomplish*ment."
> —Ralph Waldo Emerson

Must Standards become most powerful when visualized and personalized. "Must"ang Sally, for example, uses her Must Circle of Life chart to define clear standards in each domain:

- **Health & Vitality:**

    "I must exercise at least 30 minutes, five days per week, prepare home-cooked meals using whole foods most days, and get a minimum of seven hours of sleep each night."

- **Relationships:**

    "I must communicate honestly and kindly with my loved ones daily, offer at least one intentional act of appreciation each day, and set and honor healthy boundaries."

- **Career/Professional:**

    "I must show up prepared for every meeting, invest in at least one skill-building activity per month, and deliver work that reflects my highest standard of quality while mentoring others when possible."

- **Financial Well-Being:**

    "I must save a set percentage of my income, avoid impulsive purchases, review my budget monthly, and make informed decisions that build long-term security."

- **Personal Growth & Learning:**

    "I must dedicate time daily to reading or learning, reflect nightly in my journal, and embrace new challenges as opportunities to grow."

- **Spirituality/Inner Peace:**

    "I must begin each day with a brief spiritual or reflective practice, express gratitude each evening, and engage in a weekly ritual that nourishes my soul."

- **Community/Legacy/Environment:**

    "I must contribute time each week to community impact, support causes I believe in, and make sustainable choices in my daily habits."

Sally writes these standards into her Must Circle of Life, creating a visual blueprint and daily reminder of her commitments. She revisits and updates them as life evolves, ensuring that her actions remain aligned with her deepest values and aspirations.

As you create your own Circle of Life with domain-specific standards, remember: your standards are not just limits; they are launchpads for becoming the person you truly want to be. Integrated across your Circle of Life, they offer direction, clarity, and a living testament to your commitment to authentic, purposeful achievement.

Must Circle of Life: My Personal Standards

Fill in three Must Standards for each of the seven domains below. Use this as your living blueprint for goal-aligned action.

Domain	Must Standard #1	Must Standard #2	Must Standard #3
Health & Vitality			
Relationships			
Career/Work			
Finances			
Growth/Learning			
Spiritual/Inner			
Community/Legacy			

Reflect

Which of these standards excites or energizes you now? Where might a raised standard offer the biggest opportunity for growth? Revise and recalibrate your standards regularly as you deepen your practice of Must-aligned goal setting.

Chapter Recap: The Foundation of Our Must Standards Aligned for Our Goal Setting

Your goal-setting foundation now rests on four pillars—Must Mindset, Must Core Beliefs, Must Core Values, and explicit Must Standards—each woven into every domain of your life and brought to life by the I AM SMART TO ACT model.

Must Standards are not idealized hopes; they are concrete, daily benchmarks that govern your choices in health, relationships, work, finances, growth, spirituality, and community. They transform self-knowledge into sustained achievement, turning abstract values into engines that power measurable, life-changing goals.

Personalization is power. You ensure that every new goal you set is both meaningful and achievable by defining and mapping your highest standards within the Must Circle of Life. Writing and revisiting these standards deepens accountability and continually raises the bar for each area of your journey, turning them into a compass that guides you toward new possibilities while keeping you aligned with your identity and purpose.

When I Raised My Own Standard

Early in life, it was easy to assume that working hard and meeting obligations meant having high standards. In reality, many routines were simply familiar, not transformative.

A turning point came after a season of burnout. It became clear that external expectations were being met, but there was no true Must Standard for personal well-being. A new nonnegotiable emerged:

"I must get seven hours of sleep each night and say no to late-night work, even on big cases."

Enforcing that standard felt uncomfortable at first. Old patterns of overwork resurfaced, and there was a real fear that saying no might cost opportunities. Yet within weeks, the difference was undeniable: greater resilience, clearer thinking, better decisions, and more effective leadership. That single standard quietly improved results in every domain.

Now, before setting or reviewing a goal, one question comes first: "What is the Must Standard here—and am I honoring it, or just performing for others?" The gap between burnout and sustainable excellence, between good and exceptional, often begins with that choice.

Reflection

- Think of one result or habit in your life that no longer meets your standards or supports your well-being.
- What new Must Standard are you willing to set, and how would honoring it consistently change your results?
- What support, reminders, or adjustments will you need to make this standard your true baseline?

As you update your Must Circle of Life and your standards, notice how each domain becomes a launchpad for deeper growth, fulfillment, and sustained achievement.

CHAPTER 7

Must Purpose: Defining Your Why for Authentic Goals

"There is one quality which one must possess to win, and that is definiteness of purpose—the knowledge of what one wants, and a burning desire to possess it."
—Napoleon Hill

"The mystery of human existence lies not in just staying alive, but in finding something to live for."
—Fyodor Dostoevsky

Vulnerability and the Birth of Purpose

True purpose often emerges through vulnerability—those moments when nothing is left but what matters most, or when love and pain intersect. For years, a sense of direction eluded me until I witnessed my mother's gritty resilience after devastating family loss. That night, her courage sparked the realization that purpose is forged not in comfort, but in struggle and love's resolve.

When my mother lost her second husband to suicide, our family's world was shattered overnight. She faced unimaginable pain and uncertainty—alone with two children and a future full of questions.

Through the depths of grief, an unwavering sense of purpose emerged: "My children will not only endure this but thrive. I must give them security, love, and examples of resilience." Her purpose wasn't born of ambition or recognition, but from a quiet decision to transform suffering into a promise that we would heal, grow, and rise together.

Every decision she made was anchored to that single Must. She worked tirelessly, shielded us from the harshest storms, and modeled the belief that life's darkest moments could still spark hope and meaning. Again and again, she led with love and faith, teaching us not just how to survive, but why we must live for one another.

Her story remains the clearest model in my life of how purpose, forged in hardship and vulnerability, can guide daily choices and inspire lasting transformation—for ourselves and for those we love most.

Reflection

Reflect on a time when adversity or loss revealed a deeper purpose within you or those you love.

- What was the "must" that emerged from that season of struggle?
- How did it change daily decisions, relationships, or future goals?
- What core commitment from your own journey do you want your goals and actions to honor right now?

Purpose is not just an idea—it grows from dreams, passions, mentors, and the hard-won lessons of adversity. Scientific research shows that reflecting honestly on both passion and pain enables the construction of a personal narrative that reveals genuine purpose and direction.

Dan McAdams' groundbreaking work on narrative identity further confirms that actively crafting and revising your life story fosters resilience, deep meaning, and sustained motivation for growth and achievement (McAdams, 2013).

Additionally, research by Eric Klinger reveals that our most persistent goals and dreams often emerge from subconscious patterns, guiding us to more profound commitment, creative ideation, and life direction (Klinger, 2013).

A *Must Purpose* is more than wishful thinking. It is your unwavering, nonnegotiable reason for living and doing—tightly linked to your beliefs, values, experiences, and hard-won wisdom. This "why" operates as both an internal compass and a wellspring of resilience, fueling your energy and reinforcing the meaning of every goal you pursue.

Action:

- Briefly describe a dream, passion, or story of overcoming. What threads connect them?
- How can you honor these core elements in the goals you set now, so your actions reflect your true purpose?

When you clarify your *Must Purpose*, you shift from generic ambitions to goals anchored in authenticity. This ignites fulfillment and positive impact across all areas of life.

Angela Duckworth's research on grit shows that sustained passion and perseverance for long-term goals predict success beyond talent alone (Duckworth et al., 2007; Duckworth, 2016). Her work also emphasizes that grit is domain-specific, not a one-size-fits-all trait—a reminder that true endurance comes from purpose-driven consistency, not mere stubbornness.

The Two Faces of Grit: Adaptive vs. Blind Perseverance

Not all persistence leads to progress. Good grit is balanced: you push forward with passion but also check in with mentors, solicit feedback, and adjust course when evidence or life shifts. "Stupid grit" means stubbornly persisting even when a method, job, or goal damages your health or no longer aligns with your Must self. Create a feedback ritual: ask trusted people to hold up a mirror and periodically review whether your perseverance is fueling healthy growth—or keeping you stuck. Being willing to adapt or let go is resilience at its best.

Understanding Our Purpose

Purpose is not a checklist goal—it is the foundation beneath all meaningful action, shaping who we become through our choices, relationships, and contributions. Research consistently shows that when goals and actions align with personal values, identity, and purpose (known as "self-concordance"), people experience more well-being, resilience, and motivation. Sheldon and Elliot's Self-Concordance Model demonstrates that authentic, value-driven goals produce sustained motivation and well-being (Sheldon & Elliot, 1999). This self-concordance principle is echoed in identity-based motivation theory, which explains that people act in ways consistent with who they believe they are (Oyserman, 2009).

This phenomenon is pioneered by Sheldon & Elliot's Self-Concordance Model, which demonstrates that people whose goals resonate with their deeply held values and interests show higher sustained motivation, greater well-being, and stronger perseverance. Their empirical research suggests that authentic, value-driven goals produce profound psychological and practical benefits, beyond mere achievement (Sheldon & Elliot, 1999).

Purpose may feel like an inspiration—spiritual or secular—emerging from authentic self-reflection and lived values. Whatever the language, true purpose sits at the intersection of your **Must Mindset, Beliefs, Values, Narrative, and Standards**. Doubt and uncertainty are a natural part of this journey. Clarity often appears during challenge, crossroads, or reflective pauses; these are not failures, but invitations to greater wisdom.

A Universal Principle: *Ikigai* and *Must Purpose*

In Japanese culture, the experience of deep purpose is described as "*ikigai*"—meaning a reason for being. **Ikigai** represents the convergence of what you love, what you are good at, what the world needs, and what can reward you (Garcia & Miralles, 2017). This aligns closely with the **Must Purpose** philosophy: when your purpose unites passion, skill, service, and meaning, every goal becomes an embodiment of who you are meant to be.

Purpose, at its deepest, is always connected to something larger. This broadens your motivation, building the kind of resilience that sustains action through setbacks and change.

The Fluid Nature of Purpose

Purpose evolves. What is meaningful in one season can shift as you grow in wisdom, experience, and new roles. The world's greatest traditions agree that fulfillment is found not by clinging to yesterday's purpose, but by regularly reflecting and adjusting as you grow.

- When has your sense of purpose changed during a life transition?

- Does your current purpose match your values, roles, and passions—or is something new emerging?

Embrace this evolution—identity-anchored goals adapt because authentic living demands ongoing review and refinement.

Discovering and Evaluating Your Authentic Purpose

True purpose is an alignment between beliefs, values, and lived experience—never simply inherited or imposed. If you reach achievements but feel empty, consider whether those successes truly reflect your deepest meaning or were externally motivated. Authentic fulfillment blooms when values, story, and direction are coherent.

Purpose is about coherence. Simon Sinek's *"Start with Why"* and neuroscience both affirm: motivation, resilience, and joy follow when people "live inside-out," letting purpose steer all meaningful efforts. Sinek's work emphasizes how purpose-driven action enhances motivation and fulfillment (Sinek, 2009).

Adjusting and Refining Your Purpose

As life unfolds, even a once-meaningful purpose may fade or need recalibration. When that happens:

- Review your Must Standards, Values, and Beliefs; allow new insights to prompt an update.
- Use spiritual guidance, mentorship, or deep reflection to clarify what matters now.

Purpose needn't be grand. Simple intentions—raising a kind family, contributing to a community, or spreading everyday kindness—are enough if they align deeply with who you are. The only true measure is resonance: does your current purpose match your evolving self?

Living in Alignment with Your Purpose

Knowing your purpose is the first step; living it is the ongoing challenge. Alignment demands not just reflection, but action—and the willingness to make difficult choices. The I AM SMART TO ACT Goals model brings purpose from insight to implementation: every "M" (Meaningful) goal must pass the purpose test before it stands.

Action: When setting new Must Goals, ask: "Does this goal clearly serve my current purpose?" Only those that pass become true *Must Goals*.

If your actions drift from your stated purpose, pause and course-correct. Review your Declaration of Purpose, Must Standards, and values. For the spiritually minded, trust your purpose to unfold in seasons, moving forward even when the path ahead isn't clear.

The Profound Impact of Purpose

Purpose is not only motivation; it boosts health, happiness, and resilience. Research confirms that people with clear, value-driven purpose live longer, rebound faster from setbacks, and report higher life satisfaction than those without this anchor.

Alignment between goals, values, and purpose doesn't just bring personal joy—it creates a powerful ripple effect, lifting communities, inspiring others, and forging legacy.

Defining Your Purpose

Find purpose not in external validation, but by tracking moments of deep engagement, passion, and challenge. Patterns in these stories reveal your unique "why," the foundation for authentic *Must Goals*.

Action

- Which moments or roles bring energy and deep involvement?
- What hardships have most shaped your values or direction?
- When have you been so engaged that time seemed to stop? Capture these and look for the unifying theme.

Crafting Your DECLARATION OF PURPOSE

Writing your purpose statement is more than a journaling exercise—it is an active step of commitment, like signing a personal *Declaration of Independence*. The words you choose become the foundation for how you lead yourself and serve others. As with any important contract, writing your purpose down gives it both clarity and power.

When you draft your ***Declaration of Purpose***, you are identifying the self-evident truths of your life—the values, beliefs, and priorities that you hold most dear. Your statement should be concise, specific, and personal: a living document to revisit and revise as you grow.

Your purpose statement is your contract with your own potential. By writing and signing it, you transform purpose from a vague ideal into a guiding force for everyday choices, habits, and relationships. This act of naming and claiming your purpose turns it into a practical compass, keeping your **Must goals** aligned with what matters most.

Instructions:

- Write your ***Declaration of Purpose*** in your own words. Focus on who you are, what you stand for, and the impact or legacy you wish to create.
- Sign it, date it, and keep it visible—on your workspace, journal, or a prominent place at home.
- Revisit and revise as your understanding of purpose evolves.

Example:

"To create, serve, and lead with integrity—using my knowledge, experience, and compassion to empower others and make a lasting, positive difference."

This living statement is your North Star and your contract for action. By signing it, you are not only honoring what is meaningful but also pledging to craft your future with intention, integrity, and courage. Let it guide your daily life, reminding you of the commitment you've willingly made to live authentically and with purpose.

Purpose as the Foundation for Your I AM SMART TO ACT **Goals**

Before every new goal, check: Does this directly support your Declaration of Purpose? If not, either refine the goal or revisit your purpose statement for updated guidance.

STEPHEN RUE

Date: ───────────────────────

My Declaration of Purpose:

Signature: ───────────────────

MUST GOALS

My purpose is: _____

My current Must Goal is _____

because it advances that purpose in the real world.

The Shadow Side of Goals: Ethics, Grey Zones, and Must Identity Alignment

Misaligned goals can produce impressive results on the outside and deep damage on the inside. Research on motivation, well-being, and organizational behavior consistently shows that when goals are driven primarily by status, comparison, pressure, or fear—rather than authentic values and purpose—they increase stress, undermine integrity, and erode relationships over time. This is the "shadow side" of goal setting: you can win the game and lose yourself while playing it.

Psychologists distinguish between intrinsic goals (growth, connection, contribution) and extrinsic goals (status, image, approval, money as an end in itself). People who chase mostly extrinsic, status-driven goals report lower life satisfaction, more anxiety and depression, and are more likely to drift into ethically questionable "grey zones" in the name of success, especially in highly competitive environments. This does not mean you are unethical or would break the law; it means that intense focus and ambition can create a kind of tunnel vision, where subtle harms or compromises are easy to miss in the twilight zone of ethical ambiguity. In organizations, cultures that worship metrics and short-term wins above all else are more vulnerable to burnout, toxic politics, and reputational crises, even when performance looks strong on paper. In personal life, externally imposed goals—living out someone else's script—often lead to quiet resentment, self-betrayal, and a nagging sense of emptiness after big achievements.

Must Goals are designed as the antidote to this shadow side. By grounding goals in your beliefs, values, standards, and purpose, you are repeatedly asked, "Success at what cost—and to whom?" before you commit. Instead of asking only "Can I hit this target?", Must Goals ask "Does this target honor who I am, how I want to treat people, and the kind of life and legacy I want to create?" This section is meant to act as both a guardrail and a bridge: a guardrail that protects you from misaligned, harmful goals, and a bridge that carries you from inner foundations into powerful goal-setting tools without losing your integrity along the way. This alignment harnesses the motivational power of clear goals while protecting your well-being, relationships, and ethics from becoming collateral damage.

You can use a simple test to expose the shadow side of any goal:

- Would I still pursue this if no one else ever knew about it?
- If I achieve this in a way that brushes against my values, will I still be proud of who I became to get there?
- Who might be harmed—directly or indirectly—if I chase this goal without restraint?
- Does this goal expand or shrink the kind of person I am becoming?

If your honest answers trouble you, that is not a reason to abandon goal setting; it is a reason to realign it. Refining or replacing a misaligned, status-driven, or externally imposed goal with a Must Goal is an act of protection and integrity, not weakness. In a world that often celebrates results at any cost, choosing Must alignment means you are not only aiming for success, but you are also insisting on becoming someone you respect on the way there.

LIVING YOUR PURPOSE: A COMMITMENT TO YOUR AUTHENTIC SELF

Your purpose is already present within you—ready to be discovered, rekindled, or refined. As you declare your purpose and align it with your authentic self (and, for those with faith, with God's greater plan), you turn intention into a living commitment.

Move forward with clarity, passion, and integrity. Use your Declaration of Purpose as your daily guide—not just a statement, but a contract you hold with yourself. Let every decision, habit, and Must goal flow from this foundation.

This is where meaning becomes real: as you embrace your purpose and translate it into essential actions, you move from dreaming to becoming.

Now is the moment to take what you've written—and live it, one purposeful action at a time. Your purpose is not only your anchor but also your springboard, shaping your path and your impact, day after day.

Chapter Recap: Purpose as the Foundation for Aligned Goals

- **Purpose is Core**: It anchors all Must-aligned goal setting—giving every achievement direction and gravity.
- **Purpose Evolves**: Expect purpose to shift with seasons of growth. Review regularly.
- **Alignment and Action**: Living your purpose means embedding it in every I AM SMART TO ACT goal and decision.
- **The Ripple Effect**: Purposeful living uplifts you and all those around you.
- **Declaration of Purpose**: By capturing your purpose in writing, you transform your motivation into a living contract—guiding habits and Must goals with clarity, accountability, and vision.

Integrating Purpose: The Upgraded *Must Circle of Life*

With this chapter, your *Circle of Life* has gained a profound, energizing layer. By weaving your *Must Purpose* directly into the center of the Circle—*alongside Must Mindset, Core Beliefs, Values, Standards, and Narrative*—you now possess a fully aligned, inside-out map for authentic achievement.

The *Upgraded Must Circle of Life* visually and practically unites every foundational element of your identity. It's no longer a static wheel: it's a living, evolving guidance system. As you continue, use it as your personal compass, reviewing and re-centering each domain so your next goals remain both deeply authentic and powerfully purposeful.

Let your enhanced *Must Circle of Life* serve as both anchor and launchpad—a visual declaration that your *Must Purpose*, and every **I AM** fundamental, drives not just what you hope for, but every step you take toward a life of meaning, coherence, and lasting success.

CHAPTER 8

Must Identity Map (My "I AM")

Use this page to collect the core discoveries from Part 1—your **Must mindset, beliefs, values, standards, personal narrative, and purpose**—into a single, personalized map. This reference anchors your identity ("**I AM**") in the foundational elements that will shape every *Must Goal* you set. Return to your *Identity Map* regularly to refresh your self-awareness, reinforce your intentions, and ensure that every new action or decision aligns with your true self and what matters most. Completing this map makes your growth and progress both visible and actionable—your starting point for authentic, lasting change.

My Must Foundations at a Glance

(Part 1 Summary Worksheet)

Complete or revisit this page as you finish Part 1 and prepare to move forward into designing your identity-rich goals.

Element	My Personalized Foundations
I AM Statement (Identity):	
Must Mindset:	
Must Core Beliefs:	1. 2. 3.
Must Core Values:	1. 2. 3.
Must Narrative (My Story):	(1-2 key lines that anchor your updated personal narrative)
Must Standards:	(Choose 1 3 for up to 3 life domains, or list your most important standards overall)
Must Purpose Statement:	
Biggest Recent Insight/Growth:	

Now that you have explored your identity, beliefs, values, narrative, and purpose, you are ready to translate them into Must Goals and Must Actions.

PART TWO

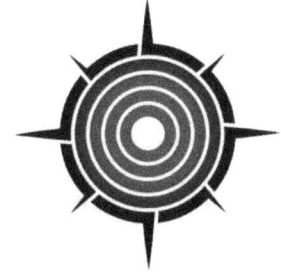

IMPLEMENTATION: CREATING MUST GOALS AND ACTIONS FOR RESULTS

Unleashing Your Potential: Activating the Power Within

You've done the deep work—the reflection, the self-assessment, the alignment. You've explored your Must Mindset, refined your Must Core Beliefs, clarified your Must Core Values, reclaimed your Must Personal Narrative, raised your Must Standards, and ignited your Must Purpose. But reflection, as important as it is, is only the beginning.

The next step—your next Must—is activation.

This chapter is the bridge between who you've become on the inside and what you will now build on the outside. Potential is not something you find; it's something you unleash when your beliefs, values, and purpose converge into decisive action.

Just as a seed already contains the blueprint for the tree it will become, you already hold within you the design for your own greatness. The work of Exploration was to uncover that design—to reveal and align your inner architecture. Now, the work of Implementation begins: turning that inner clarity into external creation.

The Nature of Potential

Potential is not power held in reserve; it is power waiting to be released. Many people never experience their full potential because they mistake awareness for progress. They learn more about themselves, but never act on what they know.

In the Must philosophy, potential turns into progress only when inner alignment meets intentional action. Knowledge without expression creates frustration; purpose without movement creates restlessness. Both are signs that your potential is asking to be set free.

Your potential expands when belief meets behavior—when your Must Core Beliefs fuel purposeful habits, and your Must Mindset transforms obstacles into opportunities. The fusion of these elements creates what I call Must Energy—the momentum that arises when your internal alignment and external focus are perfectly synced.

> "Your problem is to bridge the gap which exists between where you are now and the goal you intend to reach."
> —Earl Nightingale

The Moment of Activation

There is a moment in every transformation when clarity demands movement. Once you see the truth of who you are, remaining stagnant is no longer an option.

This moment of activation usually begins quietly—an inner nudge that says, You've learned enough. It's time to live it.

You may feel both excitement and fear in equal measure, but that tension is the birthplace of potential. It's the sign that your inner world is expanding beyond its previous limitations.

To unleash your potential means to trust your preparation enough to step forward boldly, even when the next step isn't fully visible.

A Real-World Activation Moment

Years ago, I worked with a client named Carla, a public-school teacher who had spent a decade holding quiet dreams inside. She loved her work, but felt invisible in the system—her ideas for reaching struggling students went unheard, and she told herself her voice wasn't strong enough to make a difference. Every time she thought about speaking up, a wave of old self-doubt would surface, reminding her of mistakes in her past as if they were proof she shouldn't try.

Carla's turning point came on a rainy October morning. Sitting in her car before work, she stared at the steering wheel, feeling frustration building with nowhere to go. Then she saw a small handprint on the inside of the passenger window—a mark left by a child she'd comforted the day before. In that fleeting image, she felt the weight of all the times she'd silenced her ideas "for safety," and the quiet cost it had exacted on both her and the kids she cared about.

That day, for the first time, she walked into the principal's office not to complain, but to offer a vision. She shared her dream for a reading circle for at-risk students, her voice trembling at first, but steadier as she realized she was finally living as the advocate her story had always hinted she could be. Within weeks, not only was the reading group in motion—Carla was mentoring other teachers, and her sense of possibility grew with each step she took. The single act of choosing courage over perfection, of letting action lead the way, changed her trajectory and sent ripples far beyond what she'd expected.

What most surprised Carla in the months that followed wasn't how hard the work was—but how each act of stepping forward drew out new reserves of capability she'd never seen before. Her story is a reminder: potential is unleashed not in grand gestures, but in the ordinary courage to show up differently—one moment, one decision, at a time.

Reflection: Your Activation Moment

Take a moment to pause and consider:

When in your life have you felt the quiet nudge to step forward, even if it felt risky or unfamiliar?

Was there a "handprint on the window"—an ordinary moment that called you to speak up, try something new, or leave the comfort of silence behind?

Jot down a memory or situation where you noticed your own latent strength rising, even if it was just for a moment. What helped you act, or what held you back? How might you respond if a similar moment came again?

Aligning Energy with Action

Living your potential requires a shift from intention to integration. Every insight gathered in Part One must now be expressed through consistent behavior. You'll start by applying your Must Mindset to the real-world domains of your life—what this book calls the Circle of Life:

Health and Vitality

Relationships and Love

Career and Calling

Finances and Abundance

Personal Growth and Learning

Spirituality and Inner Peace

Community and Legacy

Each of these areas is an arena where your potential will be tested, refined, and expanded through tangible goals. This is where the science of goal-setting meets the art of self-leadership.

Remember: your potential isn't revealed by perfection—it's revealed by persistence. Each goal you set and pursue is an experiment in growth, an opportunity to further embody your Must Self.

Living in the Must

To live fully in your Must is to live moment by moment in conscious alignment—with clarity of thought, consistency of action, and courage in pursuit of purpose.

Unleashing your potential is not a single decision you make once; it is a rhythm of living in which every choice reaffirms your commitment to the life you are creating.

You are now ready to channel your preparation into purpose-driven movement. The pages ahead will give you the structure, the science, and the strategies to set and achieve goals that honor your beliefs, values, and purpose.

This is more than setting goals—it's about living your life as an expression of your Must.

Your potential is ready.

Your clarity is set.

Now it's time to act.

Welcome to Part Two: Implementation — Turning Your Musts into Measurable Goals.

CHAPTER 9

The Bridge: From "I AM" to Implementation

"The vast majority of goal-setting books available today move straight to the mechanics of achievement, offering tips, routines, and systems while almost entirely omitting the most essential question: Who are you, truly? Without intentional introspection, exploration, and alignment with your deepest identity, even the most well-orchestrated goals may place you on a path that is merely adjacent to your authentic calling, rather than directly toward it. It is only by anchoring every ambition in the core of your being—through unflinching self-examination and the non-negotiable pursuit of your highest self—that you ensure your aims are not simply effective, but profoundly meaningful. Unless the compass of our truest self guides our goals, we risk impressive effort that still misses the destination where our genuine fulfillment, significance, and flourishing truly reside."

—Stephen Rue

Crossing the Bridge

Ashley was an achiever who set goal after goal—yet after years of chasing milestones, she felt unfulfilled. It wasn't until she paused to reconnect with her core identity and values—building a bridge from her "I AM" to her "I will"—that her goals began to bring both success and satisfaction. The bridge between insight and action is the difference between empty achievement and fulfillment.

Visual Anchor: *Inside-Out Flow Bridge*

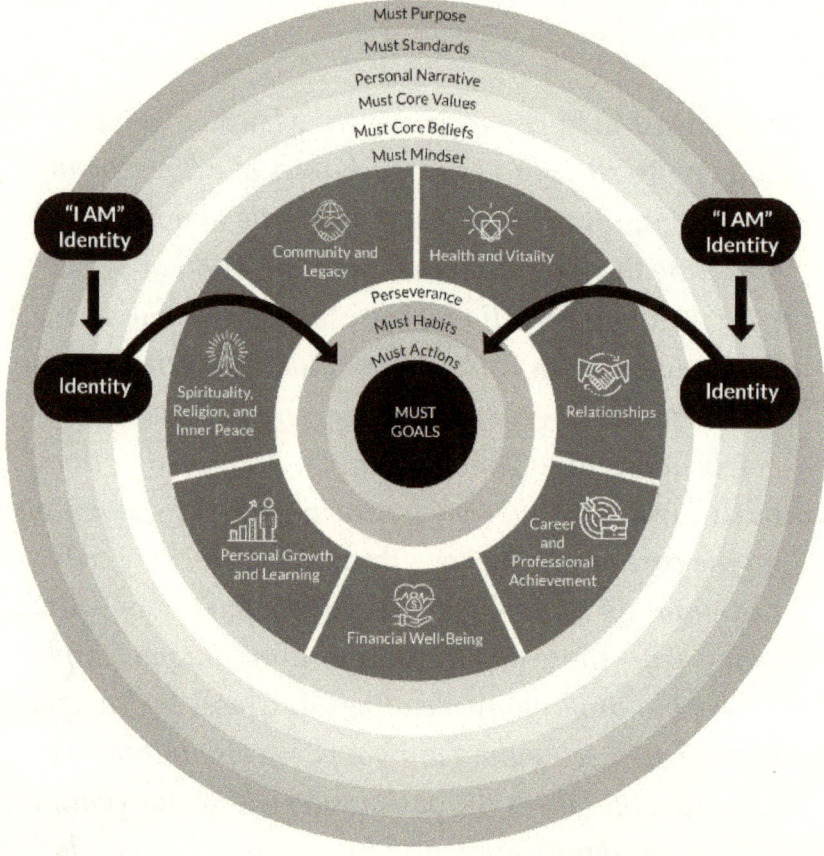

MUST GOALS

Note: Here, the graph shows the "bridge "which is the path from *Inner Identity* → Mindset → Beliefs → Values → Narrative → Standards → Purpose →to our *Outer Goals* → Habits → Tenacity → *Results*.

Pause here. Look at how far you've come—from discovering your truth to envisioning your future. Every authentic goal you set must now cross this bridge, built from self-understanding.

Reflection

- What part of your identity have you ignored or overlooked in setting goals in the past?
- How will you do it differently this time?
- Write your new "I AM Declaration" below:

Single Worksheet Reminder

Turn to your *"Must Foundations at a Glance"* worksheet from the end of Part 1. This is your reference map for everything you'll create moving forward.

If you haven't completed it yet, do so now. Bringing clarity to your identity is the most important step before moving ahead.

Activation & Affirmation

- **Activation:**

    Read your *"Declaration of Purpose"* out loud.

    Declare:

    "I cross the bridge—I build every meaningful goal from the truth of who I am."

- **Affirmation:**

    "This bridge is my power: from insight to action, from clarity to creation. My goals now flow from the deepest part of me—no longer random, but real."

The Bridge to Part 2

You are ready. Every system and tool ahead—SMART goals, ideation, planning, and habit-building—will help you translate who you are into the results you want. Cross the bridge with confidence.

Recap: The Must Pathway from Identity to Result

"To flourish, our goals must be the true bridge between who we are and who we are meant to become. Only when our aims align with our deepest self, do we consistently hit the target that fulfills us."

—Stephen Rue

CHAPTER 10

Unlimited Goal Ideation: Dreamstorming for Possibilities

Introduction: The Power of Unlimited Possibility

Every breakthrough begins at the edge of imagination—the moment when you let go of limits and allow yourself to explore the wildest possibilities for your life. Here, in the space between alignment and action, you'll discover the practices that expand your capacity to imagine, ideate, and ultimately pursue the most authentic, energizing goals (Christoff et al., 2018; Isaksen, 1998).

> *"The best way to have a good idea is to have lots of ideas."*
> —Linus Pauling (Osborn, 1953)

Recent psychological and neuroscientific research confirms that when you let your mind run free and avoid judging your ideas, you come up with more and better goals. The more ideas you allow yourself to write down—without worrying if they are too big or too wild—the more you open the door to real breakthroughs and exciting possibilities. That is how real change gets started (Christoff et al., 2018; Isaksen, 1998).

From Seminar to System: The Vision That Sparked *Must Goals*

As a young professional and aspiring attorney, one of the most transformative experiences in my life was attending a Tony Robbins seminar. It was there that I heard Joseph McClendon III—Doctor of Neuropsychology, master coach, and authority in neuroscience-based performance—share a message that fundamentally shifted how I thought about goals and possibilities.

McClendon urged us to write down every dream, desire, and extraordinary wish we held, as though there were no limitations, no barriers, and no fear of judgment standing in the way. He spoke of how open, uncensored possibility sets the stage for authentic transformation—a concept he had honed through neuropsychology and decades of coaching with leaders across the globe.

That night, inspired by the energy in that room and McClendon's call to possibility, I wrote down goals I had once thought impossible. Among them: *"Stand on a global stage, helping thousands unlock their best selves."*

That one exercise in boundless ideation became the catalyst for everything that followed—years of resilience, discovery, and ultimately the creation of the *Must Goals* system and this very book.

What began as a private spark has since become the framework I am honored to share with you—the life-tested, research-backed process for moving your wildest possibilities from imagination to identity to real-world action. Now, my own deepest goal is to help you unlock and achieve your "musts"—with all the energy, science, and creativity this method can provide.

Reflection

- What is one dream or goal—however unlikely—that you once dismissed or set aside? Write about where it came from and why it might still matter today.

Why Start with Unlimited Possibility?

Scientific Rationale:

Real change starts when you let yourself think bigger and take away your usual limits. Osborn's "brainstorming" idea was about listing as many dreams and ideas as possible, without criticizing or holding back—even if they seem wild. Today, brain science shows that this "no limits" thinking helps your mind imagine new futures and connect ideas in creative ways (Andrews-Hanna et al., 2018; Christoff et al., 2018; Osborn, 1953).

Isaksen's research found that generating many ideas leads to better results, and that people are much more creative when they feel safe to share anything—even wild ideas. When you let go of judging yourself or your ideas, you are much more likely to discover your most exciting and meaningful dreams (Isaksen, 1998).

Blue-Sky Thinking: Radical Possibility for Breakthroughs

"*Blue-sky thinking*" invites you to imagine freely—without limits, boundaries, or practicality. It is the creative space where anything is possible. In creativity research, this approach is known to activate **divergent thinking**, the brain's ability to generate many ideas and uncover possibilities that usually stay buried under everyday constraints (Sawyer, 2012).

As you *dreamstorm*, experiment with this question:

- **"What would I pursue if absolutely anything were possible?"**

Suspend judgment. Ignore the how. Let your imagination stretch beyond the edges of your current life and identity. Blue-sky thinking often reveals the **larger, bolder, more authentic** ambitions that later become your *Must Goals*—visions that only emerge when the mind is truly free.

Once the sky has opened, *then* you can refine, shape, and structure those ideas into aligned, actionable goals.

Blue-sky first. Strategy second.

The Dreamstorming Steps

Dreamstorming is your dedicated space to imagine without limits—where possibility takes the lead and practicality waits its turn. Use these steps to unlock your boldest ideas and uncover the goals your deeper self is already reaching for.

1. Set Apart Space

Give yourself 10–15 minutes without interruptions.

2. Choose Your Medium

Pick the format that helps you think most freely:

- Free-writing
- Sketching
- Voice-recording
- Mind-mapping

There is no "right way"—only the way that unleashes ideas.

3. Drop All Censorship

For this window, write down every dream, every idea, every outrageous wish.

No filtering. No practicality. No "how."

Impossible ideas welcome.

4. Use Expansive Thinking

Spark new pathways by asking questions rooted in your values, desires, and untapped potential.

These questions bypass logic and speak directly to imagination.

5. Cluster by Theme

When time is up, gently scan what you wrote.

Sort or circle ideas by:

- Excitement
- Your *Must Circle of Life* Domain (health, relationships, finance, etc.)
- Emotional pull or resonance

But still—no critique. Only recognition.

6. Highlight the Energy Points

Circle ideas that spark emotion—these are your true "musts

A flowchart illustrating the Dreamstorming process:

DREAMSTORM WORKFLOW
—From Dump to Decision

1. Unfiltered Dump:
10-15 minutes of free writing
No Limits, no logic, no edits
Capture every idea and desire

⬇

2. Cluster By Energy/Theme
Group ideas by excitement, circle of life domain, or emotional pull
Still no critique - just sorting

⬇

3. Prioritize Resonance
Highlight ideas that spark joy, fear, longing, or curiosity
These "energy hits" hint at your authentic Must Goals

⬇

4. First Action Steps
Select 1-2 top ideas
Break them into Micro-Goals
Start with simple actions to build momentum

A Micro-Goal (as more fully discussed later) is a small, manageable, and clearly defined action step that contributes directly to achieving a larger, long-term goal. Micro-goals break ambitious aspirations into actionable tasks that you can start right now, making progress feel possible and building momentum through quick, measurable wins.

Emotional Connections: Why Feelings Matter

Emotion is what transforms a mere possibility into a compelling goal. Science shows goals become "sticky" and memorable when they're emotionally charged. If you feel excitement, hope, or even fear about a goal, you're far more likely to pursue it persistently.

THE GOLDEN BUCKET EXERCISE

Unlock Your Wildest, Wisest Goals

Purpose:

To free your imagination from limits so your deepest desires can surface—unfiltered, unedited, and uncensored.

Instructions:

- Set a timer for 10 minutes.
- Write without judging or stopping, using this prompt:

    "If absolutely anything were possible—what would my ideal life look like in health, relationships, career, finances, creativity, lifestyle, spirituality, and legacy?"
- No idea is too large or improbable. Let it all pour out.

Why It Works:

This exercise bypasses the inner critic, taps imaginative neural networks, and reveals the desires your identity is already leaning toward.

Remember:

Do not edit *the* gold as it comes.
Just let the bucket fill.

> **The 20-Idea Method**
>
> Try generating 20 solutions to a single challenge or question. Only after the obvious ideas are recorded do the most creative solutions appear

Visualization for Motivation

Vividly imagine yourself moving toward a seemingly unreachable goal. Engage the senses—what do you see, hear, feel? Science confirms that visualizing the process (not just the finish line) builds motivation and confidence.

Why Visualization Works:

Studies show that engaging your senses and picturing yourself taking real steps toward a goal "trains" your brain for action, lowers anxiety, and releases dopamine to boost energy, focus, and long-term commitment (Pham & Taylor, 1999; Townsend & Liu, 2012). This effect is strongest when you imagine the process, not just the prize.

Table: Dreamstorm by Must Circle of Life Domain

Domain	Sample Prompts
Health	"If my body had no limits, what would I do or experience?"
Relationships	"If I could deepen one connection, what would that look like?"
Career	"If I could pursue any career or project, regardless of risk, what is it?"
Finances	"If money were infinite, how would I use it meaningfully?"
Personal Growth	"If I could learn one new skill instantly, what would it be?"
Spirituality	"If I could embody one virtue fully, which would I choose?"
Community	"If I could change one thing for my community, what would it be?"

Quick Self-Review

- Review your dreamstorming notes.
- Highlight the ideas with the strongest emotion.
- Prepare your top 3 "must" goals for the next chapter, where prioritizing and refining begin.

Chapter Recap: Unlimited "Goal Ideation" and "Dreamstorming"

Big Idea

Exploring unlimited possibilities through science-based dreamstorming lets you generate goals that truly match your values, energy, and dreams—rather than settling for what others say you "should" want. This chapter took you from uninhibited brainstorming to practical, emotionally charged ideas you can pursue.

Key Insights:

Unlimited Possibility

- Free-flow brainstorming removes limits and unlocks creativity.
- Quantity matters—more ideas lead to better breakthroughs and higher chances of success.

Dreamstorming Method

- Use timed "idea dumps," value-based prompts, and a "no self-censorship" rule to surface your best ideas.
- Organize and refine ideas visually, such as mind maps or flowcharts, to move toward action.

Guided Imagination

- Curated prompts for every life domain (health, relationships, career, finances, etc.) ensure a well-rounded exploration.
- Track which ideas spark your strongest emotional reactions, and prioritize what excites you most.

Visualization for Energy and Motivation

- Picture your goals step-by-step—see yourself in action, not just enjoying the end result.
- Reinforce results using journaling, vision boards, and affirmations for ongoing momentum.

Emotional Connections

- Emotion transforms "possible" into "must"—linking your goals to your story, identity, and motivation.
- Use journaling to connect feelings with your biggest dreams and recognize which ones matter most.

Integration and Next Steps

- Reflect and sort your top ideas—focus on the ones with the most energy and meaning.
- Get ready for the next chapter: filtering, ranking, and defining your true Must Goals.

Quick Self-Review Table

Section	My Top Learning/Idea	Prompts That Resonated	Most Exciting Goals	Possibility
Dreamstorming				
Imagination				
Visualization				
Emotion				

Action Steps

- Review your dreamstorming notes—highlight goals with the strongest emotion and meaning.
- Identify up to three "must" goals for deeper work in the next chapter.
- Schedule a time for daily visualizations and quick reflections.

Having generated your biggest dreams and ideas, now we'll turn those into foundation-aligned, practical goals using the **"I AM SMART TO ACT goal setting method."**

CHAPTER 11

Must Goal Setting Foundations

"Setting goals is the first step in turning the invisible into the visible."
—Tony Robbins

"The great danger for most of us lies not in setting our aim too high and falling short; but in setting our aim too low, and achieving our mark."
—Michelangelo

As a young man, I was in the audience when Zig Ziglar, with the warmth of his charming southern drawl, captivated us with this story.

> In a quaint village nestled among rolling hills, there lived an archer of great renown. Wherever he went, he amazed the locals with his seemingly supernatural ability to hit the bullseye every single time. People would gather from far and wide to witness his incredible feats of marksmanship.
>
> The archer would stride confidently into the village square, bow in hand, and a quiver of arrows slung

across his back. With a flourish, he'd pull an arrow, draw his bow, and let it fly. Thwack! The arrow would embed itself in a nearby tree, barn, or fence post. From a distance, the crowd would hold its breath in anticipation. Then, with a mischievous twinkle in his eye, the archer would saunter over to where his arrow had landed. He'd pull out a small cloth from his pocket and carefully wipe the area around the arrow, claiming he was cleaning off any debris that might have affected his shot. The villagers would nod in appreciation of his attention to detail.

This went on for years, with the archer's reputation growing with each perfect shot. People marveled at his consistency and skill, never questioning how he managed to hit the bullseye every time, regardless of the target.

One day, a wise old woman in the village decided to follow the archer after one of his performances. As she watched from afar, she saw him pull out a small pot of paint and a brush from his pocket. With great ceremony, he carefully painted a perfect, brilliantly red bullseye circle around the arrow he had just shot.

The old woman couldn't help but chuckle at the clever deception and the villagers' willingness to believe in this "magical" accuracy. She realized that the archer had been creating his own false success all along, adjusting his targets to match his results rather than truly improving his skill.

Zig Ziglar used the archer's story to illustrate a profound point about how many of us approach goal setting in our lives. He observed that, unfortunately, most of us treat our goals much like the deceptive archer in the tale. We often believe we have clear objectives in mind, but in reality, we're simply painting targets around wherever our arrows of effort happen to land. Different versions of this story have been told throughout the millennia. In fact, one version dates to the *Huainanzi*, a Chinese philosophical text from the second century BCE. This ageless wisdom still applies today.

This approach to life and goal setting is haphazard at best. We convince ourselves we're living with intention and purpose when, in fact, we're merely justifying our random actions after the fact. By doing so, we fail to take control of our destiny or aim for specific, meaningful targets in life.

The Archer's Illusion: A Lesson on Real Goal Setting

To avoid the trap of painting targets around random results, every Must Goal must be clear, specific, and measurable—so we pursue what truly matters and know with certainty when we've reached it.

Ziglar emphasized that true success requires a different approach. Instead of retroactively defining our goals based on our actions, we need to develop the necessary skills in goal setting. This involves carefully contemplating our true desired destinations before we take action. By clearly defining our targets first, we can then align our efforts and develop Must Skills needed to hit those marks consistently.

Must Skills are the critical abilities and knowledge you must acquire to hit your targets and fulfill your purpose consistently. They are more than desirable—they are essential for aligning your actions with core values and purpose. By identifying and mastering these skills, every step you take moves you closer to authentic growth, transforming your goals from mere aspirations into requirements for your life's journey.

By integrating your *musts* into your goal-setting process, you transform your goals from mere aspirations into essential components of your life's journey, propelling you toward a future that is authentic, meaningful, and purposeful. This approach to goal setting is not just about achieving success; it is about living a life that reflects your deepest aspirations and values, where every action and decision aligns with your Must Purpose.

Ziglar urges us to be more deliberate and proactive in shaping our lives. By mastering the art of goal setting, we can take control of our destiny and ensure that our efforts are directed toward achieving the specific outcomes we truly desire rather than simply rationalizing whatever results we happen to achieve. Ziglar asks us this profound question: "How can we hit a target that we do not have?"

Goals are the beacons that guide our actions, infusing our lives with direction and purpose. They are the bridge between our present state and the future we aspire to create. In this chapter, we will explore the profound impact of goal setting on our lives, drawing from the wisdom of historical studies, contemporary thought leaders, and scientific research. We will also reflect on how to integrate these principles into every aspect of our lives, as reflected in the Circle of Life. Despite compelling evidence that proper goal-setting strategies can significantly enhance one's life across all areas, surprisingly few people take advantage of this powerful tool. This paradox stems from various factors, including a lack of awareness, fear of failure, and comfort with the status quo, perceived complexity, and lack of self-belief.

This chapter will help you overcome these obstacles and join the elite group of goal-setters who consistently achieve their most ambitious aspirations. We will equip you with the knowledge and tools to harness the full potential of goal setting by addressing common barriers and providing practical strategies. You will learn how to transform goal-setting from a potentially daunting task into a natural, empowering practice that not only gives you a competitive advantage in life but also aligns your actions with your deepest purpose. Through this process, you will discover how to use goal setting as a compass for personal growth and professional success and, ultimately, to become the person you are meant to be.

Effective Goal Setting

To elevate your results, effective goal setting cannot exist in isolation—it must be grounded in who you are and who you aspire to become. This means integrating your Must Mindset, Must Core Beliefs, Must Personal Narrative, Must Values, Must Standards, and Must Purpose from the outset. When your goals are deeply rooted in this foundation, they become authentic drivers of growth and transformation, not just arbitrary targets.

Understanding the theoretical "why" of goal setting—its scientific support and proven impact—is essential. However, power lies not only in knowing but in doing. You bridge the gap between intention and transformation by tying knowledge to Must Actions, ensuring goals move from lofty aspirations to specific, measurable steps. In the end, fulfillment and change only unfold through action, not just imagination.

Set Goals That Reflect Your Must Values

For each Must Value, set a goal that actively demonstrates how you will embody that value in your daily life. For example, if excellence is a Must Value, a related goal might be to continuously improve your professional skills through targeted learning or seeking mentorship. If compassion is core, you might set a goal to volunteer regularly or to practice daily empathetic interactions.

Each goal should be specific and actionable, with clear steps that directly connect to your values and identity.

Review and Reflect

After setting these goals, step back and consider how they fit with your overall sense of purpose:

- "Are these goals helping me become the person I want to be? Do they resonate with my purpose and direction?"

Make adjustments as needed to ensure alignment. This reflective step keeps your goals from becoming mere to-do items and helps them remain authentic commitments grounded in who you are.

Ongoing Alignment and Adaptive Change

True value-driven goal setting is not a one-time event, but a life-long process. As you evolve, revisit your goals regularly—monthly or quarterly—and reflect on whether they still honor your Must Values and authentic aspirations.

Release or revise goals that have lost meaning or no longer serve your highest aims, as recommended by Arthur Brooks and supported by the latest psychological research. Letting go of goals that no longer align is not failure—it's necessary adaptation. This intentional disengagement frees up energy for new growth and further aligns your path with your deepest priorities (Brooks & Winfrey, 2023; Wrosch et al., 2007).

The Science of Goal Setting

Goal setting is rooted in centuries of wisdom: ancient philosophers like Aristotle spoke of telos, our ultimate aim, while Epictetus urged, "First say to yourself what you would be; and then do what you have to do." Today, modern science confirms what the ancients intuited—clear, purposeful goals drive meaningful achievement.

Though stories of famous Yale and Harvard goal-setting studies persist, neither institution has any record of such studies ever taking place. Instead, credible research comes from Dr. Gail Matthews at Dominican University. Her study found that people who wrote down their goals and shared them with others were 42% more likely to achieve their goals, underscoring the power of written intention and social accountability (Matthews, 2015).

Further, Locke and Latham's foundational research demonstrates that specific, challenging goals lead to higher performance than vague or easy ones, as long as individuals are committed and capable. Ambitious but clear targets energize effort and sustain motivation across work, life, and learning (Locke & Latham, 1990, 2002, 2013).

Beyond performance goals, learning goals—focused on skill acquisition and growth—are especially powerful when facing new or complex challenges. Studies show that mastering new abilities through process goals not only boosts results but also builds resilience and adaptability (Grant Halvorson, 2010; Dweck, 2006; Seijts & Latham, 2012, 2019).

Key ingredients to successful goal pursuit include:

- Writing down goals for clarity and focus.
- Regularly monitoring progress and adjusting as needed (Harkin et al., 2016).
- Using feedback and accountability to stay on track.
- Combining outcome goals with learning goals for long-term fulfillment and adaptability.

Recent research (Bird et al., 2023) confirms that effective goal achievement is a dynamic, personalized process of setting targets, tracking progress, and adapting along the way—not a rigid formula. Neuroscience adds that making progress toward a goal activates the brain's reward system, providing the drive and satisfaction needed to keep going.

Across all fields, professional, academic, or personal, goal-setting offers a proven path to greater success, satisfaction, and personal growth. When you set goals rooted in your values and take intentional steps, you unlock the science-backed potential for lasting achievement.

Group Goals and Collaborative Success

Beyond personal goal setting, research shows that establishing shared goals within teams or organizations significantly boosts motivation, effort, and alignment. When everyone works toward clear, collective objectives, accountability and progress naturally improve (Locke & Latham, 2019). Effective collaboration is further strengthened by open communication—regularly sharing updates, challenges, and feedback—so group members can coordinate efforts, learn from one another, and adapt together (Salas et al., 2017). By setting measurable team-level goals and facilitating ongoing feedback and recognition, organizations harness their collective strengths and build high-performing, resilient teams (Lee et al., 2015).

The High-Performance Cycle

Long-term success is built not on isolated actions, but on a continuous process of goal setting, action, feedback, and reward—a cycle known as the High-Performance Cycle (Locke & Latham, 2019). Setting clear goals prompts purposeful effort, while regular feedback enables learning and adjustment. Achieving goals creates both external rewards and a sense of satisfaction, which then fuels fresh motivation and commitment. By deliberately tracking milestones and celebrating progress, you create a positive feedback loop that drives sustained high performance, adaptability, and growth (Vogel & Büsch, 2021).

Best Practices in Goal Setting

Research and real-world wisdom show that effective goal setting is rooted in a few core practices: clarity, commitment, and identity alignment. Here is what science and top experts recommend:

Write Down Your Goals

Numerous studies—including Dr. Gail Matthews's 2015 research—prove you are 42% more likely to achieve goals that are written down. Productivity expert Brian Tracy also champions the daily writing and review of goals, emphasizing that this habit crystallizes your intent, strengthens your focus, and keeps your objectives front and center. If goals shift, update your list immediately and recommit each day for lasting alignment and progress (Tracy, 2006, 2015, 2025).

Be Specific and Measurable

Vague goals like "be successful" are weaker than concrete aims, such as "increase my annual income by 20% in the next year." Following the SMART framework—Specific, Measurable, Achievable, Relevant, Time-bound—makes your goals actionable and trackable, as first articulated by George Doran in 1981.

Link Goals to Meaning

Recent frameworks and thought leaders, including Michael Hyatt, remind us that goals are not just about compliance—they should stretch us, inspire us, and reflect our most important values. Clarity on your "why" boosts intrinsic motivation and fuel for long-term achievement (Deci & Ryan; Hyatt, 2021).

Use the I AM SMART TO ACT Goals Method

The **I AM SMART TO ACT Goals Method** you learned earlier is your guiding framework here. Begin from your "I AM" identity, then shape each Must Goal using that structure so it stays aligned, specific, and ready to act on.

Visualization: Making Goals Come Alive

Visualization—mentally rehearsing success before it happens—is a science-backed practice that enhances performance, focus, and goal achievement. By vividly imagining your goals as already achieved, you engage your brain's neural pathways and reticular activating system (RAS), making success feel more natural and priming you to notice relevant opportunities. Elite athletes, artists, and entrepreneurs—including Olympic swimmers like Michael Phelps and leaders like Oprah Winfrey—credit visualization as a cornerstone of their success.

Best Practices

- Be specific and sensory: Visualize not just the outcome, but the key steps. Engage all your senses to make the vision as genuine and emotionally meaningful as possible.

- Imagine in the present: Picture your goal as if it is happening now to build confidence and drive motivated action.

- Repeat consistently: Regular practice strengthens neural connections, builds confidence, and conditions your mind for success.

- Pair with affirmations: Combine visualization with identity-based statements (for example, "I am prepared and capable") to reinforce belief and drive.

- Use a vision board: Creating a visual representation of your goals keeps them top of mind and boosts accountability. Research indicates that people who write down their goals and keep them visible are significantly more likely to achieve them.

Scientific studies suggest that process-focused visualization—mentally rehearsing the key actions and strategies—produces better results than visualizing only the final outcome. This approach increases motivation, reduces anxiety, and prepares you to succeed in high-pressure situations, from public speaking to competition.

Visualization is not a substitute for action, but a powerful complement. You continuously align your brain, habits, and environment with the outcomes you truly desire by making your vision concrete and pairing it with daily effort.

The Power of Affirmations: From Satire to Science

Affirmations often evoke both inspiration and skepticism. One iconic example is Al Franken's Saturday Night Live character, Stuart Smalley, who looks in the mirror and earnestly declares: "I'm good enough, I'm smart enough, and doggone it, people like me!" This skit humorously exaggerates the use of affirmations and pokes fun at self-help culture, but it also raises a serious question: do affirmations help us achieve our goals?

The Science Behind Affirmations

When practiced intentionally, affirmations are more than feel-good slogans—they are grounded in the principles of cognitive behavioral therapy (CBT). Regularly repeating realistic, positive statements helps rewire thought patterns and reinforces new beliefs through neuroplasticity. Studies have shown that affirmations can reduce stress, increase resilience, activate the brain's reward centers, and improve performance, especially when combating negative self-talk or building new habits.

For best results, affirmations should be realistic and believable. Ground your statements in qualities and behaviors you can grow into. For example, try "I am building my confidence each day" instead of "I am a millionaire," especially if that does not feel authentic to you.

How to Use Affirmations Effectively

1. **Be Specific and Positive:** Focus on the result you want, framed positively. For instance, "I am resourceful and resilient in challenges."
2. **Align with Values and Goals:** Make your affirmation meaningful by connecting it to your Must Values and long-term aspirations.
3. **Use Present Tense:** Phrase statements as if they're true now: "I am learning and improving daily."
4. **Repeat Consistently:** Practice daily to reinforce these beliefs, just as you would with visualization or any skill.
5. **Pair With Visualization:** Visualize yourself living your affirmation—see yourself as a capable leader, a caring friend, a skilled communicator, etc.—to amplify the effect.

When you choose believable, value-driven affirmations and use them regularly, you harness both humor and science to foster genuine growth and resilience.

PERSISTENT ACTION: REPEAT, REVISE, REFINE

Tracy asserts that the key to achieving any goal is a consistent daily action. He encourages setting aside time each day to work on your most important goals, no matter how small the step. This persistent effort, compounded over time, leads to significant results. Tracy reminds us that obstacles and setbacks are inevitable, but persistence is what separates those who achieve their goals from those who do not.

It's essential to recognize that setting goals is only the first step in achieving success. The real challenge lies in creating a plan to achieve those goals and maintaining the momentum needed to see them through to completion. This is where persistent action comes into play—a crucial process that involves not only setting goals but also consistently revisiting and refining them as progress is made. By embracing this mindset, you ensure that your goals remain aligned with your evolving aspirations and that every step you take moves you closer to realizing your vision.

In this final part of our goal-setting journey, we will delve into the strategies that make persistent action effective. This includes reverse engineering your goals to break them down into manageable steps, setting micro goals that provide immediate motivation and feedback, and establishing stretch goals that challenge you to grow beyond your current limits. By integrating these techniques into your goal-achieving process, you create a dynamic framework that adapts to your growth and ensures that every effort you make is purposeful and impactful. This approach transforms goal setting from a static exercise into a living, breathing process that propels you toward your highest potential.

Persistent Action: Repeat, Revise, Refine

Brian Tracy teaches that the key to achieving any goal is persistent, daily action. Even small efforts, compounded over time, lead to extraordinary results. True achievers are not those who never face setbacks, but those who consistently move forward despite them. Setting goals is only the beginning; success comes from turning aspirations into daily practices, adapting your approach, and keeping momentum alive.

The Power of Micro Goals

Micro goals are the daily, manageable steps that turn overwhelming ambitions into achievable realities. These tiny wins fuel motivation, reinforce good habits, and create immediate feedback loops. For example:

e, writing a book becomes possible when you set a micro goal of writing just 500 words each day. In fitness, micro goals could include a 10-minute walk or preparing one healthy meal per day. The value lies in the daily repetition and attainable scale—each completed micro-goal builds confidence and creates momentum.

Why Micro Goals Work:

- They reduce overwhelm and remove the excuse of not having time or bandwidth.
- Each completion delivers a dopamine "win," making you want to repeat the positive behavior.
- Tracking and celebrating micro progress keeps your focus sharp and your motivation high.

The Impact of Stretch Goals

While micro goals provide the building blocks, stretch goals are the catalysts for real transformation. Stretch goals are ambitious, sometimes audacious targets designed to push beyond your comfort zone and spur creative thinking. They require you to develop new skills and adopt innovative strategies.

Why Stretch Goals Are Crucial:

- They ignite creativity—forcing you to find new ways and resources.
- Even if partly reached, they drive you further than safe, easily attainable goals.

- They test your limits, strengthen resilience, and unlock hidden potential.

Example:

In business, a stretch goal might be to double annual revenue in one year. If you are a writer, it could be landing a national speaking slot. Even if you fall short, the effort will spark unforeseen growth and connections.

Goal Stacking and Sequencing: Making Your Must Goals Work Together

Once you have a set of clear Must Goals, the next challenge is deciding what to do first and how they can support each other. Not all goals should be pursued at the same intensity at the same time. Some work best as foundations that make other goals easier.

A simple way to do this is to think in terms of sequencing and stacking:

- Sequencing means choosing the order: Which Must Goal comes first, second, and third.
- Stacking means designing goals so that progress on one creates momentum for others (keystone goals).

Ask yourself:

- Which Must Goal, if achieved or significantly advanced in the next 3–6 months, would make progress in other domains easier?
- Which daily or weekly habit would act as a keystone—a small change that improves multiple areas at once (for example, better sleep, improving health, mood, focus, and relationships)?
- Which goals are truly time-sensitive, and which can be deliberately placed in a "next wave" without guilt?

From there, you can:

1. Choose 1–3 primary Must Goals as your current focus.
2. Identify supporting habits or "stacked" goals that naturally ride along with those primaries.
3. Consciously park the rest as later-wave goals, not abandoned, but scheduled for a future season.

Goal stacking and sequencing protect you from overload. Instead of trying to do everything at once, you are designing a wise order in which your Must Goals build on each other and your effort compounds over time.

Goal stacking and sequencing can become more complex as the number of Must Goals grows and your life circumstances change. For additional guidance and a practical worksheet to map and prioritize your own Must Goals over time, visit *MustGoals.com/Resources*.

Caution: Avoiding Goal Setting Overload

Goal setting can be exciting, but it's easy to fall into the trap of taking on too much at once. Trying to change everything in every area can quickly lead to overwhelm, frustration, or even burnout.

Remember: Lasting progress comes from focus, not from scattering your energy.

What to do instead:

- Choose just one or two "Must" goals to prioritize in this season.
- Focus your actions and reflection on these chosen goals until you feel real momentum and confidence.
- Use the other domains as inspiration, and map them for later—resist the urge to tackle everything now.

When you feel tempted to add more, pause and ask: "Is this the right time? Will adding another goal dilute my commitment to what matters most?"

Clarity and commitment lead to real change. Protect your focus and give your best energy to a single, meaningful change before moving on.

Bringing It All Together

- **Reverse Engineer:** Visualize your ultimate goal, then break it into milestones and micro goals—each a daily or weekly step.
- **Micro Goals:** Make progress every day, create and track micro wins, and celebrate small achievements.
- **Stretch Goals:** Challenge yourself to reach higher, think bolder, and act bigger than your comfort zone allows.
- **Persistent Review:** Regularly assess your steps and results, revising your approach to adapt to new information and keep advancing.
- **Must Actions**: Ensure all actions are aligned with your core values and standards, making progress meaningful and sustainable.
- **Goal Stacking and Sequencing:** Intentionally choose which Must Goals come first, which can wait for a later season, and which keystone habits will make progress in multiple domains easier at the same time.

Do This Now – Micro and Stretch Practice

- Choose one Must Goal you have already written and define a single Must Micro-Goal you can complete today or within the next 24 hours.
- Schedule that micro-goal on your calendar at a specific time, as if it were a nonnegotiable appointment.

- Write one Stretch Goal connected to the same Must Goal—something that feels bold but exciting—and note one first step you will take toward it this week.

_____

_____

_____

By weaving persistence, micro goals, and stretch goals into your daily practice, you create a dynamic, adaptive framework for outstanding achievement—and ensure your journey always moves in the direction of your biggest vision

Navigating Obstacles: Common Pitfalls in Goal Setting

Goal setting is a proven roadmap for growth, but the journey is rarely smooth. Recognizing and addressing common pitfalls increases your odds of success and keeps you on track, no matter what challenges arise.

Vague Goals: The Trap of Ambiguity

One of the biggest mistakes is setting goals that are too vague—like "be healthier" or "find success." Without specificity, you cannot measure progress or maintain motivation. To fix this, use the **I AM SMART TO ACT** criteria: turn "be healthier" into "exercise 30 minutes, five times a week," or "reduce sugar intake by 50% in three months." The clearer your target is, the clearer your steps—and the greater your chances of achievement.

Lack of Flexibility: The Rigidity Dilemma

Persistence is vital, but so is adaptability. Life changes, obstacles arise, or your priorities may shift. If you hold too rigidly to outdated goals, frustration and burnout can set in. Tracy teaches that regular goal reviews allow you to adapt—refining or even replacing goals so they stay relevant and motivating. Flexibility is a strength: it keeps you resilient, aligned with your values, and open to new opportunities.

Overemphasis on Outcomes

Focusing only on the result can undermine your progress, especially when setbacks occur or success takes longer than expected. Outcome obsession ignores the value of consistent daily action—the process that ultimately creates results. Instead, embrace a process-oriented mindset: celebrate micro wins, learn from setbacks, and find satisfaction in the journey as much as the destination. This approach keeps you motivated, fosters growth, and helps you thrive even when challenges arise.

By confronting and correcting these pitfalls—aiming for clarity, practicing flexibility, and embracing daily process—you turn obstacles into stepping stones on the path to meaningful achievement.

Bridging Identity and Purpose: Your Next Steps

As you have discovered, the real power of goal setting comes from blending creative vision with clear, structured action—rooted in your authentic identity. The I AM SMART TO ACT framework starts with "I AM" (who you are and what you stand for), and applies the SMART criteria to ensure each Must Goal is truly actionable and measurable, not just inspirational.

Before you create goals for each domain of your life, permit yourself to dream expansively. You will be guided through structured "Dreamstorming" and powerful goal ideation exercises in Chapter 9, where you will learn how to capture your wildest aspirations, then clarify and organize them for maximum impact.

As we move into the next part of this journey, you will explore Must Goals across each of the seven core domains in the Must Circle of

Life—such as health, relationships, career, finances, growth, spirituality, and community. This holistic approach empowers you to achieve meaningful, lasting change in every area that matters.

Reflection and Personal Integration

Take a moment to reflect: Are your goals clear, intentional, and aligned with your deepest values and Must Purpose? Are you using visualization, affirmation, and persistent action to prepare for both the challenges and opportunities ahead? Remember that balanced, whole-person goal setting creates not just achievement, but a life of meaning and fulfillment.

In the words of Brian Tracy, "Your ability to set goals is the master skill of success." Let this foundation chapter inspire you to set purposeful goals in all areas of your life and pursue them with clarity, creativity, and disciplined action—transforming who you are, what you do, and the legacy you create.

Chapter 10 Recap:
The Foundations of Goal Setting

Key Insights:

- Unclear, "painted-target" goals keep us stuck—clarity, specificity, and measurement unlock real results.
- Success begins with who you are—root your goals in your Must Mindset, values, and purpose, then turn intention into measurable Must Actions.
- Science shows: writing down goals, regularly reviewing progress, and using feedback dramatically boost achievement.
- Balance outcome focus with daily process—celebrate micro goals, build momentum, and adapt flexibly as life changes.
- Visualization and affirmations reinforce your identity and prime your mind and actions for achievement.
- Meaningful goals are not static—to flourish, continually review, release, and realign your goals with your deepest aspirations and current reality.

Best Practices:

- Write detailed, value-driven, time-bound goals and review them often.
- Take persistent daily action—use micro goals for momentum and stretch goals for growth.
- Use visualization, affirmations, and vision boards to activate your subconscious and sustain motivation.
- Turn setbacks into learning moments by focusing on process, not just the end result.

Your Next Step:

- Leverage the I AM SMART TO ACT method to translate your wildest dreams into actionable, identity-aligned Must Goals.

- Prepare to apply this process—starting with Health & Vitality—in each domain of your Must Circle of Life.

Do This Now

- Write three Must Goals using the I AM SMART TO ACT Goals Method, each in a different life domain from your Circle of Life.

- Choose one of those three to focus on first in this season, and star it in your notes.

- Break that starred Must Goal into a single Must Micro-Goal you can complete in the next 24 hours.

Reflection

- Are your current goals clear, measurable, and rooted in your authentic self?

- What is one micro action you'll take today to move a Must Goal forward?

"Your ability to set goals is the master skill of success."
— Brian Tracy

Use this recap to anchor your understanding and as a launching pad for setting truly transformative Must Goals across every area of your life.

CHAPTER 12

Must Health & Vitality Goals – The Energy of Excellence

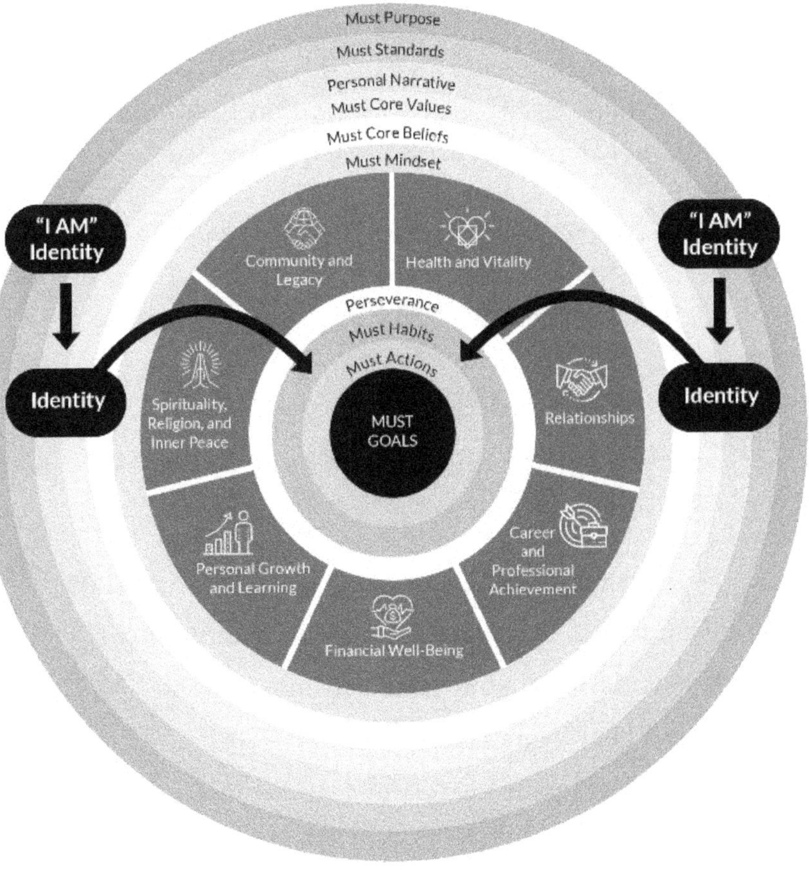

Health & Vitality Goals – The Energy of Excellence

Health is not just about fitness or appearance—it's about creating a body that sustains your purpose. Without energy, even your biggest dreams can't take shape. In the Must System, health means aligning your daily actions with the mission your soul is called to live. When your body is energized, your mind is sharper, and your confidence is high.

Quick Tip: Access free journaling templates at www.MustGoals.com/Resources and www.MustBook.net/Resources to help you track this process.

The Must Lens on Health

In this system, health is about purposeful discipline—not perfection or guilt. Your Must Health Goals should flow from who you decide you must be, not from comparison or outside pressure.

This chapter helps you clarify the building blocks of your health goals. Reflect on each foundational area, connect it to your vision, and shape goals that are truly authentic.

Kickstart Your Health Today

Ready for change? Start now—one small step is all it takes. Choose at least one action below and do it today:

- **Drink a full glass of water first thing this morning.**
- **Take a brisk 10-minute walk (indoors or outdoors).**
- **Set an alarm for your ideal bedtime tonight.**
- **Prep a healthy meal or snack.**
- **Write down your top health value or intention on a sticky note and place it where you'll see it.**
- **Take five slow, mindful breaths whenever you feel tense.**

Why this works:

The science is clear: small, doable steps build real momentum. The key isn't perfection, it's movement. Each success makes the next choice easier and more automatic.

Tip:

Check the box once you complete your action and celebrate the win! Your Must Health journey starts now—with energy, confidence, and simplicity.

Jenna's One-Day Turnaround

Jenna always felt stuck when it came to health. She worried that making lasting changes required drastic routines and endless motivation. Inspired by the Must Goals "Kickstart" box, she chose one simple step: going to bed 30 minutes earlier three nights in a row.

What happened next surprised her. "I woke up more refreshed—and it gave me the push I needed to go for a morning walk," Jenna says. "Something shifted. That first small win—just changing my bedtime—made me believe a bigger change was possible."

Jenna didn't overhaul her life overnight. She stacked small wins: a glass of water in the morning, a mindful meal at lunch. Each action made the next one easier. "Now I review my goals every Sunday with my daughter. We celebrate progress, talk about setbacks, and just keep going."

Takeaway:

Real change starts with one doable step. Even the smallest action can spark the momentum for larger, lasting results. Celebrate each win—progress is built, one choice at a time.

Reflect and Align: Your Must Foundations

Must Core Beliefs

Reflect and jot down your beliefs about your health and potential:

- What do I believe about my ability to live with sustained energy?
- What old beliefs no longer serve me, and which new ones am I ready to claim?
- How do my beliefs reflect my Must identity?

Must Core Values

Identify the values that guide your care and energy:

- Which values matter most for my health (strength, discipline, self-respect, resilience)?
- Do my habits honor these values?
- What boundaries will help protect my energy?

Must Personal Narrative

Rewrite your health story for possibility:

- What story have I been telling myself?
- How has this limited my progress?
- If I write a new story of strength and possibility, what will change?

Must Standards

Set your nonnegotiable floor for self-care:

- What basic practices should always be proper for my health?
- How will I hold myself accountable, and realign when I slip?

Must Purpose

Connect effort to meaning:

- How does my physical health support my greater purpose?
- What becomes possible if I treat my health as a sacred trust?

You'll avoid repetition and move efficiently from reflection into meaningful action by focusing on these foundations. Every section ties directly to identity, energy, and daily choices—making this chapter concise, engaging, and practical for Must readers.

Your Health Vision: Unlimited Possibility Exercise

After reflecting on your Must Foundations, give yourself a moment of creative freedom. Imagine that there are no barriers—no limits of time, money, energy, or possibility.

Ask yourself:

If anything were possible, what would health and vitality look and feel like in my life?

What kinds of experiences, states, or achievements would I create for myself?

Now, write freely—no censoring, no self-doubt, no "buts" or "can'ts." List absolutely everything you want in the arena of health and vitality, even if it seems bold, big, or unconventional.

This is your Golden Bucket—a pool of all potential dreams and desired experiences in this domain.

Turning Vision into Aligned Action

1. **Review:**

    Look over your Golden Bucket list. Highlight the ideas that resonate most strongly with your core beliefs, values, personal narrative, standards, and purpose.

2. **Prioritize:**

    Choose which goals align most directly with the life you want and need to build now.

3. **Transform:**

    Take the top priorities and convert them, one by one, into I AM SMART TO ACT goals:

Identity alignment

I AM - Identity alignment

S: Specific

M: Measurable

A: Achievable

R: Relevant

T: Time-bound

TO ACT – Take your first step today.

Remember: Progress is made through small daily steps. When your actions are aligned with your Must Self, your goals become expressions of truth—not just willpower or ambition.

Pause to Reflect

Before you move forward:

- Picture what living at your healthiest, most vital feels like.

- Ask: How would increased health and energy strengthen my greater purpose?
- What ONE action can you commit to today that honors your health and supports your alignment?

(Examples: Go to bed 15 minutes earlier, take a walk outdoors, drink more water, plan a nourishing meal, practice mindful breathing.)

Health is not a distant achievement—it's the foundation you live from each day. As you honor your energy, you expand your purpose and create the capacity for all other successes.

Science Spotlight: Small Steps, Big Results

Recent studies in health psychology show that even modest, regular changes—like adding 10–20 minutes of daily movement—can significantly improve energy, mood, and cognitive performance, often more sustainably than sporadic intense workouts.

Research on sleep and nutrition confirms that small shifts, such as getting an extra hour of sleep or increasing daily fruit and vegetable intake, reduce stress, inflammation, and long-term disease risk while boosting well-being.

The takeaway: sustainable progress comes from stacking small wins, not grand gestures. Every healthy choice you make today creates a measurable, positive ripple—for your mind, your body, and your future.

Avatar Walkthrough: Mustang Sally—Health & Vitality

1. Must Mindset

Sally decides her health must change—she adopts a nonnegotiable mindset centered on possibility and believes she can improve.

Example: "I now believe my health and vitality are possible to transform—and I commit to lasting well-being with no excuses."

2. Must Core Beliefs

She identifies three essential beliefs that empower growth:

- "I am capable of getting stronger and more energetic at any age."
- "My body responds to what I practice each day."
- "Change is not just possible—it's expected when I act with intention."

3. Must Core Values

Sally chooses her top three values for this domain:

- Resilience
- Balance
- Self-care

4. Mustang Sally's Personal Narrative

Sally recognizes her old story was rooted in doubt, learned helplessness, and excuses. She consciously rewrites it:

Old narrative: "Nothing works; it's just my genetics."

New narrative: "Every small healthy choice builds a new story of energy, confidence, and self-respect."

5. Health and Vitality Standards

She sets nonnegotiable standards, such as:

- "I must exercise 30 minutes, five days per week."
- "I must prepare healthy meals at home at least five days a week."
- "I must sleep at least seven hours nightly."

6. Must Purpose

Sally defines her purpose for health as:

"To sustain vibrant energy so I can serve my family, express my creativity, and live with freedom—well into the future."

7. Dreamstorming

She unleashes a list of bold, limitless health possibilities:

- Run a 5k for the first time.
- Wake up energized and pain-free every day.
- Learn to cook nourishing meals she truly enjoys.

8. I AM SMART TO ACT Health Goals (Three Examples)

Must Goal 1: Health & Vitality (Walking)

"I am an energetic walker who values consistency, family leadership, and self-respect. I will walk at least 7,000 steps each weekday, tracked daily with my smartwatch, for the next 90 days. After every week, I will review my step totals and celebrate each completed week with a small reward—like listening to my favorite podcast, enjoying a special tea, or marking my tracker in a bold color. At 30 and 60 days, I'll pause to assess what's working, adjust anything that isn't, and recommit for the next month. If I miss a day, I'll pause, reflect on what happened, learn from the setback, and return to my goal the next morning with self-compassion—not judgment. By doing this, I will feel more energetic, build lasting confidence, and show my loved ones that belief and commitment bring transformation—for myself and those I influence."

I AM SMART TO ACT Breakdown:

- **Specific:** Walk 7,000 steps each weekday.
- **Measurable:** Steps tracked with smartwatch; weekly and monthly reviews.
- **Achievable:** Sally has time, equipment, and a manageable routine.
- **Relevant:** Increases daily energy, models commitment, and leadership in family health.
- **Time-bound:** For the next 90 days, with progress checkpoints at 30 and 60 days.
- **TO ACT:** Sally schedules her first intentional walk today.

Tip for Celebration:

- Each week you achieve your step goal, pick one way to celebrate—take a podcast walk, enjoy a nourishing snack, or highlight your tracker with your favorite color.

Bounce Back Plan:

- If life interrupts your routine, pause and reflect: What happened? What can you learn and adjust? Restart your steps the next day with kindness; the goal is progress, not perfection.

Must Goal 2: Health & Vitality (Nutrition)

"I am a creative home chef who prioritizes nourishment, family connection, and self-care. For the next 60 days, I will prepare a home-cooked dinner with vegetables at least four times per week. I will keep a simple dinner journal to record my progress and new recipes I enjoy. If meal planning gets tough, I will batch-cook on Sundays or ask for help. Each Sunday, I'll review my dinners, celebrate my successes by sharing my favorite dishes with family, try a

new recipe, or give myself a moment of gratitude for my effort. At 30 days, I'll assess what's working, refine my process if needed, and recommit for the following month. If I miss a night or get off track, I'll reflect without judgment, learn, and return to my plan the next day with self-kindness. By doing this, I will nourish my body, live my values, and inspire those I love as a healthy leader in my home."

I AM SMART TO ACT Breakdown:

- **Specific:** Prepare a vegetable-filled home-cooked dinner four nights per week.
- **Measurable:** Track each dinner in a journal; weekly and mid-point reviews.
- **Achievable:** Sally's meal-planning and batch-cooking make this doable.
- **Relevant:** Boosts self-care, family connection, and nutritional wellbeing.
- **Time-bound:** For 60 days, with a milestone review at 30 days.
- **TO ACT:** Sally plans this week's four dinners today.

Tip for Celebration:

- After a successful week, celebrate by trying a new recipe, inviting family to help cook, or sharing your favorite meal online.

Bounce Back Plan:

- If you miss dinner, pause and ask: What made this hard? What can I adjust for next week? Return to your cooking with kindness; the goal is steady nourishment.

Must Goal 3: Health & Vitality (Rest and Renewal):

"I am a well-rested person who values balance and recovery. For the next four weeks, I will be in bed with devices off by 10:30 PM at least five nights a week, tracked using a sleep log. I will check my progress every Saturday and, if I fall off, reset my bedtime routine with an evening wind-down alarm and a relaxing activity. Each week, I will reflect on how my improved sleep is boosting my daytime energy, so I continue to protect my rest and prioritize my wellbeing."

I AM SMART TO ACT **Breakdown:**

- **Specific:** Bedtime at 10:30 PM, devices off.
- **Measurable:** Tracked nights per week.
- **Achievable:** Sally can adjust her evening routine.
- **Relevant:** Enhances energy/balance.
- **Time-bound:** For four weeks
- **TO ACT:** Sally sets her wind-down alarm and prepares her bedtime routine tonight.

Transition: Now It's Your Turn

Having seen Mustang Sally's journey, you can now build your own path. Use the same structure to shape your foundational beliefs, values, story, standards, purpose, and measurable health goals.

Your Health & Vitality Must Goals

1. Must Mindset

My new, nonnegotiable mindset for health and vitality:

2. Must Core Beliefs Regarding Health & Vitality

a. _____

b. _____

c. _____

3. Must Core Values for Health & Vitality

a. _____

b. _____

c. _____

4. My Upgraded Health Narrative

Old story: _____

New narrative: _____

5. Health & Vitality Standards

a. _____

b. _____

c. _____

6. Must Purpose

My purpose for prioritizing health is:

_____

7. Dreamstorm (Bold Visions)

_____

_____

_____

8. My I AM SMART TO ACT Health Goals (3):

Goal 1: _____

Goal 2: _____

Goal 3: _____

Tip:

Remember to set weekly reviews to track progress, celebrate each win (big or small), and use your bounce-back plan whenever you need to reset—with self-kindness and renewed commitment. For more resources and printable templates, visit <u>www.MustGoals.com/Resources</u>.

The Power of Peer Support

Peer Support: Multiply Your Must Momentum

Building lasting change is easier—and more enjoyable—when you have someone in your corner. Consider sharing your top Must Health Goals with a friend, family member, coach, or community group. Invite them to join you, check in weekly, or simply offer encouragement.

- **Why it helps:**

    Research shows that sharing your goals and progress with others dramatically increases motivation, persistence, and follow-through.

- **How to do it:**

    Send a message outlining your health goal and why it matters to you.

    Invite someone to be your accountability partner: share wins, troubleshoot obstacles, and celebrate together.

    Join an online Must Goals community for prompts, feedback, and group energy.

    Schedule a monthly check-in—by text, call, or in person.

Tip:

You don't need a large group. One supportive person can make all the difference on the journey to Must.

Health & Vitality Recap: Keys to Lasting Energy

- Your purpose is powered by your health.
- Must Foundations (mindset, beliefs, values, standards, purpose) give clarity and strength to your goals.
- Small steps—hydration, rest, movement—build momentum and resilience.
- I AM SMART TO ACT goals turn vision into action.
- Celebrate wins, use support systems, and treat setbacks with compassion.
- Keep your focus on progress, not perfection.
- Your health journey fuels every other area of life—start today, honor your daily actions, and keep moving forward.
- Next: Moving into meaningful relationships—because energy shared is energy multiplied.

Health: The Foundation for All That Follows

In the Must Circle of Life, health and vitality aren't just isolated goals—they are the foundation for success, joy, and growth in every other domain. Physical energy enables you to build meaningful relationships, pursue purposeful careers, learn, serve your community, and live with emotional and spiritual clarity.

When you invest in your health—through rest, movement, nourishment, and self-care—you empower all other aspects of your life. Intellectual growth, emotional resilience, strong relationships, and service to others are fed by the energy and confidence that come from caring for your body.

Holistic well-being means tending to every part of who you are. As you strengthen your health, you make every other domain of life possible and more vibrant. In the Circle of Life, each domain is interconnected.

As you continue through the following chapters, notice how health underpins your capacity to love deeper, learn more, contribute meaningfully, and live a purposeful, flourishing life.

CHAPTER 13

Must Relationship Goals – Building Meaningful Connection

Relationships & Love – Building Meaningful Connection

Meaningful relationships are the heart of a fulfilled life. In the Must System, love and connection are not left to chance; they are built, nurtured, and deepened with intention. Connection fuels your well-being, supports your growth, and amplifies your resilience in every season of life.

Quick Tip:

Access free journaling and communication templates at www.MustGoals.com/Resources and www.MustBook.net/Resources.

The Must Lens on Relationships

Just like health, the quality of your relationships begins with conscious choice—not accident or old habits. Your Must Relationship Goals are shaped by who you must become, not by comparison, insecurity, or social pressure.

MUST GOALS

This chapter helps you clarify the building blocks of connection. Reflect on each foundational area, align them with your vision, and shape goals that are truly authentic.

Kickstart Deeper Connection Today

Start with one simple step. Choose at least one action below and do it today:

- Send a kind message to someone you care about.
- Schedule a real conversation—no devices, just presence.
- Express genuine gratitude to a partner, friend, or colleague.
- Plan a shared experience: a walk, a meal, or a call.
- Write down your top relationship value on a card and place it where you'll see it.
- Listen deeply—without interrupting—for five full minutes.

Why this works:

Small gestures, offered with presence, cultivate trust and warmth. One positive interaction can spark a bigger change in how you give and receive love.

Tip:

Check the box once you complete your action and celebrate the win! Your Must Relationship journey starts now—with intention, warmth, and simplicity.

Mason's Weekly Reset

Mason felt distant from his closest friends after years of work and family demands. Inspired by the "Kickstart Connection" box, he scheduled a weekly 30-minute call with his best friend from college.

"At first, I worried we'd have nothing to say," Mason admits. "But after just two calls, we were laughing like old times—and I felt lighter. It reminded me why connection matters."

Mason didn't stop there. He started a monthly dinner tradition with neighbors and began checking in with family more intentionally. "Now I protect that time. My relationships fuel everything else I do."

Takeaway:

Real connection starts with one intentional act. Even the smallest effort—repeated—can rebuild trust, deepen bonds, and bring joy back into your life.

Reflect and Align: Your Must Foundations

Must Core Beliefs

Reflect and jot down your beliefs about relationships and connection:

- What do I believe about my ability to build trusting, loving relationships?
- What old beliefs or fears have held me back from a deeper connection?
- Which new beliefs am I ready to claim that reflect my Must identity?

Must Core Values

Identify the values that guide your connections:

- Which values define my ideal relationships (honesty, kindness, loyalty, respect, vulnerability)?
- Do my habits and words honor these values?
- What boundaries will protect and strengthen my relationships?

Must Personal Narrative

Rewrite your relationship story for possibility:

- What story have I been telling myself about love, trust, or connection?
- How has this limited my relationships?
- If I write a new narrative of openness and strength, what will change?

Must Standards

Set your nonnegotiable floor for connection:

What practices keep my relationships strong (weekly check-ins, honesty, presence)?

How will I hold myself accountable and repair when I fall short?

Must Purpose

Connect effort to meaning:

- How do meaningful relationships empower my greater purpose?
- What becomes possible when I nurture authentic, loving connections?

Your Relationship Vision: Unlimited Possibility Exercise

After reflecting on your Must Foundations, give yourself a moment of creative freedom. Imagine that there are no barriers—no limits of time, distance, fear, or past hurt.

Ask yourself:

- If anything were possible, what would my relationships look and feel like?
- Who would I connect with, and how would I show up authentically?

Now, write freely—no censoring, no self-doubt, no "buts." List absolutely everything you want in the arena of relationships and love, even if it seems bold or unconventional.

This is your Golden Bucket—a pool of all potential dreams and desired experiences in this domain.

Turning Vision into Aligned Action

1. **Review:**

   Look over your Golden Bucket list. Highlight the ideas that resonate most strongly with your core beliefs, values, personal narrative, standards, and purpose.

2. **Prioritize:**

   Choose which goals align most directly with the life you want and need to build now.

3. **Transform:**

   Take the top priorities and convert them, one by one, into **I AM SMART TO ACT** goals:

   I: Identity alignment

   A: Aligned with values and purpose

   M: Meaningful

   S: Specific

   M: Measurable

   A: Achievable

R: Relevant

T: Time-bound

TO ACT: Take action—commit to the first step today

Remember: Progress is made through small daily steps. When your actions are built on alignment with your Must Self, your goals become expressions of truth—not just effort or obligation.

Pause to Reflect

Before you move forward:

- Picture what living with deep, authentic connection feels like.
- Ask: How would stronger relationships expand my capacity to live my Must Purpose?
- What ONE action can you commit to today that honors your relationships and supports alignment?
  (Examples: Send a text, schedule a call, listen deeply, express gratitude, set a boundary with love.)

Connection is not a distant goal—it's the foundation you live from each day. As you nurture your relationships, you expand your purpose and create the capacity for all other success.

Science Spotlight: The Power of Connection

Research in psychology and neuroscience shows that positive social interaction doesn't just boost happiness, it also improves physical health, immune function, and longevity. Studies show that regular, meaningful conversations reduce stress hormones and increase oxytocin, the "bonding hormone."

Even small acts of kindness, listening, or appreciation trigger measurable positive shifts in both giver and receiver. The takeaway? Sustainable, joyful relationships are built on small, repeated acts of presence and care—not grand gestures.

Avatar Walkthrough: Mustang Sally—Relationships & Love

To make your journey through this domain practical and personal, follow Mustang Sally as she models every step of the Must Goals process. After Sally's example, you'll create your own path with a fill-in-the-blank format.

1. Must Mindset

Sally decides her relationships must deepen—she adopts a nonnegotiable mindset centered on authentic connection and believes she can grow closer to those she loves.

Example: "I now believe meaningful, trusting relationships are possible for me—and I commit to showing up with honesty, kindness, and intention."

2. Must Core Beliefs

She identifies three essential beliefs that empower connection:

"I am worthy of love and capable of deep connection."

"Relationships grow stronger when I show up authentically."

"Conflict and repair are natural parts of lasting love."

3. Must Core Values

Sally chooses her top three values for this domain:

Honesty

Presence

Compassion

4. Mustang Sally's Personal Narrative

Sally recognizes that her old story was rooted in fear of vulnerability and patterns of withdrawal. She consciously rewrites it:

Old narrative: "I'm better off keeping my guard up. People always leave."

New narrative: "When I show up fully, I create space for real connection. Love grows when I risk being seen."

5. Relationship Standards

She sets nonnegotiable standards, such as:

"I must check in with my partner at least three times per week with full presence."

"I must listen without interrupting or planning my response."

"I must repair quickly after conflict—with honesty and care."

6. Must Purpose

Sally defines her purpose for relationships as:

"To build a life rich with trust, laughter, and support—so I can give and receive love fully, and model healthy connection for my children."

7. Dreamstorming

She unleashes a list of bold, limitless relationship possibilities:

Have weekly meaningful conversations with my partner.

Reconnect with old friends I've lost touch with.

Create family traditions that build closeness and joy.

Practice vulnerability and share my true feelings more often.

8. I AM SMART TO ACT Relationship Goals (Three Examples)

Must Goal 1: Relationships & Love (Weekly Quality Time)

"I am a present, loving partner who values deep connection. For the next 90 days, I will schedule one distraction-free 'date night' with my partner each week—whether at home or out—tracked on our shared calendar. Every Sunday, I'll reflect on what went well and celebrate our time together by writing one thing I appreciated in a gratitude journal. At 30 and 60 days, I'll check in with my partner about how this is strengthening our bond and adjust as needed. If life interrupts, I'll reschedule within 48 hours and remind myself that consistency, not perfection, builds love. By doing this, I will deepen trust, model intentional love for my family, and create a relationship built on presence and joy."

SMART TO ACT Breakdown:

- **Specific:** One distraction-free date night per week.
- **Measurable:** Tracked on shared calendar; gratitude journal entries.
- **Achievable:** Sally can schedule and protect this time.
- **Relevant:** Strengthens partnership, models connection for children.
- **Time-bound:** For 90 days, with check-ins at 30 and 60 days.
- **TO ACT:** Sally schedules the first date night today.

Tip for Celebration:

After each date night, write down one moment you cherished, or share a favorite memory with your partner over breakfast.

Bounce Back Plan:

If you miss a week, pause and ask: What got in the way? Reschedule within 48 hours and return with intention—connection is built through repair, not perfection.

Must Goal 2: Relationships & Love (Reconnection)

"I am a loyal friend who values meaningful connections across time. For the next 60 days, I will reach out to one old friend each week—via call, text, or video—and track it in my phone notes. Each Sunday, I'll review my outreach and celebrate reconnection by journaling about what I learned or enjoyed. At 30 days, I'll assess which friendships feel energizing and worth deeper investment. If scheduling is tough, I'll send a voice message or plan a short 10-minute call. By doing this, I will rebuild trust, combat loneliness, and create a network of support that enriches my life and theirs."

SMART TO ACT Breakdown:

- **Specific:** Reach out to one friend per week.
- **Measurable:** Tracked in phone notes; weekly journal reflections.
- **Achievable**: Sally has time for calls or messages.
- **Relevant:** Builds community, reduces isolation, strengthens joy.
- **Time-bound:** For 60 days, with a review at 30 days.
- **TO ACT:** Sally texts her first friend today.

Tip for Celebration:

Share a favorite story from your reconnection with your family, or treat yourself to a favorite coffee while journaling.

Bounce Back Plan:

If you skip a week, ask yourself: Was I overwhelmed, or avoiding? Adjust the format (shorter calls, texts instead), then reach out the next day with kindness.

Must Goal 3: Relationships & Love (Listening with Presence)

"I am a compassionate listener who values understanding over being right. For the next four weeks, I will practice active listening in at least five conversations per week—pausing, making eye contact, and reflecting what I hear before responding. I'll track these moments in a simple tally on my phone. Every Saturday, I'll review my progress and celebrate by acknowledging one conversation where I truly connected. If I interrupt or check out, I'll notice without judgment, apologize if needed, and try again in the next interaction. By doing this, I will deepen trust, reduce conflict, and make others feel seen and valued."

SMART TO ACT Breakdown:

- **Specific:** Practice active listening in five conversations per week.
- **Measurable**: Daily tally on phone; weekly Saturday reflection.
- **Achievable:** Sally can pause and listen intentionally.
- Relevant: Strengthens all relationships, reduces misunderstandings.
- Time-bound: For four weeks.
- **TO ACT:** Sally commits to listening fully in her next conversation today.

MUST GOALS

Tip for Celebration:

After a week of strong listening, reward yourself with quiet reflection time, a favorite meal, or sharing your progress with a trusted friend.

Bounce Back Plan:

If you interrupt or zone out, pause, acknowledge it kindly ("Sorry, let me listen better"), and return to presence. Growth is in the return, not the perfection.

Transition: Now It's Your Turn

Having seen Mustang Sally's journey, you can now build your own path. Use the same structure to shape your foundational beliefs, values, story, standards, purpose, and measurable relationship goals.

Your Relationships & Love Must Goals

1. Must Mindset

My new, nonnegotiable mindset for relationships and love:

_____

2. Must Core Beliefs Regarding Relationships & Love

a. _____
b. _____
c. _____

3. Must Core Values for Relationships & Love

a. _____
b. _____
c. _____

4. My Upgraded Relationship Narrative

Old story:

New narrative:

5. Relationship Standards

a. _____

b. _____

c. _____

6. Must Purpose

My purpose for prioritizing relationships is:

_____

7. Dreamstorm (Bold Visions)

_____

_____

_____

8. My I AM SMART TO ACT Relationship Goals (3):

Must Goal 1: _____

Must Goal 2: _____

Must Goal 3: _____

Tip:

Remember to set weekly reviews to track progress, celebrate each win (big or small), and use your bounce-back plan whenever you need to reset—with self-kindness and renewed commitment. For more resources and printable templates, visit www.MustGoals.com/Resources.

The Power of Relational Support

Multiply Your Connection Momentum

Building lasting relationships is easier—and more joyful—when you share the journey with others. Consider inviting a friend, partner, or group to join you in setting relationship goals together.

Why it helps:

Research shows that shared commitment to connection increases follow-through, accountability, and satisfaction.

How to do it:

- Share your top relationship goal with someone you trust.
- Invite someone to join you in weekly check-ins or shared growth practices.
- Join an online Must Goals community focused on relationships.
- Schedule monthly reviews with your partner or close friend.

Tip:

You don't need a large group. One committed companion can make all the difference.

Relationships & Love Recap: Keys to Meaningful Connection

- Your relationships fuel every other domain of life.
- Must Foundations (mindset, beliefs, values, standards, purpose) give clarity and strength to your connection goals.
- Small acts—listening, gratitude, presence—build trust and resilience.
- I AM SMART TO ACT goals turn vision into action.
- Celebrate wins, use support systems, and treat setbacks with compassion.
- Keep your focus on progress, not perfection.
- Your relationship journey enriches every area of life—start today, honor your daily actions, and keep moving forward.

Relationships: The Next Layer of the Circle of Life

In the **Must Circle of Life**, relationships and love aren't just isolated goals—they are the foundation for joy, resilience, and shared success. Meaningful connections empower you to pursue purposeful work, serve your community, learn, grow spiritually, and live with emotional and intellectual clarity.

When you invest in your relationships—through presence, honesty, and care—you empower all other aspects of your life. Strong bonds feed creativity, health, confidence, and contribution.

Holistic well-being means tending to every part of who you are. As you strengthen your connections, you make every other domain of life richer and more vibrant. As you continue through the following chapters, notice how relationships underpin your capacity to lead, serve, learn, and live a purposeful, flourishing life.

CHAPTER 14

Must Career & Professional Development Goals

Career & Professional Growth – Building Your Must Work Life

Your career is more than a paycheck—it's a platform for purpose, growth, and contribution. In the Must System, professional success isn't about comparison or external validation, it's about aligning your daily work with who you are meant to become and the value you are called to create.

Quick Tip:

Access free career planning and goal-setting templates at www.MustGoals.com/Resources and www.MustBook.net/Resources.

The Must Lens on Career

Just as health and relationships begin with conscious choice—not accident, obligation, or fear—so does career fulfillment. Your Must Career Goals are shaped by who you must become and the impact you want to make, not by titles, salaries, or societal pressure.

This chapter helps you clarify the building blocks of meaningful work. Reflect on each foundational area, align them with your vision, and shape truly authentic career goals.

Kickstart Your Career Growth Today

Start with one simple step. Choose at least one action below and do it today:

- Update one section of your resume or LinkedIn profile.
- Reach out to a mentor, colleague, or industry contact.
- Sign up for one skill-building course, webinar, or podcast.
- Write down your top career value or aspiration on a card and place it where you'll see it.
- Block 30 minutes this week to research a role, company, or opportunity that excites you.
- Identify one small improvement you can make in your current work today.

Why this works:

Small, intentional career actions build clarity and confidence. Each step forward—no matter how minor—creates momentum toward meaningful work.

Tip:

Check the box once you complete your action and celebrate the win! Your Must Career journey starts now—with clarity, intention, and courage.

Carlos's Pivot

Carlos felt stuck in a job that paid well but drained his energy. Inspired by the "Kickstart Career Growth" box, he decided to reach out to a former colleague working in a field he'd always been curious about.

"That one coffee meeting changed everything," Carlos says. "I learned about opportunities I didn't know existed—and realized my skills were transferable. Within six months, I'd made the leap to a role that energizes me every day."

Carlos didn't overhaul his life overnight. He took small steps: informational interviews, online courses, networking. "Now I wake up excited about my work. I wish I'd started sooner."

Takeaway:

Real career change starts with one intentional conversation or small action. Clarity and opportunity grow when you move toward what matters, one step at a time.

Reflect and Align: Your Must Foundations

Must Core Beliefs

Reflect and jot down your beliefs about work and professional growth:

- What do I believe about my ability to build a fulfilling, impactful career?
- What old beliefs or fears have held me back from pursuing meaningful work?
- Which new beliefs am I ready to claim that reflect my Must identity?

Must Core Values

Identify the values that guide your career decisions:

- Which values define my ideal work (creativity, impact, leadership, flexibility, service)?
- Do my current work habits honor these values?

- What boundaries will protect my professional well-being and integrity?

Must Personal Narrative

Rewrite your career story for possibility:

- What story have I been telling myself about my work, skills, or potential?
- How has this limited my career growth?
- If I write a new narrative of capability and purpose, what will change?

Must Standards

- Set your nonnegotiable floor for professional excellence:
- What practices keep me performing at my best (learning, networking, boundaries)?
- How will I hold myself accountable and realign when I slip?

Must Purpose

Connect effort to meaning:

How does meaningful work empower my greater purpose?

What becomes possible when I align my career with my values and identity?

Your Career Vision: Unlimited Possibility Exercise

After reflecting on your Must Foundations, give yourself a moment of creative freedom. Imagine that there are no barriers—no limits of education, experience, money, or fear.

Ask yourself:

- If anything were possible, what would my ideal career look and feel like?
- What kind of work would I do, and how would I show up?

Now, write freely—no censoring, no self-doubt, no "buts." List absolutely everything you want in the arena of career and professional growth, even if it seems bold or unconventional.

This is your *Golden Bucket*—a pool of all potential dreams and desired experiences in this domain.

Turning Vision into Aligned Action

1. **Review:**

    Look over your Golden Bucket list. Highlight the ideas that resonate most strongly with your core beliefs, values, personal narrative, standards, and purpose.

2. **Prioritize:**

    Choose which goals align most directly with the career you want and need to build now.

3. **Transform:**

    Take the top priorities and convert them, one by one, **into I AM SMART TO ACT** goals:

    I: Identity alignment

    A: Aligned with values and purpose
    M: Meaningful

    S: Specific
    M: Measurable

A: Achievable

R: Relevant

T: Time-bound

TO ACT: Take action—commit to the first step today

Remember: Progress is made through small daily steps. When your actions are aligned with your Must Self, your goals become expressions of truth—not just ambition or obligation.

Pause to Reflect

Before you move forward:

- Picture what working with purpose, impact, and alignment feels like.
- Ask: How would a fulfilling career expand my capacity to live my Must Purpose?
- What ONE action can you commit to today that honors your career and supports alignment?
  (Examples: Reach out to a mentor, update your skills, set a work boundary, explore a new opportunity, improve one deliverable.)

Career fulfillment is not a distant goal—it's the foundation you build from each day. As you align your work with your identity, you expand your purpose and create the capacity for all other success.

Science Spotlight: The Power of Purpose-Driven Work

Research in organizational psychology shows that employees who find meaning in their work experience higher engagement, creativity, resilience, and job satisfaction. Studies show that aligning work with personal values reduces burnout and increases performance by up to 30%.

Even small steps—like reframing daily tasks to connect with larger goals or seeking feedback from mentors—can dramatically improve motivation and career trajectory. The takeaway? Purposeful careers are built on intentional, values-aligned choices, not luck.

Avatar Walkthrough: Mustang Sally— Career & Professional Growth

To make your journey through this domain practical and personal, follow Mustang Sally as she models every step of the Must Goals process. After Sally's example, you'll create your own path with a fill-in-the-blank format.

1. Must Mindset

Sally decides her career must evolve—she adopts a nonnegotiable mindset centered on growth, purpose, and impact.

Example: "I now believe a fulfilling, purpose-driven career is possible for me—and I commit to aligning my work with my values and strengths."

2. Must Core Beliefs

She identifies three essential beliefs that empower professional growth:

- "I am capable of learning new skills and adapting to new opportunities."
- "My work has value, and I deserve to be compensated fairly."
- "Career growth is a journey, not a destination—and I can shape it intentionally."

3. Must Core Values

Sally chooses her top three values for this domain:

Creativity

Impact

Integrity

4. Mustang Sally's Personal Narrative

Sally recognizes that her old story was rooted in fear of failure and limiting beliefs about her qualifications. She consciously rewrites it:

Old narrative: "I'm not qualified enough. I should just be grateful for what I have."

New narrative: "My skills, experiences, and passion make me valuable. I can build a career that aligns with who I am."

5. Career Standards

She sets nonnegotiable standards, such as:

- "I must dedicate at least 2 hours per week to skill development."
- "I must protect boundaries around my work hours to prevent burnout."
- "I must seek feedback and mentorship regularly to grow."

6. Must Purpose

Sally defines her purpose for her career as:

"To use my creativity and skills to create meaningful impact—while modeling professional growth and balance for my family."

7. Dreamstorming

She unleashes a list of bold, limitless career possibilities:

- Lead a project that makes a real difference.
- Transition into a role that energizes and challenges me.
- Build a side business or creative venture.
- Earn a certification or advanced skill in my field.
- Mentor others and contribute to my professional community.

8. I AM SMART TO ACT Career Goals (Three Examples)

Must Goal 1: Career & Professional Growth (Skill Development)

"I am a lifelong learner who values growth and mastery. For the next 90 days, I will dedicate 2 hours each week to learning a new skill relevant to my career—tracked on my calendar and completed via online courses, books, or mentorship. Every Sunday, I'll review my progress and celebrate by journaling one insight or breakthrough. At 30 and 60 days, I'll assess what I've learned and adjust my focus if needed. If I miss a week, I'll identify what got in the way, adjust my schedule, and restart the next week with self-compassion. By doing this, I will increase my confidence, expand my opportunities, and model continuous growth for those around me."

SMART TO ACT Breakdown:

- **Specific:** 2 hours per week on skill development.
- **Measurable:** Tracked on calendar; weekly journal reflections.
- **Achievable:** Sally can carve out time and access resources.
- **Relevant**: Builds expertise, opens doors, aligns with career goals.

- **Time-bound:** 90 days, with checkpoints at 30 and 60 days.
- **TO ACT:** Sally enrolls in her first course today.

Tip for Celebration:

After each week of learning, reward yourself by sharing one insight with a colleague or friend, or treat yourself to something you enjoy.

Bounce Back Plan:

If you skip a week, pause and reflect: What got in the way? Adjust your schedule or method (e.g., shorter sessions, a different format), then restart with kindness.

Must Goal 2: Career & Professional Growth (Networking)

"I am a connector who values relationships and community. For the next 60 days, I will reach out to one professional contact each week—via email, LinkedIn, or coffee—tracked in a networking journal. Each Friday, I'll review my outreach and celebrate by noting what I learned or who inspired me. At 30 days, I'll assess which connections feel most valuable and explore deeper collaboration. If scheduling is tough, I'll send a thoughtful message or share an article. By doing this, I will expand my network, open new opportunities, and build a community of support and growth."

SMART TO ACT Breakdown:

Specific: One professional outreach per week.

Measurable: Tracked in journal; weekly Friday reflections.

Achievable: Sally can send messages or schedule brief calls.

Relevant: Builds network, opens opportunities, strengthens career resilience.

Time-bound: 60 days, with a review at 30 days.

TO ACT: Sally sends her first message today.

Tip for Celebration:

After reaching out consistently for a month, celebrate by treating yourself to a favorite coffee or reflecting on how your network has grown.

Bounce Back Plan:

If you miss a week, ask: Was I avoiding or overwhelmed? Adjust your approach (shorter messages, different contacts), then reach out the next day.

Must Goal 3: Career & Professional Growth (Work-Life Boundaries)

"I am a professional who values balance and sustainable excellence. For the next four weeks, I will leave work on time at least four days per week—setting a firm end-time alarm and closing my laptop—tracked on my phone. Every Saturday, I'll review my boundary-keeping and celebrate by doing something I love outside of work. If I slip, I'll reflect on what pulled me in and adjust my workflow or delegation strategy. By doing this, I will protect my energy, prevent burnout, and model healthy work habits for my team and family."

SMART TO ACT Breakdown:

Specific: Leave work on time four days per week.
Measurable: Tracked daily on phone; weekly Saturday reflections.
Achievable: Sally can set alarms and plan her workday accordingly.
Relevant: Prevents burnout, protects relationships, sustains long-term performance.
Time-bound: Four weeks.

TO ACT: Sally sets her end-time alarm today.

Tip for Celebration:

After a week of honoring boundaries, reward yourself with a hobby, a walk, or quality time with loved ones.

Bounce Back Plan:

If you work late, pause and ask: What derailed me? Adjust your schedule, delegate, or communicate boundaries more clearly—then restart the next day.

Transition: Now It's Your Turn

Having seen Mustang Sally's journey, you can now build your own path. Use the same structure to shape your foundational beliefs, values, story, standards, purpose, and measurable career goals.

Your Career & Professional Growth Must Goals

1. Must Mindset

My new, nonnegotiable mindset for career and professional growth:

_____

2. Must Core Beliefs Regarding Career

a. _____
b. _____
c. _____

3. Must Core Values for Career

a. _____
b. _____
c. _____

4. My Upgraded Career Narrative

Old story: _____

New narrative: _____

5. Career Standards

a. _____

b. _____

c. _____

6. Must Purpose

My purpose for prioritizing career growth is:

_____

7. Dreamstorm (Bold Visions)

_____

_____

_____

8. My I AM SMART TO ACT Career Goals (3):

Goal 1: _____

Goal 2: _____

Goal 3: _____

Tip:

Remember to set weekly reviews to track progress, celebrate each win (big or small), and use your bounce-back plan whenever you need to reset—with self-kindness and renewed commitment. For more resources and printable templates, visit www.MustGoals.com/Resources.

The Power of Professional Support

Multiply Your Career Momentum

Building a fulfilling career is easier—and more rewarding—when you have support. Consider sharing your career goals with a mentor, colleague, coach, or mastermind group.

Why it helps:

Research shows that mentorship and peer accountability dramatically increase career growth, satisfaction, and goal achievement.

How to do it:

- Share your top career goal with someone you trust.
- Invite a mentor or peer to join you in quarterly career check-ins.
- Join a professional community or online Must Goals group.
- Schedule monthly progress reviews with an accountability partner.

Tip:

You don't need an extensive network. One supportive mentor or colleague can make all the difference.

Applying Must Goals to Your Team, Business, or Organization

If you lead others, you can extend Must thinking beyond your own life and into your team, business, or organization. The same foundations that shape your personal Must—beliefs, values, standards, and purpose—also show up at scale as culture: what your group truly believes, rewards, and tolerates over time.

Two common tools used in organizations are **OKRs** (Objectives and Key Results) and **KPIs** (Key Performance Indicators).

- **OKRs** are ambitious goals paired with a few measurable results that define what success looks like over a set period.
- **KPIs** are the core metrics you track regularly to see how well the business or team is performing.

A simple way to connect Must Goals, culture, and OKRs/KPIs:

- **Clarify your shared Must and culture**: Name the core beliefs, values, standards, and purpose that define your team, business, or organization at its best. This is the collective version of your personal identity work.
- **Set Must-aligned Objectives**: Use that shared Must and culture to shape a small number of clear, inspiring Objectives (the "O" in OKRs) that express who you are together and what you are here to do.
- **Choose Key Results and KPIs that fit:** Let Key Results and KPIs measure what matters most for those Objectives—so the numbers you track are direct evidence that you are living your shared Must, not just chasing superficial targets.
- **Review for culture alignment, not just performance:** In regular reviews, ask not only "Are we hitting our numbers?" but also "Do these goals, behaviors, and metrics still reflect our shared beliefs, values, standards, and purpose?"

Used this way, your personal identity foundations and your organization's culture are working in parallel: Must Goals provide the "who we are and why it matters," while OKRs and KPIs provide the "what we aim to achieve and how we will know."

Together, they align people, culture, and performance around what truly matters

Must Career & Professional Development Recap: Keys to Meaningful Work

Your career fuels your purpose and your capacity to contribute.

Must Foundations (mindset, beliefs, values, standards, purpose) give clarity and strength to your career goals.

Small steps—learning, networking, boundaries—build momentum and resilience.

I AM SMART TO ACT. Goals turn vision into action.

- Celebrate wins, use support systems, and treat setbacks with compassion.
- Keep your focus on progress, not perfection.
- Your career journey enriches every area of life—start today, honor your daily actions, and keep moving forward.

Career: The Next Layer of the Circle of Life

In the **Must Circle of Life,** career and professional growth aren't just isolated goals, they are platforms for purpose, contribution, and identity. Meaningful work empowers you to serve your community, support your family, pursue personal growth, and live with confidence and clarity.

When you invest in your career—through learning, networking, and boundaries—you empower all other aspects of your life. Professional fulfillment feeds creativity, health, relationships, and service.

Holistic well-being means tending to every part of who you are. As you strengthen your career, you make every other domain of life richer and more vibrant.

As you continue through the following chapters, notice how career underpins your capacity to lead, love, learn, and live a purposeful, flourishing life.

CHAPTER 15

Must Financial Well-Being Goals: Creating Abundance Through Alignment

Your Financial Goals: Creating Abundance Through Alignment

Financial wellness is not just about accumulating wealth, it's about stewardship, freedom, and purpose. In the Must System, your financial goals reflect your ability to create, sustain, and multiply resources in ways that honor your beliefs, standards, values, and mission. Prosperity here is measured by the peace, freedom, and impact your resources enable—not just numbers in an account.

Quick Tip:

Access financial journaling and templates at www.MustGoals.com/Resources.

The Must Lens on Finances and Abundance

Just like health and relationships, financial mastery begins with conscious choice—not comparison or inherited habits. Your Must Financial Goals are shaped by who you must become and the legacy you're called to build, not by fear, shame, or outside approval.

Kickstart Your Financial Transformation Today

Start with one small step. Select and complete one action today:

- Check your account balances and note where you're strongest.
- Automate a transfer to your savings.
- Track your expenses for one day or a week.
- Cancel one unused subscription.
- Give to a cause that inspires you—even a tiny amount.
- Write down your top financial value or giving goal and post it visibly.

Why this works:

Progress in finances begins with awareness and small wins. Money is managed best in bite-sized, repeatable steps.

Tip:

Check the box after your action and celebrate your awareness—your Must Money journey starts now, with clarity, discipline, and hope.

Taylor's Savings Shift

Taylor used to dread looking at her bank accounts. After reading the "Kickstart" box, she decided to automate $20 a week into a savings account. "It felt so minor, but for the first time, I felt in control," she says. "Every month the savings grew, and it motivated me to learn more. Now I regularly give to charity and have an emergency fund. The hardest part was starting."

Takeaway:

Real financial transformation starts with one easy habit—doable, visible, and repeatable. Each step builds momentum for greater abundance and generosity.

Reflect and Align: Your Must Foundations

Must Core Beliefs

- What do I believe about wealth, abundance, and my ability to generate it?
- Are there limiting beliefs from my upbringing or past setbacks?
- What new beliefs will support wise stewardship and expansion?

Must Core Values

- Which values—security, freedom, generosity, discipline, growth—should shape my financial habits?
- Are my current financial actions honoring these values?
- What boundaries protect or expand my wealth and giving?

Must Personal Narrative

- What stories do I tell myself about money?
- Whose voices shaped these stories, and do they still serve me?
- What would a new narrative of opportunity and abundance sound like?

Must Standards

- What practices are nonnegotiable for my financial integrity (savings rate, budgeting, giving)?
- How do I stay accountable and return to my standards after setbacks?

Must Purpose

Why does financial abundance matter to me, beyond comfort?

What mission or impact does my wealth empower?

How does my financial life amplify my purpose, values, and legacy?

Your Financial Vision: Unlimited Possibility Exercise

After reflecting on your Must Foundations, picture a life without money fears or limits. Ask yourself:

What financial outcomes bring real peace, freedom, optimism, and impact?

How would I steward resources if constraints and doubts vanished?

Who would benefit from my abundance—family, community, causes?

What would my day-to-day financial life look and feel like?

Write your "**Golden Bucket**"—every wish, dream, or vision for prosperity, security, and contribution. This is the foundation for your goals.

Turning Vision into Aligned Action

1. **Review:** Highlight the dreams from your "Golden Bucket" that connect most to your beliefs, values, and legacy.
2. **Prioritize:** Rank by immediacy (healing, stability, legacy).
3. **Transform:** Turn your top priorities into three **I AM SMART TO ACT** Must Financial Goals:

   I: Identity alignment

   A: Aligned with values and purpose
   M: Meaningful

S: Specific
M: Measurable
A: Achievable
R: Relevant
T: Time-bound

TO ACT: Take action—start one step today.

Remember: Abundance grows from small, consistent actions—aligned with your Must Self.

Pause to Reflect

- How does financial discipline support my values and mission?
- What new belief or habit can increase my freedom to give, save, or invest?
- Which outdated money story am I ready to release?
- What's one action I'll take today to anchor my new financial identity?

Science Spotlight: The Returns of Small Steps

Neuroscience shows that even small, automated money behaviors (like rounding up purchases and saving the difference or tracking spending) rewire our decision pathways and reduce financial anxiety. Studies prove that people who set specific, values-aligned giving or saving targets are far more likely to reach them. Each action builds resilience, confidence, and future abundance.

Avatar Walkthrough: Mustang Sally—Finances & Abundance

1. Must Mindset

Sally commits to abundance with purpose, shifting from scarcity to stewardship.

Example: "I now believe I am capable and worthy of building wealth for security, freedom, and impact through daily, values-driven choices."

2. Must Core Beliefs

- "I am capable of earning, saving, and giving in ways that multiply purpose."
- "Wealth is a tool for both security and service."
- "Changing my habits changes my future."

3. Must Core Values

- Generosity
- Discipline
- Legacy

4. Mustang Sally's Financial Narrative

Old narrative: "Money is always tight. I'll never catch up."

New narrative: "I can master my money and create opportunities—for myself and others—through smart, aligned actions."

5. Must Standards

- "I must save at least 15% of every paycheck."
- "I must update my budget monthly and track all major expenses."

- "I must give a portion of my income to causes aligned with my purpose."

6. Must Purpose

"To build security, generosity, and opportunity—for my family, my future, and the causes I believe in."

7. Dreamstorming

- Debt-free living.
- Funding family travel or education dreams.
- Building a charitable giving fund.
- Leaving a multigenerational legacy.
- Owning a home or investment property.

8. I AM SMART TO ACT Financial Goals (Three Examples)

Must Goal 1: Emergency Savings

"I am a prudent steward who values security and responsibility. For the next 12 months, I will save $10,000 in my emergency fund by setting aside $834/month, tracked with an automatic transfer and monthly review. Every month, I celebrate progress—reviewing wins, adjusting my budget, or rewarding myself with a small treat. If I miss a month, I analyze what happened and restart next month without shame. By doing this, I build peace of mind, model responsibility for my loved ones, and increase my freedom to give and take new risks."

SMART TO ACT Breakdown:

Specific: $834/month saved

Measurable: Track with automatic transfer/monthly review

Achievable: Sally's budget supports these savings

Relevant: Security for family, foundation for giving/investing

Time-Bound: 12 months

TO ACT: Sally sets up her automated transfer today

Tip for Celebration: After each deposit, look at your growing balance and celebrate your discipline.

Bounce Back Plan: If you skip a month, review your spending, adjust, and begin again. Progress, not perfection.

Must Goal 2: Purposeful Giving

"I am a generous giver who values impact. For the next six months, I will give at least 5% of my net income to causes aligned with my values, tracking it through my bank app and a gratitude journal. Each month, I reflect on the difference my giving made and seek stories from those I help. If finances get tight, I reduce the amount but maintain regular giving—knowing consistency builds more abundance for me and others."

(**SMART TO ACT** Breakdown follows the same format as above; TO ACT = Schedule first donation today.)

Must Goal 3: Investing for Freedom

"I am a wise investor who values freedom and growth. Each month, I will invest $250 in my chosen retirement account, with contributions tracked via online statements, for the next year. After each quarter, I review progress and celebrate with a special dinner or personal reward. If I can't invest a full amount one month, I invest what I can and adjust my plan—always returning to my standard the next month."

(**SMART TO ACT** Breakdown follows above; TO ACT = Sally sets up her investment today.)

Now It's Your Turn: Your Financial Must Goals

1. Must Mindset

My new, nonnegotiable financial mindset: _____

2. Must Core Beliefs Regarding Finances

a. _____

b. _____

c. _____

3. Must Core Values for Finances

a. _____

b. _____

c. _____

4. My New Financial Narrative

Old story: _____

New narrative: _____

5. Financial Standards

a. _____

b. _____

c. _____

6. Must Purpose

My purpose for financial abundance is: _____

7. Dreamstorm (Vision List)

_____

_____

_____

8. My I AM SMART TO ACT Financial Goals (3):

Goal 1: _____

Goal 2: _____

Goal 3: _____

Tip:

Set weekly or monthly reviews, celebrate milestones, and show yourself kindness. Money mastery is a journey.

> **The Power of Shared Stewardship**
> - Multiply Your Money Momentum
> - Managing money is easier—and more meaningful—when shared. Invite a trusted partner, advisor, or group into your money journey. Set up accountability check-ins, celebrate together, or join a financial literacy group.

Financial Recap: Keys to Abundance

- Your wealth is both a resource and a responsibility.
- Must Foundations (mindset, beliefs, values, standards, purpose) anchor true abundance.
- Small actions—saving, giving, learning—compound for freedom and impact.
- I AM SMART TO ACT goals create results.
- Celebrate progress, use support, show yourself compassion.
- Your financial journey strengthens every aspect of your life.

Closing: Finances as the Engine of Impact

Financial abundance is your engine for freedom, contribution, and legacy. As you align money with your Must, you unlock security for your family, fuel your dreams, and serve what matters most. In the **Circle of Life**, wise stewardship in this domain powers joy, confidence, and purpose everywhere.

CHAPTER 16

Must Personal Growth Goals: Becoming Your Next Self

Your Personal Growth Goals: Becoming Your Next Self

Personal growth is more than learning new skills—it is a journey of becoming the truest, boldest version of yourself. In the Must System, growth is intentional and holistic: it's about developing wisdom, resilience, and character through aligned beliefs, values, standards, and purpose. Sustainable growth is always anchored in your Must Self.

Quick Tip:

Access self-discovery journaling, course templates, and growth trackers at www.MustGoals.com/Resources.

The Must Perspective on Growth

Growth doesn't happen by accident—it starts with conscious choice, not comparison or old labels. Your Must Growth Goals reflect who you are called to become in every area of your life. This chapter helps you clarify your building blocks for meaningful, lifelong transformation.

Kickstart Your Personal Growth Today

Pick one step and do it now:

Read one page of a personal growth book.

Write down one quality you'd love to strengthen.

Enroll in a course, webinar, or workshop that excites you.

Ask a friend or mentor for honest feedback on one area you care about.

Journal about a past challenge and the wisdom it taught you.

Try a new skill for 15 minutes—no expectation, just curiosity.

Why this works:

Every micro-action builds momentum and confidence. The smallest investment in learning ignites lasting progress.

Tip:

Celebrate your action today—growth begins with bold curiosity.

Reader Spotlight: Maya's Learning Streak

Maya felt stuck at work, but craved meaning. She began a streak of reading one new book each month. "At first it was just curiosity," she says, "but soon my confidence, career, and relationships improved. Reading that first book triggered bigger changes—eventually, I signed up for a certification and started mentoring others."

Takeaway:

Any growth journey begins with one act of courage or curiosity. Repeated regularly, these steps stack powerfully over time.

Reflect and Align: Your Must Foundations

Must Core Beliefs

What do I believe about my ability to grow, learn, and transform?

Does fear, failure, or the past limit me?

What bold, empowering beliefs will unlock my highest potential?

Must Core Values

Which values (curiosity, discipline, kindness, resilience, adventure) truly fuel my growth?

Are my habits reflecting those values, or are they drifting from them?

What boundaries or commitments do I need to protect my focus and dream?

Must Personal Narrative

What story have I told myself about my capacity for change?

Is this story outdated or energizing?

Create your new narrative: "I am a lifelong learner and creator of my own evolution."

Must Standards

What nonnegotiable behaviors will I commit to for growth? (Example: daily reading, weekly feedback, monthly learning goals)

How will I maintain and revisit these standards?

Must Purpose

Why does personal growth matter to me?

What impact will my evolution have on my family, work, and community?

What legacy do I hope to inspire?

Your Growth Vision: Unlimited Possibility Exercise

Imagine living in total alignment with your growth musts—fear and limitation dissolved.

Ask yourself:

What qualities, skills, or wisdom will define my next self?

How would I show up in life, in relationships, and in my contribution?

Who else would benefit from my journey?

Journal or sketch your "Golden Bucket" of growth—the habits, skills, character, and experiences that call to your highest self.

Turning Vision into Aligned Action

Review: Highlight visions that match your Must beliefs, values, standards, and purpose.

Prioritize: Rank as immediate, mid-term, or transformation goals.

Transform: Create your top 3 I AM SMART TO ACT Must Growth Goals:

I: Identity alignment

A: Aligned with values and purpose

M: Meaningful

S: Specific

M: Measurable

A: Achievable

R: Relevant

T: Time-bound

TO ACT: Take concrete action today.

Remember: Lifelong transformation is the result of aligned, repeated action.

Pause to Reflect

What belief, value, or habit could most accelerate my growth?

Which outdated story or comfort zone must I outgrow?

What habit, commitment, or relationship will I invest in next?

What step can I take now to honor my becoming?

Choose your Must Action and begin—today's step is tomorrow's transformation.

Science Spotlight: The Power of Lifelong Learning

Neuroscience confirms that the adult brain has remarkable plasticity: every new learning effort strengthens neural connections and delays cognitive decline. Research shows that goal-directed self-development increases happiness, adaptability, and impact—at every age. Regular reflection and new challenges are proven to multiply your progress and sense of purpose.

Avatar Walkthrough: Mustang Sally— Personal Growth & Becoming

1. Must Mindset

Sally embraces growth, believing that her best self is yet to come:

Example: "I now believe that every challenge teaches wisdom and every day brings a chance for renewal."

2. Must Core Beliefs

"I can learn, adapt, and improve at every stage."

"Mistakes are teachers, not verdicts."

"I am worthy of growth for its own sake and for the benefit of others."

3. Must Core Values

Curiosity

Resilience

Service

4. Mustang Sally's Growth Narrative

Old narrative: "Some people are just born with it. I'm not."

New narrative: "My capacity for growth and wisdom is unlimited as long as I stay open, brave, and willing to act."

5. Must Standards

"I dedicate 20 minutes every day to reading, journaling, or practicing a new skill."

"I seek feedback each month to calibrate my path."

"I set one growth challenge every quarter."

6. Must Purpose

"To become my next self, so I can serve, inspire, and lead change in my community."

7. Dreamstorming

Master public speaking or storytelling.

Start a creative project or side business.

Cultivate daily meditation or gratitude practice.

Mentor others through a shared challenge.

Learn a new language or advanced skill.

8. I AM SMART TO ACT Growth Goals (Three Examples)

Must Goal 1: Public Speaking

"I am a courageous communicator who values growth and empowerment. Over the next 90 days, I will practice public speaking by recording a weekly two-minute video and presenting once a month at my local group, tracked in my journal. Each Friday, I reflect on progress and celebrate courage with a favorite meal. If I miss a week or feel fear, I reset intentions and try again, knowing every step builds skill and confidence."

SMART TO ACT Breakdown:

Specific: Weekly video; monthly talk

Measurable: Journal, tally tracker

Achievable: Time is scheduled

Relevant: Builds impact, aligns with purpose

Time-bound: 90 days

TO ACT: Record the first video today

Must Goal 2: Discipline & Daily Reading

"I am a lifelong learner who values curiosity and discipline. For the next 30 days, I'll read 10 pages of a personal growth book each morning, tracked on my calendar. Each week, I write down one insight and celebrate progress with a small treat or affirmation. If I miss a day, I resume the next without guilt—progress is cumulative."

Must Goal 3: Growth Mentorship

"I am an evolving mentor who values service. Over the next six months, I'll connect monthly with a mentee or a learning group to share experiences and learn together, with each session tracked in meeting notes. I celebrate each session with gratitude journaling and adjust if schedules conflict. By doing this, I contribute to others' growth and deepen my own purpose."

Now It's Your Turn: Your Personal Growth Must Goals

1. Must Mindset
My growth mindset declaration: _____

2. Must Core Beliefs

a. _____
b. _____
c. _____

3. Must Core Values

a. _____
b. _____
c. _____

4. My New Growth Narrative
Old story: _____
New narrative: _____

5. Growth Standards

a. _____
b. _____
c. _____

6. Must Purpose

My purpose for growth is: _____

7. Dreamstorm (Vision List)

_____

_____

_____

8. My I AM SMART TO ACT Growth Goals (3):

Goal 1: _____
Goal 2: _____
Goal 3: _____

Tip:

Set regular review times, reward courageous steps, and treat setbacks as learning. Growth is your birthright.

Learning In Community

Share and Expand

Journey is richer with others. Invite a friend or group to set growth challenges, trade progress check-ins, or share insights. Join a book circle or mastermind for shared energy and support.

Growth Recap: Keys to Lifelong Becoming

- Growth is the continual discovery and creation of yourself.
- Foundations (beliefs, values, narrative, purpose) make change meaningful and sustainable.
- Small steps, tracked over time, change your trajectory.
- I AM SMART TO ACT goals keep you moving from vision to mastery.
- Every bit of progress is worthy of compassion and celebration.

Closing: Growth Multiplies Every Domain

Personal growth is the engine of all change. As you grow, every other area—health, wealth, relationships, and purpose—expands in possibility. Your willingness to learn, challenge, and evolve shapes not just your future, but the future of everyone you influence.

CHAPTER 17

Your Spiritual and Peace of Mind Goals

Your Spiritual & Peace of Mind Goals: Living in Alignment With Spirit

Spirituality and inner peace are the roots that nourish every other domain of life. Whether through faith, meditation, service, or mindful living, authentic spiritual practice brings meaning, strength, and resilience—enabling you to meet life's challenges with hope and equanimity. Here, your Must Goals will cultivate not just belief, but daily peace, presence, and a deeper connection to what matters most.

Quick Tip:

Access reflection prompts, spiritual practice trackers, and service templates at www.MustGoals.com/Resources.

The Must Lens on Spirituality and Peace

True spiritual growth is about love, acceptance, and conscious alignment—not fear, guilt, or comparison. Your spiritual and peace goals are shaped by who you must become, and the legacy of hope and healing you wish to leave.

Kickstart Your Spiritual Growth Today

Pick and complete one step today:

Spend five minutes in quiet reflection, prayer, or meditation.

List three things you feel grateful for right now.

Express compassion to yourself or another—by listening, forgiving, or offering help.

Light a candle, read an inspiring text, or walk in nature.

Reach out to someone for support or to share hope.

Set aside one device-free moment for presence.

Why this works:

Inner calm grows with intentional focus and small acts of presence. Even a moment rooted in peace can restore and reset your entire day.

Tip:

Mark your action and notice the inner shift—a peaceful life is built choice by choice.

Reader Spotlight: Naomi's Return to Stillness

Naomi's life was noisy and rushed. She started with a daily "two minutes of breathing"—no phone, just silence. "It felt odd, but quickly became my foundation. Soon, I found myself responding to stress more calmly and even reconnected with my faith." Over time, Naomi joined a community group and began volunteering. "Each small act of presence led to more peace, not less."

Takeaway:

The path to spiritual mastery starts with the smallest habits. Stillness expands from simple, repeated moments.

Reflect and Align: Your Must Foundations

Must Core Beliefs

What do I believe about spirit, faith, peace, or higher meaning?

Are these beliefs shaped by freedom, curiosity, and hope—or guilt and fear?

What empowering beliefs align me with a loving and wise life?

Must Core Values

Which values ground my spiritual journey—faith, compassion, wisdom, gratitude, service, humility?

Do my daily rituals reflect these values, or do they need reevaluation?

What boundaries/moments protect my peace and deepen my practice?

Must Personal Narrative

What story have I told myself about faith, strength, or my spiritual growth?

Is my story empowering or limiting? Whose voice have I included or excluded?

Write a new narrative: "I am on a journey to wholeness, guided by faith and love."

Must Standards

What essential habits nurture my faith and calm (prayer/meditation, reflection, weekly gathering, acts of kindness)?

How will I return to these standards in busy or challenging times?

MUST GOALS

Must Purpose

Why is spiritual wellness vital to me?

How does inner peace strengthen my body, relationships, work, and legacy?

What do I want my spiritual life to model or inspire others?

Your Spiritual Vision: Unlimited Possibility Exercise

Imagine your life filled with peace, presence, and purpose—where faith is vibrant, and serenity is your foundation.

Ask:

What would total inner peace and connection with the divine feel like?

What habits, rituals, or community would nurture my spirit?

How would my growth benefit my family, my work, and my wider circles?

Write your "Golden Bucket"—spiritual and peace-of-mind desires, rituals, and values that make your spirit sing.

Turning Vision into Aligned Action

Review: Highlight the dreams most aligned with your beliefs and values.

Prioritize: Sequence goals as immediate (peace), deepening (practice), or legacy (service).

Transform: Choose your top 3 and create I AM SMART TO ACT Spiritual Goals:

I: Identity alignment

A: Aligned with deepest values

M: Meaningful (rooted in purpose)

S: Specific

M: Measurable

A: Achievable

R: Relevant

T: Time-bound

TO ACT: Set the action—begin today

Remember: Inner peace, like any mastery, grows from small acts rooted in deep intention.

Pause to Reflect

Which belief or practice could most renew my sense of peace?

What boundary or habit will keep me centered in the face of a challenge?

What old story or wound am I ready to release?

What one step will I take today to deepen my spirit or stillness?

Science Spotlight: Peaceful Practices & Wellbeing

Research confirms that even brief daily meditation, gratitude, or prayer changes the brain—lowering stress hormones, reducing anxiety, and boosting emotional resilience. Social and faith-based practices increase feelings of belonging and hope, especially in times of adversity.

Avatar Walkthrough: Mustang Sally— Spirituality & Peace of Mind

1. Must Mindset

Sally commits to daily spiritual grounding, leaving guilt and comparison behind.

Example: "I now believe spiritual peace is possible every day, no matter the chaos."

2. Must Core Beliefs

"I am always connected to wisdom and hope."

"Inner peace is a skill I can strengthen."

"Faith, not fear, is my compass."

3. Must Core Values

Compassion

Gratitude

Presence

4. Mustang Sally's Spiritual Narrative

Old narrative: "I'm only at peace when everything is perfect."

New narrative: "True peace is my practice—I can cultivate it in any moment, for myself and others."

5. Must Standards

"I must journal at least three times a week on gratitude and reflection."

"I practice five minutes of silence or prayer before bed nightly."

"I volunteer monthly in a community of shared values."

6. Must Purpose

"To embody hope, wisdom, and compassion so I can uplift my family and all I serve."

7. Dreamstorming

Meditate daily with joy, not obligation.

Reconcile or forgive an old hurt.

Attend a spiritual or support group regularly.

Perform quiet acts of kindness or mercy.

Create a gratitude ritual with family.

8. I AM SMART TO ACT Spiritual Goals (Three Examples)

Must Goal 1: Daily Centering

"I am a soul at peace who values presence and gratitude. For the next 90 days, I will meditate or pray for 10 minutes every morning, tracked on my habit app. Each Sunday, I reflect and celebrate my streak by sharing gratitude aloud. If I miss a day, I restart the next morning—each fresh return counts and builds peace for myself and my family."

(SMART TO ACT breakdown and TO ACT = schedule tomorrow's meditation.)

Must Goal 2: Compassion & Service

"I am a compassionate presence who values giving. For the next 8 weeks, I will volunteer or perform a deliberate act of kindness weekly—recorded in my journal. Each month, I celebrate by reflecting on someone's story or sharing appreciation. If I skip a week, I note the why and return without guilt—every act is progress."

(TO ACT = sign up for next service day.)

Must Goal 3: Healing & Forgiveness

"I am a healer who values connection and freedom. By the end of this year, I'll work to forgive one past hurt—journaling, seeking counsel, or practicing release. Each month, I mark emotional progress and celebrate with self-acknowledgment. If it's hard or slow, I bring compassion and return to my intention—knowing peace is a journey."

(TO ACT = write the first forgiveness letter or reflect today.)

Now It's Your Turn: Your Spiritual & Peace Must Goals

1. Must Mindset

My spiritual mindset declaration: _____

2. Must Core Beliefs

a. _____

b. _____

c. _____

3. Must Core Values

a. _____

b. _____

c. _____

4. My New Spiritual Narrative

Old story: _____

New narrative: _____

5. Spiritual Standards

a. _____

b. _____

c. _____

6. Must Purpose

My purpose for peace of mind and spirit: _____

7. Dreamstorm (Vision List)

_____

_____

_____

8. My I AM SMART TO ACT Spiritual Goals (3):

Goal 1: _____

Goal 2: _____

Goal 3: _____

Tip:

Reflect and revisit every week—even small steps nourish a spiritual life.

Community for the Spirit

Multiply Peace Together

Invite a friend, faith partner, or group into your journey. Share struggles and hope, create gratitude or forgiveness rituals together, or join a spiritual support circle. Shared spirit multiplies peace.

Mantra: Progress, Not Perfection in Spirit

"I honor presence, not performance."

"My spirit can begin again, every moment."

"Brokenness can be transformed into blessing."

"Compassion is my anchor and my strength."

Spiritual Recap: Keys to Peace & Purpose

Spirituality and peace are the roots of all domains of life.

Must Foundations align your deepest beliefs with daily rituals.

Small acts—reflection, gratitude, service—build an inner sanctuary.

I AM SMART TO ACT goals create and sustain spiritual progress.

Celebrate every effort, and honor the journey's rhythm.

Closing: Spirit Flows Through All

Inner peace and faith are the wells that feed your health, relationships, work, and legacy. As you align spirit and purpose, your life radiates hope and meaning—lighting the path for others.

CHAPTER 18

Your Community & Legacy Goals

Your Community, Contribution, and Legacy Goals: Elevating Life Through Service

True legacy is not what you accumulate, but the lives you touch and the positive impact you leave behind. In the Must System, community and contribution represent the expression of your highest values and capacities. Service and legacy are how you plant seeds—today and for generations—that reflect what mattered most about your time here.

Quick Tip:

Access legacy planning prompts, service trackers, and impact journaling sheets at www.MustGoals.com/Resources.

The Must Lens on Community, Contribution, and Legacy

The outward flow of your Must Self transforms aspiration into action and impact. Whether you serve through coaching, volunteering, mentoring, philanthropy, or everyday kindness, what you give becomes the story the world tells about you. Your Must Contribution

Goals are built on intention, not accident or obligation—they are about living your values in community.

Kickstart Your Service and Legacy Today

Choose and complete one action:

Reach out to a local organization or community group to offer help.

Donate your time, money, or expertise to a cause you care about.

Mentor or encourage someone who's one step behind you.

Write an open letter or share your story with a community.

Thank someone who made an impact in your life.

Start a legacy project—archive family stories, plant a tree, or launch an initiative.

Why this works:

Each intentional act ripples outward and multiplies. Legacy is grown in the soil of daily, purposeful action.

Tip:

Celebrate your impact, however small. Every contribution counts and builds the foundation of your lasting story.

Reader Spotlight: Omar's Ripple Effect

Omar wanted to make a difference, but doubted how much one person could do. He began mentoring one student per year in his field. "Over time, those students became leaders, changing their communities for the better," he shares. "It became clear that consistent giving made an exponential impact—my small ripple turned into a wave."

Takeaway:

Legacy isn't built in one grand gesture—it's the sum of intentional, repeated acts of giving, mentoring, or service.

Reflect and Align: Your Must Foundations

Must Core Beliefs

What do I believe about my power to serve or create change?

Are there limits, doubts, or past experiences that kept me from contributing fully?

How can I adopt a belief that, "My actions matter at every scale?"

Must Core Values

What values will shape my service—compassion, justice, creativity, leadership, stewardship?

Do my routines honor these, or is it time for renewal?

What boundaries let me give without burning out?

Must Personal Narrative

What story have I told myself about my role in the world?

Do I see myself as a bystander, or as an agent of positive change?

Write a new story: "My legacy will be defined by the lives I lift and the world I help build."

Must Standards

What principles will keep me giving—showing up, volunteering, advocating, mentoring, or staying informed?

How do I embody consistency even when the outcome isn't immediate?

Must Purpose

Why do service and legacy matter to me?

How does my impact connect to family, community, or the planet?

What message do I want my actions to send to future generations?

Your Contribution and Legacy Vision: The Unlimited Possibility Exercise

Imagine a life where your service and legacy are fully realized—no barriers, no doubts. Ask:

What kind of positive change, from the smallest kindness to broad initiatives, do I wish to nurture?

What lasting influence or project would make me most proud?

How would I like to be remembered?

Who would benefit now or in the future?

Journal your "Golden Bucket" of aspirations—these are the seeds of your legacy.

Turning Vision into Aligned Action

Review: Highlight ideas that reflect your core values and beliefs.

Prioritize: Sort goals by what can be started immediately, built in the next few months, or as your long-term legacy.

Transform: Create three I AM SMART TO ACT Must Contribution Goals:

I: Identity alignment

A: Aligned with purpose

M: Meaningful

S: Specific
M: Measurable
A: Achievable
R: Relevant
T: Time-bound

TO ACT: Commit to an action step today

Remember: Every lasting legacy is built on small, deliberate actions.

Pause to Reflect

Which belief or value could expand my positive impact?
What story of service and legacy do I want my life to tell?
What daily or weekly action will seed a future I'm proud of?
What Must Action can I take now to be a force for good?
Record your answers and start with one tangible act.

Science Spotlight: The Legacy Effect

Research shows that consistent, value-aligned service or giving increases wellbeing, enhances social connection, and even extends lifespan. Legacy-building habits, from mentorship to philanthropy, foster resilience and empathy across generations.

Avatar Walkthrough: Mustang Sally—Community & Legacy

1. Must Mindset

Sally commits to making a difference, however small or large.

Example: "I believe I am a force for good, and my actions—big or small—matter for the future."

2. Must Core Beliefs

"My story matters, my actions multiply."

"Service is not separate from success—it defines it."

"Every talent can serve the greater good."

3. Must Core Values

Compassion

Stewardship

Empowerment

4. Mustang Sally's Legacy Narrative

Old narrative: "I'm just one person—what can I really change?"

New narrative: "My daily actions create ripple effects; every contribution, seen or unseen, is part of my legacy."

5. Must Standards

"I must volunteer or serve in my community monthly."

"I support a cause I care about each quarter—through giving, advocacy, or skills."

"I share my story and lessons with the next generation."

6. Must Purpose

"To leave my community brighter and more hopeful, multiplying the gifts I've received for others to enjoy."

7. Dreamstorming

Launch a scholarship fund for local youth.

Document and share family or community stories.

Organize an annual clean-up or health event.

Mentor three future leaders in my field.

Advocate for a policy or cause that matters.

8. I AM SMART TO ACT Community Goals (Three Examples)

Must Goal 1: Monthly Volunteering

"I am a committed neighbor who values connection and service. Starting now, I will volunteer three hours each month at a local food bank for the next 12 months, tracked in my calendar. Each month, I'll reflect on my impact and celebrate by writing a gratitude letter. If I miss a month, I'll find another opportunity or double up next time. Step by step, I'm building a legacy of hands-on service."

Must Goal 2: Mentorship Program

"I am an empowering mentor committed to growing others. Over the next year, I will guide two young professionals by meeting monthly to share insights and feedback, which will be tracked in a mentorship log. Each quarter, I'll celebrate with a get-together or progress review."

Must Goal 3: Legacy Project

"I am a steward of family history and hope. By next year, I will record and digitally archive the stories, photos, and lessons of my parents' and grandparents' generation, sharing them with my family at a reunion. Each milestone, I'll invite reflections from others and honor our shared journey."

Now It's Your Turn: Your Community & Legacy Must Goals

1. Must Mindset

My service/legacy mindset: _____

2. Must Core Beliefs

a. _____

b. _____

c. _____

3. Must Core Values

a. _____

b. _____

c. _____

4. My New Contribution Narrative

Old story: _____

New narrative: _____

5. Contribution Standards

a. _____

b. _____

c. _____

6. Must Purpose

My purpose for service/legacy: _____

7. Dreamstorm (Vision List)

_____

_____

_____

8. My I AM SMART TO ACT Community Goals (3):

Goal 1: _____

Goal 2: _____

Goal 3: _____

Tip:

Set regular times to review your impact and celebrate every step—legacy is built by consistency, not perfection.

Service Is a Team Sport

Multiply Impact Together

Invite loved ones, friends, or colleagues to join your service. Legacy initiatives empower, connect, and energize teams. Shared effort not only multiplies results, but builds lasting relationships and memories.

Legacy Recap: Keys to Enduring Impact

Legacy and service multiply as you share, mentor, teach, or help.

Must Foundations keep giving aligned, consistent, and meaningful.

Small contributions compound over time into lasting change.

I AM SMART TO ACT goals ensure every act is intentional and actionable.

Your life becomes both a lesson and an inspiration for those who follow.

Closing: You Are the Legacy

You are the gift. Through daily actions, stories, and consistent contribution, you craft a community and legacy that outlive you. As you plant seeds of hope, service, and wisdom, you inspire others to grow and give—creating a future that echoes with your purpose.

CHAPTER 19

Measuring Progress and Implementing Systems: Tracking and Achieving Must Goals

"You can't improve what you don't measure."
— Peter Drucker

What you measure, you multiply. When you track your progress with clarity and kindness, you turn vague hopes into visible momentum. Measurements and systems are not about judgment; they are about giving your Must Goals a reliable path to walk on every day.

Why Systems Matter for Must Goals

Must Goals are identity-anchored commitments, not casual wishes. Without simple systems, even the most aligned goals can get lost in busy weeks, shifting emotions, and constant demands. Systems create a bridge between your I AM SMART TO ACT declarations and your lived days.

- Systems protect your Must from moods and distractions by pre-deciding how and when you act.

- Measurement turns invisible effort into visible progress, which research shows significantly increases motivation, self-efficacy, and persistence over time.

When you combine Must identity with small, repeatable systems, your goals stop depending on bursts of willpower and start riding on structure.

From Must Goals to Must Metrics

Every I AM SMART TO ACT Must Goal needs 1–3 simple ways to see progress. Think of these as Must Metrics: clear indicators that show whether you are honoring your identity in action.

To define a Must Metric, ask three questions for each goal:

1. **What is the key behavior?**
    - Example: "Walk 8,000 steps at least 5 days each week" key behavior: daily walking.
2. **How will I know it happened?**
    - Step count, minutes, sessions, reps, dollars, pages, conversations, or yes/no completion.
3. **How often will I check it?**
    - Daily log, weekly review, or 12-week cycle summary.

Keep metrics behavioral and under your control. Instead of "lose 20 pounds," track "days I completed my movement and nutrition Must Habits." Instead of "find a dream job," track "applications sent," "networking conversations," or "skills practiced." This keeps your attention on actions that express your Must identity—regardless of short-term outcomes.

Try This Now

- Choose one Must Goal in any domain.
- Write one Must Metric you can track this week, in clear, simple language.
- Ask: "Does this metric measure my alignment with my Must identity, or only external results?" Adjust until it reflects who you are becoming, not just what you are chasing.

Simple Identity-Aligned Tracking Tools

Tracking does not have to be complex. The best system is the one you will actually use. Start with tools that match your personality and season of life.

Three low-friction options:

1. **Habit Grid or Check-Box Calendar**
    - Draw a simple grid: days across the top, Must Habits down the side. Each day you act, make an X or color a square.
    - This visual streak taps into the power of small wins and makes consistency satisfying.
2. **Daily or Weekly Log**
    - Use a notebook, notes app, or spreadsheet to record: "Must Goal," "Must Habit," "Did I act today?" "One sentence about what helped or hindered."
    - This adds reflection, which supports self-awareness and course correction.
3. **One-Glance Must Dashboard**
    - Create a simple page with your seven life domains (the Must Circle of Life) and list your #1 Must Metric for each domain.

- Review this dashboard weekly to see where you feel strong, stretched, or neglected.

Whatever format you choose, link it back to your I AM and your Must Standards. You are not just checking boxes; you are voting for the person you have chosen to become.

Feedback Loops and the Weekly Must Review

Progress accelerates when you regularly pause, notice, and adjust. You already use reflective questions elsewhere in this book; here, you gather them into a simple Weekly Must Review.

Once a week, ask:

What worked?

- Where did I live my Must Goals and standards in real actions this week?

What needs adjusting?

- Which habits, times of day, or environments made alignment difficult? What tiny change would help?

How do I feel about my progress?

- Not just numbers—energy, peace, stress, joy. Are my systems supporting my well-being across the Circle of Life?

What is my Must Focus for next week?

- Choose one Must Goal or habit to emphasize, so your effort is focused, not scattered.

Use your answers to refine your Must Habits and Must Micro-Goals, not to attack your worth. The purpose of the review is recalibration, not self-criticism.

Try This Now

- Pick one time in the next seven days (for example, Sunday evening).
- Schedule a 15-minute Weekly Must Review and protect it as firmly as any meeting.
- Use the downloadable Weekly Must Review template at MustGoals.com/Resources to guide your reflection and tracking.

The Must 12-Week Cycle

Big ambitions need time, but motivation thrives on nearer horizons. Many high-performers use 12-week or quarterly cycles to bring urgency and focus to their goals. You can adapt this idea as a Must 12-Week Cycle.

Step 1: Choose Your Vital Few

For the next 12 weeks:

- Select 1–3 Must Goals that would create the most significant positive ripple across your life in this season.
- Ensure they are fully aligned with your Must Mindset, Core Beliefs, Core Values, Standards, and Purpose.

Step 2: Define Weekly Milestones

Ask for each goal:

- "If this goal were on track 12 weeks from now, what would need to be true each week?"
- Translate that into small, measurable targets (for example, "3 strength workouts," "2 connection conversations," "save $X," "practice skill Y for 90 minutes").

Step 3: Track and Review Weekly

- Use your Must Metrics and Weekly Must Review to see whether you are honoring your commitments.
- Adjust process, not identity—keep the Must intact while experimenting with different actions or schedules.

Step 4: Celebrate and Recalibrate at Week 12

At the end of 12 weeks:

- Name achievements, strengths, and invisible gains (confidence, boundaries, self-trust).
- Ask, "Given who I am now, how do my next Must Goals need to evolve?"
- Choose the subsequent 12-week cycle with fresh clarity.

This simple rhythm keeps your Must Goals alive in time, prevents endless "someday" goals, and builds a habit of regular celebration and renewal.

Using OKRs and KPIs as Must Tools

In teams and organizations, you may encounter OKRs (Objectives and Key Results) and KPIs (Key Performance Indicators). These can become powerful extensions of your Must—if they start from identity and values, not just external pressure.

- **Objective:** A meaningful Must-aligned intention, such as "Build a culture of service-centered leadership" or "Deliver work that reflects our highest standards of integrity and excellence."
- **Key Results:** 3–5 measurable outcomes that show this is happening (for example, response times, quality scores, relationships built, specific projects delivered).

To integrate Must and OKRs:

- Begin with your Must Identity Map and Core Values—who you are as a leader, teammate, or professional.
- Set Objectives that reflect this identity.
- Choose Key Results that measure behaviors you can influence daily, using Must Habits and the Must Zone to execute.

When your workplace metrics are rooted in your Must, even corporate numbers become expressions of your authentic self rather than a source of constant misalignment.

A Simple Framework for Failure and Recalibration

No system is complete without a way to respond when goals stall, fail, or no longer fit your life. This book has already explored strategic course correction; here is a concise four-step recalibration framework you can apply any time your metrics tell you something is off.

1. **Recognize**
    - Notice patterns: repeated misses, constant dread, or data that never moves despite honest effort.
    - Admit, without shame, "The way I am pursuing this Must Goal is not working."
2. Realign
    - Recheck the foundations:
      Does this goal still align with my Must beliefs, values,
    - standards, and purpose?
    - If not, refine or release the goal. Let the Must remain; change the form.

3. **Redesign**

    If the goal is still aligned, but the system is not:
    - Shrink the step, not the standard—make today's action smaller but keep the identity intact.
    - Change timing, environment, or support (accountability partners, tools, or community).

4. **Re-engage**
    - Choose the smallest next micro-goal and act today.
    - Update your metrics and tracking to match your new plan.

Failure becomes feedback, not a verdict. Recalibration is how your ystems stay alive as your life changes.

Bringing It All Together

Measuring progress and implementing systems is not about becoming a machine; it is about giving your authentic self a practical way to show up, day after day. When your Must Goals are supported by Must Metrics, simple tracking, weekly reviews, 12-week cycles, and wise recalibration, you create an environment where alignment becomes normal and success becomes sustainable.

In the next chapter, you will step fully into the Must Zone—where these systems and measurements translate into daily, courageous action that reflects who you truly are.

CHAPTER 20

Must Actions in the Must Zone: Turning Goals into Momentum

"Without action, even the most carefully crafted, identity-aligned goals serve little purpose; only action on the goal creates the inertia and momentum that carry you to ultimate accomplishment."
— Stephen Rue

The Must Zone in Action: Where Alignment Becomes Courage

In the Must system, your **musts** are not weights or punishments—they are **beacons**. They are your most chosen, cherished values and purposes, lighting the way through life's fog, confusion, and challenge. On any courageous journey, discomfort, fear, and uncertainty will always show up—especially as you step forward in action.

The Must Zone is where those beacons meet your real life. It is the living space where identity, belief, standards, and daily choices converge, turning musts from written goals into lived movement.

The Must Zone: Your True Field of Growth

The Must Zone is the field where your deepest identity and chosen standards meet the realities of daily living. Resistance, "what if" worries, emotional lows, and old doubts are not proof that you are failing—they are direct evidence that you are moving forward. In the Must Zone, pressure is not a verdict; it is feedback that you are standing for something new.

If you feel fear, uncertainty, or challenge, you are not broken—you are in the arena of change. In this arena, your Must Actions become the bridge between who you say you are on paper and who you prove yourself to be in practice.

Fear, Doubt, and Uncertainty as Signals

Modern neuroscience and behavioral science show that discomfort and resistance are reliable indicators of growth. Whenever the brain encounters something new or identity-challenging, the threat system activates to keep you in the familiar, even when the familiar is limiting. Pressure often means, "This matters."

Seen through the Must lens:

- Discomfort is a signal that you are stretching old boundaries, not a sign that you are unworthy.
- Doubt is the "noise" of outdated narratives being challenged by new evidence.
- Uncertainty is the unavoidable companion of any path that is truly alive and aligned.

Courage, in the Must Zone, is not the absence of fear; it is taking

Must Actions in spite of fear, aligned with who you choose to be. Each courageous action helps form new neural pathways of resilience and self-efficacy, training your brain to expect that you will show up.

Objectifying Your Fears

Brian Tracy teaches that real progress requires not just admitting your fears, but listing and prioritizing them so you can deliberately address the ones holding you back the most. When you write your fears down, you transform them from vague clouds into specific targets.

This is a powerful Must move: your fears are not you—they are objects in your mental landscape, not your identity. On paper, fear becomes something you can investigate, plan around, and step toward with Must Actions, rather than a silent force that decides your future.

Must Actions: The Engine of Momentum

Must Actions are identity-aligned, value-driven, purpose-rooted steps that you treat as nonnegotiable. They are not random tasks or occasional bursts of willpower; they are deliberate efforts that directly honor your Must Mindset, Must Core Beliefs, Must Values, Must Narrative, Must Standards, and Must Purpose.

When you choose Must Actions:

- Each action answers fear with evidence: "This is who I am This mirrors the Yerkes–Dodson lawbecoming."

- Your musts begin to "weigh" more than your doubts, and your track record of showing up shrinks old obstacles.
- External uncertainty may remain, but its grip on your behavior and self-concept weakens.

Written goals can clarify direction, but only action creates inertia and momentum. A Must Goal on the page becomes a Must Life in reality only when you take the next aligned step, again and again.

Author Story: When Must Actions Became Survival

There was a season in my life when I felt deeply unhappy, weighed down by past family tragedies and personal setbacks. I slipped into a dark place of depression and a diminished personal narrative, feeling as though I was merely existing rather than truly living. The realization that this could not be my whole story was both painful and liberating—it pushed me to seek a way out of that darkness.

I knew I had to take deliberate, focused actions—what I now call **Must Actions**—to transform my life. I read voraciously, immersed myself in ancient wisdom and modern self-help, attended seminars, and learned from teachers like Tony Robbins, Les Brown, Jack Canfield, Zig Ziglar, and Brian Tracy. These actions were not optional; they felt essential to my survival and rebirth.

As I engaged in these **Must Actions**, I learned to reframe my past from burden to catalyst. My challenges became raw material for growth, and my mindset shifted from a focus on limitations to one of empowerment. That shift did not come from inspiration alone—it came from repeatedly acting in alignment with a new identity, even when fear and pain were loud.

Why the Must Zone Works: Science in Motion

Core psychological and neuroscientific principles support the Must Zone:

- Approach motivation. When action is tied to alignment and meaning, your brain releases dopamine for effort itself, not only for final success. This makes persistence more sustainable.
- **Cognitive dissonance.** When you feel discomfort yet still act for your must, your mind updates your identity to match your behavior, weakening old limiting mindsets.
- **Exposure and emotional learning.** Each time you face fear and act, your brain learns, "This is survivable and aligned," transforming old threats into signals of capability over time.
- **Neuroplasticity.** Repeated Must Actions literally rewire your brain, laying down new neural pathways that support your chosen identity, not your history.

The more you live in the Must Zone, the more natural it feels to think, choose, and act from your musts instead of your fears.

From Comfort Zone to Must Zone

Traditional advice tells you to "step out of your comfort zone," then slips you back into safety as soon as the pressure rises. The **Must Zone** offers a different model: you build a new normal where purposeful challenge is expected and desired.

In this upgraded frame:

- Challenge is expected, not avoided.
- Pressure is interpreted as meaningful, not catastrophic.

- Your comfort zone expands because growth becomes familiar and resourced, not foreign and frightening.

This mirrors the Yerkes–Dodson law: performance is highest at an optimal level of arousal—not too little challenge (boredom), not too much (overwhelm). Must Actions help you live near this optimal point: stretched, but not shattered; engaged, but not consumed.

The Must Zone also sets the stage for moments of *flow*—a state of deep, energized focus in which a meaningful challenge fully engages your skills, and time seems to fade.

Living the Must Zone in Real Life

The next time you notice:

- **Pressure** – "This is hard…"
- **Fear** – "What if I fail or look foolish?"
- **Doubt** – "Is this worth it? Am I enough?"
- **Uncertainty** – "What if the outcome isn't perfect?"

Remind yourself:

- "These are signs that I am growing. Progress is occurring."
- "This is old wiring, not new truth."
- "My must walks me through—not around—the fire."

This reframing turns the very sensations that once stopped you into cues that you are exactly where you need to be: in the Must Zone, doing the work that matters.

Mustang Sally: A Must Zone Portrait

When Mustang Sally feels nervous about starting a new health habit or questions her worth in a relationship, she does not treat these feelings as verdicts. Instead, she checks in with her Must Core Beliefs and Must Standards and asks, "What does my must call me to do here?"

Her pattern:

- She names the signal: "I feel fear and pressure."
- She re-grounds in identity: "I am a committed, resilient, loving woman."
- She shrinks the challenge into a Must Action: a 10-minute walk, a courageous conversation, a boundary respectfully stated.
- She reflects at day's end, celebrating not perfection but every time she acted because pressure showed up.

Over time, Sally's nervousness becomes less of a stop sign and more of a bell that rings every time she is close to growth.

Turning Pressure into Discipline

At first, the Must Zone can feel intense: new standards, new actions, new stories about who you are. Early on, pressure is what jolts you out of inertia—like the spark that ignites a flame.

If you keep returning to your musts:

- That raw pressure gradually transforms into structure and rhythm.
- Discipline replaces drama; consistent routines carry you when emotion fluctuates.
- Your "default self" shifts from avoiding difficulty to engaging it on purpose.

The sensations that once triggered retreat become the starting gun for disciplined forward motion—momentum born from aligned action.

If–Then Planning for Must Actions

Once you know your Must Actions, you can make them far more automatic with simple "*If–Then*" plans. Research shows that when you decide in advance exactly when, where, and how you will act, follow-through increases dramatically.

Use this structure:

- *If* [situation / cue], *then I will* [specific Must Action].

Examples:

- If it is 7:00 a.m. on weekdays, then I will walk for 20 minutes.
- If I feel the urge to procrastinate on my Must business task, then I will work on it for just 5 focused minutes.

Keep your *If–Then* plans short, concrete, and tied to real cues in your day. A few well-designed *If–Then* plans can turn your Must Goals into predictable, repeatable behavior. For a printable If–Then planning worksheet, visit *MustGoals.com/Resources*.

Risk and Scenario Planning for Big Must Goals

Big Must Goals—especially in health, business, and finances—deserve an extra layer of preparation. Instead of hoping nothing goes wrong, briefly consider what might derail you and decide how you will respond.

Use this quick scan for each major Must Goal:

1. Name the goal.
2. List 3–5 realistic risks or setbacks.
3. For each one, complete:
    - *If* X happens, *then I will* Y.

For example:

- If a significant expense hits my budget, then I will temporarily cut these three nonessential costs while still contributing something to my Must savings goal.

You do not need to predict everything; you only need enough contingency thinking to stay in motion when challenges appear. A simple Risk & Scenario Planning worksheet is available at *MustGoals.com/Resources*.

Step-by-Step: Making Your Must Your Anchor

Use this simple, repeatable sequence to stay anchored in the Must Zone:

1. **Honor Every Signal**

    Pause when you feel tension, fear, or resistance. Name it and acknowledge: "This means I've chosen something that matters."

2. **Re-ground in Iden**tity

    Reaffirm who you are and what you stand for with a present-tense declaration that links identity to action (for example, "I am a committed, resilient, creative leader—and today, I show up.").

3. **Shrink to Act**

    Ask, "What is the smallest next Must Action I can take in the next few minutes?" Then do just that. Small, aligned action is the only thing that rewrites fear's narrative.

4. **Reflect and Celebrate**

    At day's end, note where you chose Must Actions, especially when pressure was loud. Celebrate the fact that you acted because it was hard, not only when it was easy.

As this four-step loop repeats, it becomes a **habit: signal → identity → tiny action → evidence.**

Key Reminders for the Must Zone

As you integrate Must Actions and the Must Zone into daily life, keep these truths in view:

- Discomfort is not the enemy of progress—it is its proof.
- Every act aligned with your must, especially under pressure, builds a new reality and a new identity.
- Your musts, rooted in what you stand for, are always stronger than the fleeting winds of doubt—when you act on them.

The question is no longer, "How do I get rid of fear?" but, "*What Must Action will I take next, even here?*"

Bridge to Must Habits

Repeated Must Actions, especially those taken when fear or uncertainty are loudest, hardwire new ways of being. Over time, what begins as a chosen effort in the Must Zone becomes automatic: Must Habits.

These habits are the daily, reliable expression of your identity, built through countless small decisions to act from your must. In the next chapter, you will design specific Must Habits so that acting from your beacon is no longer occasional—it becomes your new normal.

Key Exercise:

Make a list of your fears connected to your goals. Circle the one that feels most limiting right now. Plan a small but intentional action to challenge it, proving to yourself that you can address, face, and move beyond it.

As John C. Maxwell eloquently puts it, "An unintentional life accepts everything and does nothing. An intentional life embraces only the things that will add to the mission of significance." This is precisely what my Must Actions were about—being intentional and focused on creating a better life.

I broke free from the cycle of suffering and created a new narrative for myself by committing to these Must Actions. I saw myself not as a victim of circumstance but as a survivor with a unique story to tell. My journey taught me that Must Actions are not just tasks; they are the deliberate efforts that drive us toward our true potential. They are the nonnegotiable steps we must take to align our lives with our deepest aspirations, our Must Values, and our Must Standards.

Must Actions are the deliberate and focused efforts that drive you forward, even when challenges arise. By consistently applying Must Actions to your daily tasks, you create a strong foundation for achieving your goals.

CHAPTER 20

Achieving Goals Through Must Habits

*"Success is the product of daily habits—
not once-in-a-lifetime transformations."*
—James Clea

Why Habits Matter in the Must System

In the Must Goals framework, habits are not just routines—they are the bridge between who you believe you can be ("I AM") and what you actually do, day after day. Habits are how your Must Mindset, Core Beliefs, Values, Narrative, Standards, and Purpose become visible in your calendar, your body, your relationships, and your results.

Goals give you direction, but habits create your trajectory. Real change lives in daily action, and habits are the structure that makes transformation sustainable, scalable, and less dependent on willpower over time.

Identity as the Root of Every Habit

Every Must Habit begins with identity. Your "I AM" statements—who you choose to be—are the root system.

- "I am a present parent."
- "I am a healthy, energetic person."
- "I am a disciplined, creative professional."

The question is not, "Can I force myself to do this habit?" but, "What does the person I am becoming naturally do?"

Confucius, the renowned Chinese philosopher, taught that people are born with similar natures, but it is their habits that carry them far apart. Virtue and excellence are not fixed traits; they are built through repeated practice over a lifetime. Every time you follow through on a Must Habit, you are doing exactly that—training your character through repetition, not waiting on talent, mood, or luck.

Every time you follow through on a Must Habit, you cast a vote for your chosen identity. Each repetition strengthens neural pathways, emotional associations, and self-trust, until the behavior becomes the easiest way to express who you are. Over time, Must Habits become the "memory of your future self in action."

Moving from Goals to Action: I AM SMART TO ACT

Earlier, you learned to craft I AM SMART TO ACT goals. Habits are how those goals come to life.

- You choose one small, meaningful action that embodies the goal.
- You do it today, and again tomorrow.
- You repeat often, making the behavior easier and less reliant on motivation.

This is Must in motion. You are no longer just writing goals—you are living them, one small, consistent action at a time.

What Makes a Must Habit Different?

A Must Habit is a simple, repeatable action you commit to daily or weekly, designed to make progress toward your Must Goal automatic and sustainable. It is:

- **Aligned with Core Identity.** It springs from your Must foundations—mindset, beliefs, values, narrative, standards, and purpose. It reflects who you want to be, not just what you want to get.
- **Driven by Repetition and Frequency.** Through consistent repetition, the habit becomes automatic, supporting your goals even when motivation dips or life gets messy.
- **A Bridge Between Action and Identity.** Your repeated choices become tangible expressions of your story and purpose. The habit is not just a tactic; it is a declaration of who you are in the world.

In short: a Must Habit is a deliberate, identity-aligned action you repeat until it becomes effortless and enduring—a proper foundation for achieving your Must Goals.

In a very real sense, we are the embodiment of our habits. Our repeated behaviors do not just fill our days; they literally reshape our brains and bodies through neuroplasticity—the brain's ability to form and strengthen neural pathways in response to what we do again and again. Each time you perform a Must Habit, you reinforce those pathways, making the behavior more automatic and natural over time. Your habits also show up in your physical health, posture, and energy. In this way, Must Habits are not just things you do; they become part of who you are, expressed in your thoughts, actions, and presence.

Must Habits are not only good for you; they are quiet blessings for others. When you build habits of kindness, generosity, and integrity, you create a ripple effect—that shapes the emotional climate of your home, your team, and your community. A consistent habit of showing up on time, listening fully, or offering a small word of encouragement can change more days and more lives than you will ever see.

The Four Pillars of Must Habit Formation

Every habit—good or bad—tends to follow the same basic loop:

1. **Cue** – The trigger that starts the behavior.

   "When I pour my morning coffee…"

2. **Craving** – The feeling or outcome you anticipate.

   "I crave the clarity and peace I feel after journaling."

3. **Response** – The small, specific action.

   "I'll write one line in my Must journal."

4. **Reward** – The immediate benefit and sense of congruence.

   "I feel grounded and check off today's action on my tracker."

Your brain is wired to repeat what feels rewarding. To make Must Habits stick, make the new behavior as satisfying as possible: choose actions you genuinely enjoy, celebrate small wins, and, occasionally, surprise yourself with a small, values-aligned treat after a streak of consistency. At the same time, gently disrupt the rewards that fuel unhelpful habits—break the link between scrolling and relaxation, or between stress and sugar—by pairing those cues with healthier, more restorative responses.

One easy way to choose a cue is to "stack" your new Must Habit onto an existing one: "After I brew my morning coffee, I'll write one line in my gratitude journal," or "After I close my laptop at work, I'll take a 5-minute walk before checking my phone."

Your role is to design this loop on purpose:

- Choose cues you can count on (existing routines, times, or locations).
- Tie cravings to identity ("I love being someone who...") rather than just external rewards.
- Make responses so small they feel almost too easy.
- Use rewards that reinforce your story—tiny celebrations, tracking, gratitude, or a brief moment of pride.

Implementation Blueprint: From Identity to Habit

Step 1: Declare Your I AM Identity

Write 1–3 identity statements connected to your Must Goals:

- "I am a grateful leader."
- "I am a lifelong learner."
- "I am a fit and energetic parent."

Not every possible habit deserves the same attention. Must Habits are the few daily or weekly behaviors that most directly express your Must Beliefs, Values, Standards, and Purpose. When you concentrate on these, you stop scattering your willpower across dozens of "shoulds" and instead build a small set of nonnegotiable practices that truly define who you are becoming.

Step 2: Set a SMART TO ACT Goal

Clarify one concrete outcome:

- "I will walk 7,000 steps a day for the next 60 days."
- "I will read 10 pages every night for 30 days."

Step 3: Translate to a Micro-Must Habit

Shrink this into the smallest repeatable action:

- "After I put my shoes on in the morning, I will walk for 5 minutes."
- "After I brush my teeth at night, I will read 2 pages before turning off the light."

If you resist the habit, make it even smaller. Micro-Musts are how you outsmart perfectionism and inconsistency.

Step 4: Build the Habit Loop

- **Cue:** "After I [existing routine]…"
- **Craving:** "I look forward to feeling like a person who honors this Must."
- **Response:** "I do the smallest version of my habit."
- **Reward:** "I mark it, smile, breathe 'thank you'—and move on."

One powerful way to lock this in is to use an "implementation intention"—a simple if–then plan such as, "If it is 7:00 a.m., then I will put on my walking shoes," or "When I feel the afternoon slump at 3:00 p.m., I will drink water and eat a piece of fruit instead of grabbing a candy bar." This kind of pre-decision links a clear cue to your chosen Must Habit and dramatically increases follow-through.

Step 5: Track, Celebrate, Adjust

- Track with a simple grid, calendar, or app—one check per day you act.
- When you miss, notice it without shame and simply return the next day. "Returning to Must" is itself a Must Habit.

- If you repeatedly forget or avoid the habit, adjust the cue, shrink the action, or connect it to a different time of day that matches your real life.

My Story: When Habits Became a Lifeline

As I reflect on my journey, I realize that Must Habits have been with me since long before I had the language for them. Growing up, after my father left and our family was shattered by tragedy, I carried a heavy sense of responsibility. I believed I had to be strong, to show up, to succeed—for my mother, my sister, and myself.

School became one place I could exert some control. I built quiet, simple habits: waking early to study, reviewing notes each evening, finishing assignments ahead of time. These were not glamorous routines, but they were Must Habits—anchored in a deep belief that doing well mattered for our future.

As I grew older, those habits evolved. I devoured personal development books, attended seminars, and sought mentors. I applied the same pattern to new goals: small, consistent actions, grounded in the identity of someone who takes responsibility for his life. That path led me through law school, business studies, and beyond—not because of talent alone, but because of habits that enabled perseverance.

Looking back, it is clear: the Must Habits I formed—discipline, daily learning, showing up when it was hard—did more than help me earn credentials. They changed who I believed myself to be. The habits became the building blocks of a life of purpose and contribution.

Eliminating Old Unhelpful Habits

Unhelpful habits—procrastination, numbing with screens, late-night snacking, constant self-criticism—are powerful precisely because they are automatic. Left unchecked, they quietly pull you away from your Must Goals. Your work is not to shame yourself, but to redesign these loops so they serve who you are becoming.

To build Must Habits, you often have to unbuild competing ones.

1. Name the Must you are protecting.

- "I must protect my energy and focus."
- "I must honor my health."

2. Make unhelpful cues invisible or rare.

- Remove apps from your home screen.
- Keep junk food out of the house.
- Avoid "just checking" email first thing in the morning.

3. Replace, don't just remove.

- Swap scrolling with a 5-minute reading or breath practice.
- Trade late-night snacking for herbal tea while you journal.
- Make unwanted behavior hard and Must behavior easy.

4. Put friction in front of the old habit (passwords, distance, time delay).

- Put support around the new one (lay out clothes, pre-fill water, open the book).
- You are not fighting yourself; you are redesigning your environment to serve who you are becoming.

Mustang Sally's Habit Cascade

Mustang Sally has learned to see habits as the daily proof of her Must identity.

- **I AM:** "I am a resilient, present friend."
- **Goal:** "I will meaningfully connect with my loved ones every week."
- **Habit:** After Sunday morning coffee (cue), Sally texts or calls one person (response), enjoys the feeling of connection (reward), and marks it off on her tracker.

When life gets busy, and she misses a Sunday, Sally does not declare herself "bad at relationships." She simply reconnects the following week. Her identity is not on trial every time she slips; it is being reinforced every time she returns.

That is how Must Habits work: not through perfection, but through loyal returning.

Troubleshooting & Evolving Your Must Habits

- **If you resist the habit, make it smal**ler.

    If you avoid a 30-minute workout, commit to 3 minutes. If you dodge writing 500 words, write 50.

- **If you forget the habit, change the** cue.

    Stack the habit onto a rock-solid routine (waking up, making coffee, brushing teeth, turning off the work computer).

- **If the reward feels flat, adjust** it.

    Add a social element (check-in with a friend), a visible marker (habit chain on the wall), or a deeper reflection ("How did this align with my Must today?").

- **If your Must evolves, update the habit.**

    As your identity, season, or priorities shift, retire or redesign habits so they match your next chapter. Old habits that once served you may no longer fit your current Must.

The True Outcome: Habits as the Foundation for Your Future

"Goals get you started; habits keep you going." In the Must system, both are essential and deeply interwoven:

- **Habits bring your "I AM" to life.** They automate the expression of your best self, even on days when motivation is low or feelings are complicated.

- **Your environment and routines are like soil and sunlight.** When you design them to nourish your Must, growth often seems to happen almost naturally.

Over months and years, Must Habits compound like interest. Small, identity-aligned actions, repeated consistently, create outsized results—greater health, deeper relationships, stronger finances, richer contribution—because they all flow from the same aligned source: who you choose to be.

From Habit to Tenacity

Once you've built new Must Habits, the journey is not over; it is entering a new phase. Some days, your habits will feel easy and natural. Other days—under stress, fatigue, or disappointment—they will feel heavy. Those are the days when tenacity, perseverance, and grit matter most.

Habits give you the structure. Tenacity keeps you walking inside that structure when storms come.

In the next chapter, you will discover how to endure, adapt, and rise—turning Must Habits and Must Actions into an unshakable way of life, no matter what challenges appear.

Must Habits: Key Takeaways

- Must Habits are small, repeatable actions that express your chosen identity ("I AM") and move your Must Goals forward automatically.
- Every repetition of a Must Habit casts a vote for who you are becoming, reshaping your brain, your body, and your relationships over time.
- Effective Must Habits use clear cues, tiny responses, and meaningful rewards—and they are often stacked onto routines you already have.
- Your work is to focus on a few high-leverage Must Habits, remove or redesign competing habits, and return to your Must each time you slip.
- Over months and years, these habits compound like interest—quietly building the health, relationships, work, and impact that match your deepest Must.

CHAPTER 21

Tenacity, Perseverance & Grit

"Never give in. Never, never, never, never—in nothing, great or small, large or petty—never give in, except to convictions of honour and good sense. Never yield to force. Never yield to the apparently overwhelming might of the enemy."
—British Prime Minister Winston Churchill

My mother's life is a testament to tenacity and perseverance. After my stepfather's tragic suicide, she became a young widow with two small children to raise. Despite her own grief and struggles, she never wavered in her commitment to provide for us and ensure we had the best possible future. She worked tirelessly as a public school teacher, often tutoring children at our kitchen table late into the night to make ends meet. Her unwavering determination to see us go through school, get a good education, and become successful and happy adults was a constant source of inspiration.

The depth of my mother's tenacity was truly remarkable. She faced countless worried days and sleepless nights, grappling with the overwhelming challenge of providing for our every need. The financial burden of ensuring we had an excellent education weighed heavily on her shoulders. Yet she never let her anxiety show, always presenting a strong and optimistic front to us. Her ultimate goal was to ensure we could depend on ourselves to advance in life as adults. This meant sacrificing her own comforts and desires, often going without so we could have the opportunities she believed we deserved. Her resilience in the face of such daunting odds was nothing short of heroic.

This spirit of tenacity and perseverance is a legacy I carry into my own life.

After I started deliberately exploring my beliefs and values, I left the law firm where I worked to pursue my own independent journey as a lawyer. I hung up my lawyer shingle and started representing people from all walks of life and in all types of cases. I wasn't making much money, but I loved what I was doing—helping people in need. One day, I passed by an old, boarded-up steak and egg restaurant that had sat vacant for years. No one wanted to buy it, because they saw the building as it once was, not as it could be. I saw a blank slate, a new canvas on which to create my future. I had little money, but I located the elderly owner of the property and told him my story. He graciously allowed me to owner-finance the property for a few years. When I first entered the building, it literally had the orange booths and decor that had been popular for that restaurant in the 1970s. The restaurant had a long steel grill that traveled the length of the back wall, and a long booth where people sat on round, orange stools.

I sold everything and gutted the place.

As I built the first building I ever owned, I had to sleep in the back room of the office for a year and a half as I couldn't afford to also get an apartment. All my income went to paying for ongoing debts, the building, construction, and advertising. I bought the biggest Yellow Pages ad, which I could not even afford. I had faith in myself and believed it would pay off. After all, I was my mother's child, and she had greater tenacity and resilience than anyone I had ever known.

When you have gone through great adversity in your life, it actually gives you a sense of freedom that you can get through anything, including the financial struggles that lie ahead, I had already endured so much more suffering in my life. With God's grace and with the determination forged from my past, over the years, I saw my law firm grow to numerous offices around the Greater New Orleans area. My law firm now stands as a well-known, established law practice where people know they are welcome and will receive the "Excellence in Action" that our core values promise.

This journey was not easy. But the tenacity and perseverance I learned from my mother, combined with my own determination to help others and stay true to my values, carried me through. It's a testament to the power of innate and learned resilience and the importance of never giving up on your dreams, no matter how difficult the path may seem.

Life is a journey marked by peaks and valleys, moments of triumph, and times of trial. As we navigate this journey, we are often faced with challenges that test our resolve, obstacles that seem insurmountable, and setbacks that threaten to derail us from our path. In these moments, it is not merely our talent or intelligence that determines our success, but our tenacity and perseverance—our ability to keep going despite the difficulties we encounter.

Take a moment to reflect on your life journey and the tremendous challenges you've already faced. Think about those pivotal moments when you stood at the crossroads of adversity and perseverance. What sense of courage did you muster from deep within? Where in the recesses of your being did you find that positive, motivating self-talk that urged you forward?

Remember the actions you took to push through, over, under, and around the walls that tried to impede your progress. What prior experiences of pain and suffering did you recall that were even worse than what you imagined might occur in the future? How did these memories comfort you, reminding you that you had already endured more, assuring you that you could survive the impending struggles?

Consider the outcomes you desired. Were they greater than the work and hardship you would encounter along the way? Think about the times when failure knocked you down once or more. Remember the ancient Japanese proverb to "fall seven times, stand up eight." Was the potential for failure insufficient to thwart the momentum of your desire to accomplish your goals? Recall that moment when the last of many so-called failures was finally followed by success.

These experiences are the crucible in which our *musts* are forged. They are the foundation of our perseverance, tenacity, and determination. As we reflect on the transformative power of embracing our *musts*, we find ourselves at a pivotal moment where the principles of mindset, core beliefs, and core values converge to guide us toward creating lasting habits.

In previous chapters, we explored how our mindset shapes our potential for growth and how identifying and aligning with our core values provides clarity and purpose. We learned that mindset is the lens through which we view challenges, while core beliefs act as the silent architects of our self-perception. Together, these elements influence everything from our daily decisions to the pursuit of our long-term goals. But this chapter asks us to go deeper. It challenges us to examine how the trials and tribulations of our past have shaped who we are today. The moments of pain and struggle—the heartbreaks, failures, and setbacks—are not just obstacles; they are the forge in which our character is tempered. These experiences have given us resilience, taught us lessons, and revealed strengths we may not have known we possessed.

This chapter builds upon the foundation laid earlier by showing how perseverance and tenacity are born from those very hardships. It connects the dots between mindset, beliefs, values, personal narrative, standards, and purpose, illustrating how they come together to fuel our determination to overcome adversity. Here we will explore how embracing our *musts* with unwavering commitment enables us to transform suffering into purpose, setbacks into stepping stones, and challenges into opportunities for growth. As you read on, consider this: What moments in your life have tested you? How have they shaped your beliefs about yourself and your capacity to persevere? This chapter is an invitation to honor those experiences, not as sources of regret or pain but as the defining moments that have prepared you for greatness. Together, we will uncover how perseverance and tenacity are not just traits but choices— choices that align with your *musts* and propel you toward becoming the person you were meant to be.

TENACITY AND PERSEVERANCE: THE PILLARS OF THE MUST ZONE

The journey into the Must Zone is not merely about optimizing daily life; it is about building a robust foundation for long-term resilience and purpose. As we embrace our *musts*—our nonnegotiable habits, mindset, and values—we simultaneously develop the mental and emotional tools necessary to face life's challenges head-on. These *musts* are not just routines; they are the crucible in which tenacity and perseverance are forged, empowering us to transform adversity into growth and setbacks into stepping stones toward greatness.

Tenacity and perseverance are essential qualities that elevate our Must Habits into a force capable of overcoming life's greatest challenges. While Must Habits provide the structure for our daily routines, tenacity and perseverance infuse these routines with the resilience and determination needed to thrive in the face of adversity. Angela Duckworth's research on grit demonstrates that sustained effort and resilience are more predictive of success than talent alone (Duckworth, 2016).

Tenacity is not merely about persistence. It is about strategic persistence—adapting and improving our approach with every setback, ensuring we grow stronger and more effective. Perseverance is the unwavering commitment to stay the course, even when obstacles seem insurmountable. Together, these virtues transform our Must Habits into tools for achieving greatness.

Our Must Habits, combined with a Must Mindset, serve as the foundation for cultivating tenacity and perseverance. We create a framework that supports resilience by integrating practices such as mindfulness, structured productivity, and a growth mindset into our lives. Mindfulness helps us maintain focus and emotional balance during difficult times; structured productivity helps us prioritize tasks effectively to avoid distractions, and a growth mindset fosters the belief that failure is an opportunity for learning and improvement. These habits allow us to approach challenges with clarity and purpose, ensuring that setbacks become stepping stones rather than roadblocks. Adversity plays a critical role in strengthening tenacity. The moments of pain, struggle, and loss shape our character and teach us invaluable lessons about resilience. These experiences—whether heartbreaks, failures, or setbacks—are not obstacles but crucibles that temper our character. They remind us that setbacks are opportunities to innovate, adapt, and grow stronger. By embracing these challenges with unwavering determination, we honor our journey and prepare ourselves for future triumphs.

Living in the Must Zone offers immediate benefits, like increased productivity, clarity of purpose, and alignment with core values. However, its true power lies in cultivating qualities essential for overcoming adversity. The discipline required to maintain Must Habits strengthens your ability to persevere through difficult times, creating a ripple effect that touches every aspect of your life. This chapter builds upon previous lessons by showing how perseverance and tenacity are born from hardships while connecting mindset, beliefs, values, personal narrative, standards, and purpose into a cohesive framework for resilience.

Consistent application of Must Zone principles leads to a compounding effect on resilience. Each day lived in alignment with your *musts* not only improves immediate well-being but also incrementally builds the strength needed to face larger life challenges. This cumulative growth in resilience is like compound interest for your personal development—small but consistent efforts yield exponential results over time.

By embracing tenacity and perseverance as essential qualities that build upon Must Habits, we ensure that every moment counts toward becoming our best selves. These virtues empower us to face life's challenges head-on while transforming suffering into purpose, setbacks into stepping stones, and challenges into opportunities for growth. As Winston Churchill said, "Success is not final; failure is not fatal: it is the courage to continue that counts." Let this courage guide you as you craft a life of purpose, resilience, and fulfillment within the Must Zone—a space where your habits align with your deepest values and fuel your journey toward greatness.

Research shows that individuals with a clear purpose are better equipped to handle stress and recover from setbacks. By defining your purpose through the Must Zone framework, you're not just improving your daily life; you're preparing yourself for future challenges. This sense of purpose acts as an anchor during turbulent times, providing stability and direction when you need it most.

Must Habits transform our choices into nonnegotiable commitments, propelling us forward despite the odds. As you reflect on these moments, recognize how they've shaped your resilience and fueled your growth mindset. These are the experiences that have prepared you for the journey ahead, equipping you with the strength to face whatever challenges may come.

At its core, tenacity is the determination to keep pursuing a goal, no matter how difficult or elusive it may be. It is the relentless drive that pushes us to continue striving for success, even when the odds are stacked against us. Perseverance, on the other hand, is the steadfastness to endure through trials and tribulations. It is the quality that enables us to weather the storms of life with grace and resilience, holding on to our vision even when the going gets tough.

These two qualities are inextricably linked. Tenacity fuels our perseverance, giving us the energy to keep pushing forward. Perseverance sustains our tenacity, allowing us to maintain our efforts over the long haul. Together, they form the backbone of any successful endeavor.

Tenacity and perseverance are not mere buzzwords; they are the bedrock of any significant achievement.

THE WRIGHT BROTHERS: THE POWER OF TENACITY AND *MUST*

As we explore the profound commitment implementing our *musts* requires, it's impossible not to draw inspiration from the story of the Wright brothers, Wilbur and Orville. Their journey from obscurity to achieving one of the most significant technological feats of the twentieth century—the first powered, controlled flight—serves as a powerful example of what it means to embrace your *musts* with unwavering determination.

The Wright brothers were not formally trained engineers or scientists; they were self-taught inventors driven by a passion for solving the mystery of flight. Their path was anything but smooth. The world at the time was skeptical, and many experts in the field doubted that powered flight was even possible. Yet the Wright brothers were not deterred. They possessed a relentless *must*—the unshakable belief of achieving human flight. This belief, goal, and purpose were not just a desire or dream; they were convictions so strong that they guided their every action.

Numerous challenges marked the brothers' journey, including technical failures, harsh environmental conditions, and even a serious injury that nearly ended Wilbur's life. Yet their unwavering commitment to their *must*—the deep purpose driving their efforts—propelled them forward. They spent years meticulously studying aerodynamics, testing countless models, and enduring repeated failures, each time returning to the drawing board with greater resolve. One of the most striking examples of their perseverance was their methodical approach to overcoming technical obstacles. When they needed a lightweight engine for powered flight but could not find one suitable, the brothers designed and built it themselves. Their first powered flight attempt stalled after three seconds and resulted in a crash that damaged the aircraft. Undeterred, they repaired the plane and tried again three days later, achieving a historic twelve-second flight that laid the foundation for modern aviation. This iterative process of failure and improvement highlighted their ability to adapt and innovate under pressure.

The Wright brothers also faced skepticism from experts and competitors with greater resources. Despite lacking formal education in aeronautics and financial backing, they relied on systematic experimentation to refine their designs. For instance, they conducted over 200 wind tunnel tests to perfect airfoil shapes and developed a groundbreaking three-axis control system that enabled controlled flight. Their persistence in addressing challenges like stability and lift efficiency set them apart from others in the field.

Even after achieving a powered flight in 1903, the brothers continued to improve their designs, demonstrating that tenacity is not just about reaching a milestone but about striving for excellence beyond it. Their ability to transform setbacks into stepping stones was rooted in their Must Mindset, which combined resilience, strategic problem-solving, and an unyielding belief in their purpose. By living in alignment with their Must Zone, they not only achieved success but inspired generations to pursue ambitious goals despite adversity. Orville Wright once remarked, "If we worked on the assumption that what is accepted as true really is true, then there would be little hope for advance." This resonates deeply with the essence of the Wright brothers' journey and the lesson it offers. The Wright brothers understood that achieving something extraordinary often requires questioning the status quo and pursuing your *musts* with a tenacity that defies conventional wisdom. They knew their success would not come from accepting limitations, but from challenging them and pushing beyond what was considered possible.

The Wright brothers' story is a testament to the idea that when we commit to our *musts*, we are not just making a choice; we are engaging in a process of continual learning, adaptation, and growth. Their success was not a sudden, singular event. It was the culmination of years of persistent effort, of small, incremental steps taken with purpose and resolve. Each experiment, each failure, and each discovery brought them closer to their goal because they remained steadfast in their commitment to their *must*.

The Wright brothers exemplify the power of embracing your *musts* with total dedication. They remind us that the path to fulfilling our purpose is rarely straightforward. It is in the daily, deliberate actions we take, no matter how challenging or uncertain, that our success is forged. Just as the Wright brothers' *must* led them to reshape the boundaries of what was possible, your *musts* have the power to redefine your life, push you beyond perceived limitations, and lead you toward extraordinary achievements.

THE SCIENCE OF TENACITY AND PERSEVERANCE

The qualities of tenacity and perseverance are not just inspirational; they are grounded in rigorous scientific research. Studies in psychology and neuroscience have demonstrated that these traits can be developed and strengthened over time, akin to muscle growth.

Understanding the underlying mechanisms can empower us to cultivate these qualities more effectively in our lives.

Recent neuroimaging research has begun to uncover the neural mechanisms underlying perseverance and goal-directed behavior. A 2019 study identified the anterior mid-cingulate cortex (aMCC) as a central hub for integrating information across multiple brain systems—such as attention, memory, emotion, and motor planning—to assess the costs and benefits of sustained effort. The researchers proposed that this region plays a critical role in "tenacity," enabling individuals to persist in challenging situations by dynamically evaluating whether continued effort is worthwhile.

The power of intentional repetitive thoughts and actions in developing perseverance is supported by neuroscience. The brain's ability to reorganize itself by forming new neural connections throughout life is enhanced when we consistently engage in persevering behaviors and thoughts; we strengthen the neural pathways associated with these traits.

Positive emotions also play a crucial role in building perseverance. According to the broaden-and-build theory, developed by psychologist Barbara Fredrickson, positive emotions expand our awareness and encourage novel, varied, and exploratory thoughts and actions. Over time, this broadened mindset helps build lasting personal resources, such as perseverance.

Fredrickson's research suggests that by cultivating positive emotions, such as joy, gratitude, and hope, we can enhance our perseverance and build a buffer against the effects of stress. Positive emotions not only make us feel good in the moment, but they also help us recover more quickly from adversity and build the psychological resources needed to face future challenges. Fredrickson eloquently cautions, "Just as water lilies retract when sunlight fades, so do our minds when positivity fades." We must maintain our positive emotions to provide fuel for our tenacity and perseverance.

These scientific insights provide a solid foundation for our practical applications of developing tenacity and perseverance. By engaging in intentional repetitive thoughts and actions that reinforce perseverant behavior, we can strengthen the neural pathways associated with these traits. This process involves setting and pursuing challenging goals, which push us beyond our comfort zones and require sustained effort as we stay in our Must Zone. As we work toward these goals, practicing positive self-talk during difficult tasks becomes crucial, helping us maintain motivation and overcome obstacles. Regularly engaging in activities that demand sustained effort further reinforces our capacity for perseverance, whether through physical exercise, learning a new skill, or tackling complex projects. Cultivating a growth mindset through education and self-reflection is equally important, as it allows us to view challenges as opportunities for growth rather than insurmountable barriers. By consistently applying these strategies, we can harness the power of neuroplasticity to enhance our capacity for perseverance and tenacity. This intentional approach to developing these traits not only strengthens our ability to overcome obstacles but also leads to greater personal and professional success, as we become more resilient and determined in pursuing our goals.

GRIT AND LONG-TERM SUCCESS

Angela Duckworth is a prominent psychologist and professor at the University of Pennsylvania who has gained widespread recognition for her research on grit. As a former management consultant and seventh- grade math teacher, Duckworth became intrigued by the disparity between student potential and actual achievement. This curiosity led her to pursue a PhD in psychology and develop her theory of grit. Duckworth defines grit as "passion and perseverance for very long- term goals." It's a combination of sustained interest (passion) and persistent effort (perseverance) toward challenging objectives. Grit goes beyond mere resilience or tenacity; it encompasses the ability to maintain focus and dedication over extended periods, often years or even decades.

Gritty individuals not only overcome obstacles but also stay committed to their objectives despite temptations to change course or give up. Duckworth's research suggests that grit is a better predictor of success in various fields than factors like IQ or talent alone. Her studies have shown grit's significance in contexts ranging from West Point military cadets to National Spelling Bee contestants.

Duckworth tells us, "Grit is living life like it's a marathon, not a sprint." This metaphor effectively conveys the long-term nature of grit, emphasizing that success often requires sustained effort over time rather than short bursts of intensity. It challenges the notion of overnight success and highlights the importance of perseverance in achieving significant goals.

CONJURING OUR OWN TENACITY, PERSEVERANCE, AND GRIT

Where do we find the tenacity, perseverance, and grit to keep going when the road becomes unbearably tough? These traits are not gifts

bestowed upon a select few; they are qualities that reside within each of us, waiting to be called upon in times of need. But how do we access them? How do we summon the strength to persevere when everything inside us screams to give up?

Our Must Mindset empowers us to see failure not as a reflection of our inherent abilities but as a stepping stone to success. It allows us to persist in the face of adversity, knowing that each setback is simply part of the journey. By cultivating a Must Mindset that compels us, we tap into an inexhaustible well of tenacity and grit, enabling us to keep moving forward, no matter how daunting the challenge.

Another wellspring of tenacity and perseverance is our sense of our purpose derived from our *must* foundations of who we are. When we are deeply connected to our purpose—when we know our "why"—we are far more likely to persevere through difficulties. Purpose gives us a reason to keep going, even when the path is hard. It fuels our determination and keeps us focused on the bigger picture.

Simon Sinek reminds us that our purpose is our motivating engine of progress. Those who understand their "why" are better equipped to inspire action in themselves and others. "Working hard for something we don't care about is called stress; working hard for something we love is called passion," Sinek explains. When we align our goals with our purpose, we transform our efforts from a burden into a mission. This sense of purpose becomes the fuel that drives our tenacity, helping us to stay the course even when the going gets tough.

The way we approach goals can also help us build tenacity. One helpful strategy is to set clear, long-term goals that are personally meaningful and break them down into smaller, achievable milestones. This strategy, known as "goal laddering," has been shown to increase motivation and persistence by up to 30 percent in longitudinal studies. Additionally, engaging in deliberate, focused practice in areas targeted for improvement is crucial.

Research indicates that individuals who dedicate at least ten thousand hours to mastering a skill demonstrate significantly higher levels of grit and expertise in their chosen field. While it may seem circular, the development of tenacity through persistent practice is a self-reinforcing process. The act of dedicating oneself to deliberate, focused practice not only builds skill but also strengthens the mental fortitude required for long-term commitment. As individuals invest time and effort into their chosen pursuits, they develop not just expertise but also resilience, perseverance, and a growth mindset. This process creates a positive feedback loop: the more one practices, the more tenacious they become, which in turn fuels their ability to engage in further practice.

It's important to note that the ten-thousand-hour rule is not a rigid benchmark but rather a representation of the substantial time investment required for mastery. The key takeaway is that consistent, purposeful effort over time not only develops skill but also cultivates the very qualities of grit and determination that enable continued growth and achievement.

Tenacity, perseverance, and grit are often strengthened by the support of others. Surrounding ourselves with a community of like-minded individuals who share our goals and values can provide the encouragement and accountability we need to keep pushing forward. Whether it's a mentor who offers guidance, a friend who lends a listening ear, or a group of peers who share our struggles, the power of community cannot be underestimated.

Research has shown that social support is a critical factor in resilience and perseverance. When we feel supported by others, we are more likely to persevere through challenges and less likely to give up when things get tough. This support helps us to maintain our motivation and stay focused on our goals, even in the face of adversity.

For example, Angela Duckworth and her colleagues conducted a comprehensive study that shed light on the significant role of social support in fostering grit among adolescents. Their research, which involved a large sample of students from diverse backgrounds, revealed a strong correlation between perceived support from teachers and peers and higher levels of grit and perseverance in academic pursuits. Specifically, students who reported feeling valued, encouraged, and supported by their educators and classmates demonstrated a 20 percent increase in grit scores compared to those who felt less supported.

Embracing challenges as opportunities for growth rather than threats is another key component in developing grit. This mindset shift, rooted in Carol Dweck's growth mindset theory, has been associated with an increase in academic performance and resilience in the face of setbacks.

Regularly reflecting on progress and celebrating small victories along the way has been linked to increased motivation and perseverance. Research indicates that individuals who engage in weekly self-reflection and acknowledge their incremental progress have an enhanced likelihood of achieving their long-term goals.

By implementing these evidence-based strategies and maintaining a growth mindset, individuals can develop the tenacity, perseverance, and grit to overcome obstacles and achieve their long-term aspirations. It's important to remember that these qualities are not innate or fixed traits, but rather skills that can be cultivated and strengthened over time through consistent effort, practice, and a supportive environment.

Overcoming Challenges Through Support and Accountability

No one maintains tenacity in isolation. Even the most committed Must Goals will encounter seasons of fatigue, complexity, or crisis, and in those moments, support and accountability become the scaffolding that keeps you standing. Resilient people do not just push harder alone; they wisely invite others into the journey.

Support and accountability work best when they are grounded in your Must identity rather than in shame or pressure. The goal is not to have someone "police" you, but to surround yourself with people who see your potential, respect your boundaries, and remind you of who you are when you temporarily forget.

Three Must Support Systems

- Mentors and Guides

    A mentor, coach, or trusted elder can help you interpret setbacks, challenge unhelpful stories, and spot when stubborn grit is drifting into misalignment. Mentors are especially valuable during major pivots—career shifts, health crises, or relational turning points—when your perspective may narrow under stress.

- Peers and Accountability Partners

    A peer or accountability partner walks beside you, not above you. Share your top one to three Must Goals, agree on simple weekly or bi-weekly check-ins, and use those conversations to review progress, apply the Failure and Recalibration steps, and celebrate small wins together. The point is mutual encouragement and honest reflection, not perfection.

- Communities and Environments

    Groups—professional networks, faith communities, online Must spaces, mastermind circles—shape your norms and expectations. Environments that normalize growth, vulnerability, and long-term purpose make it far easier to persist than environments that glorify burnout, perfectionism, or superficial success.

Using Failure and Recalibration with Others

Earlier, you learned a four-part framework for recalibrating when a goal stalls or your life context changes: Recognize, Realign, Redesign, Re-engage. Support and accountability multiply the power of that process.

- Recognize (with honest mirrors)

    Share your data and feelings with someone you trust: missed habits, emotional resistance, or recurring obstacles. Ask them, "What do you see that I might be minimizing or ignoring?" Others often spot patterns—exhaustion, over-commitment, misalignment—before you can.

- Realign (checking your Must together)

    Revisit your Must Beliefs, Values, Standards, and Purpose with a mentor or partner, asking: "Does this goal still fit who I am becoming, or has my season changed?" Let their questions help you distinguish between fear-based quitting and wise course correction.

- Redesign (co-creating better strategies)

    Invite input on new approaches: shrinking the step, changing timelines, delegating tasks, or altering your environment. Sometimes a small, outside suggestion—moving your writing time, changing your workout location, adjusting a metric—removes friction you have normalized.

- Re-engage (with shared commitment)

    Define one fresh Must Micro-Goal and tell your partner or group exactly when and how you will do it. Ask them to check in after that time. Knowing someone will ask about your next step increases follow-through without relying on sheer willpower.

Reflection and Action

- Who are the two or three people you trust to see both your courage and your blind spots?
- How could you invite them into your Must journey—not to control you, but to walk with you?
- Which current struggle or stalled goal could benefit most from one shared conversation using Recognize, Realign, Redesign, and Re-engage?

When you combine internal tenacity with external support and wise recalibration, your resilience stops being a fragile state of mind and becomes a robust way of living.

STEPHEN RUE

THE BALANCE BETWEEN SURRENDER AND PERSEVERANCE

Does surrender mean failure? When is it wise to surrender one path of pursuit and choose another one? The word "surrender" often conjures images of white flags and defeat, but true surrender can be an act of immense strength and wisdom.

The idea that surrender equals failure is a common misconception. In reality, there are times when surrender is the wisest course of action, a recognition that some battles are not meant to be fought. However, perseverance at all costs can also lead to burnout, diverting us from our true path.

Wisdom lies in knowing when to hold on and when to let go. It's about asking the tough questions: Is this pursuit enhancing my life or draining my spirit? Am I holding on out of fear or genuine aspiration? True courage comes from being honest with ourselves, confronting our fears, and living authentically.

Steve Jobs, the co-founder of Apple, exemplified this wisdom. Known for his relentless drive and vision, Jobs also understood the importance of knowing when to pivot. After being ousted from Apple, the company he co-founded, Jobs could have persisted in trying to regain his position. Instead, he chose to surrender that fight and focus on new ventures, including the creation of Pixar, which revolutionized the animation industry. His decision to let go of one battle allowed him to win another, ultimately leading to his triumphant return to Apple and the creation of iconic products like the iPhone.

Navigating the balance between surrender and perseverance requires courage—the courage to be vulnerable, to admit when we don't have all the answers, and to take the leap of faith that is required, whether in surrender or perseverance. The true measure of knowing if you are on the right path, and whether you should surrender or persevere, is whether your current path is in direct alignment with your Must Core Beliefs, Must Values, Must Standards, and thoroughly examined purpose.

THE UNBREAKABLE HUMAN SPIRIT

Your life is rich not just with sunny meadows but also with deep valleys. Your most challenging times often reveal the core of who you are, and it's from that core that you draw the strength to rise. As you traverse life's difficulties, each challenge is a stepping stone on your path to becoming the magnificent being you were always meant to be. Richard Bach, American author, proclaims, "You are never given a dream without also being given the power to make it true."

Earlier in this book, the story of my mother on her hands and knees after my stepfather's death showed what a real-life Must looks like in action. That same fierce commitment is the heart of tenacity and grit.

I pray you never have to experience such profound suffering or face a tragedy that shatters the very foundations of your world. But if you are confronted with overwhelming darkness, remember this: within you lies an untapped wellspring of strength, a reservoir of tenacity that you can rise from and that must carry you through the storm. If you have already encountered a devastating tragedy in your life, then you know you can handle whatever happens in the future. For in the end, it is not the absence of suffering that defines us, but how we choose to respond to it. Let your response be one of courage, of compassion, and of unwavering resolve. In doing so, you not only honor your own journey but also inspire others to find their inner strength in times of need.

When Tenacity Means Letting Go or Changing Direction: The Science of Strategic Course Correction

Tenacity is essential for meaningful achievement. But the research is clear: persisting with every goal at any cost is not strength; it can be a path to burnout, regret, and misalignment. Strategic course correction—choosing to adjust, pause, or even release a goal—is a core skill of wise, self-aware high performers.

Use the following questions as a simple test for course correction:

- **Progress:** Have you made honest, sustained effort over time, yet progress remains minimal or nonexistent?
- **Alignment:** Does this goal still fit your core beliefs, values, standards, and Must purpose—or has it drifted out of alignment with who you are becoming?
- **Cost:** Is continuing this goal requiring you to sacrifice your health, relationships, integrity, or other Must priorities in a way that no longer feels acceptable?
- **Opportunity**: Has a more meaningful or realistic goal appeared that better reflects your identity, current season, or responsibilities?

If several of these answers concern you, tenacity may now mean changing direction—not pushing harder in the same way. You can revise the goal (scope, timeline, approach), redefine success, or release it entirely and reclaim that energy for higher-priority Must Goals.

Letting go or changing direction is not quitting on yourself. It is choosing the goals that are truly worthy of your effort.

When Goals Collide: Navigating Goal Conflict with Wisdom

Sometimes the problem is not a single goal, but a conflict between goals—either within your own life or between your goals and the needs or goals of others. Unresolved goal conflict is a major reason people stall, procrastinate, or feel torn.

There are two common types:

- **Internal conflict:** Two or more of your goals compete for time, energy, or resources (for example, rapid career advancement vs. deep presence with family).
- **Interpersonal conflict**: Your Must Goals appear to clash with someone else's goals or expectations (a partner, boss, team, or community).

When you notice goal conflict, apply the same course-correction lens:

- Clarify which goals most fully reflect your Must mindset, beliefs, values, and purpose.
- Decide what can be delayed, delegated, scaled back, or redesigned.
- When others are involved, communicate openly: name your Must priorities, listen to theirs, and look for creative adjustments or shared solutions rather than silent resentment.

If a conflict cannot be resolved without betraying your deepest Must commitments, tenacity may again mean changing course—choosing the path that best honors your authentic identity and relationships over the long term.

When Goals Are Complete: Renewal, New Priorities, and Celebration

Reaching a Must Goal is not the end of your growth; it is a transition point. Research shows that people who pause to reflect on what they did well, what they learned, and how they grew are more likely to sustain confidence, avoid the "now what?" crash, and choose their next goals more wisely.

When you complete a goal, ask:

- What strengths, skills, and habits did this goal help me build?
- How did this journey change my identity, beliefs, or values?
- Given who I am now, what feels like the next right Must Goal or priority?

As life seasons change, your priorities will change too. Tenacity does not mean clinging to yesterday's targets; it means continually re-aiming your effort toward what matters most now. Use completions as natural checkpoints to realign your Circle of Life domains and update your Must Goals, rather than drifting into autopilot.

Finally, celebrate. Science is clear that acknowledging progress—both the outcome and the process—builds motivation, positive emotion, and a stronger sense of self-efficacy for future goals. Don't just celebrate the result you achieved; honor the consistent actions you took, the obstacles you faced, and the person you became along the way. This kind of intentional celebration closes the loop on one chapter of your growth and energizes you to write the next one.

COMMON OBSTACLES ON THE MUST PATH
How to Stay Aligned When Life Gets Hard

Every meaningful change meets resistance. Not because you are weak or broken, but because you are human. If you are pursuing Must

Goals—identity-rooted commitments that matter deeply to you—you will inevitably face seasons when progress slows, motivation drops, or life crowds your plans.

This is not a sign that your Must is wrong. It is a sign that your Must is real.

This section gathers the most common obstacles that appear across every domain—health, relationships, career, finances, growth, spirituality, and community—and offers you a simple, Must-centered way to move through them. Return here whenever the journey feels heavy. Let it remind you that struggle is not the opposite of success; it is part of it.

WHEN MOTIVATION DISAPPEARS

There will be days when your Must Goals feel distant, and your energy feels thin. You may wake up and think, I just don't feel like it today. That moment is not a verdict on your character. It is a crossroads.

On the Must path, motivation is a bonus—not the engine. Identity and alignment are the engine.

When motivation dips:

- Remember who you are, not how you feel.

  Re-anchor in your I AM statement and your Declaration of Purpose. You are not the mood of the morning. You are the person who has decided to live from Must.

- Shrink the step, not the standard.

  Keep your standard (I must care for my health, I must invest in my marriage, I must steward my finances), but make today's action as small as necessary. One glass of water. One honest conversation. One bill reviewed. Small actions keep identity intact.

- Move first, feel later.

    On many days, feelings follow movement. Commit to five minutes in the Must Zone—five minutes of writing, walking, connecting, planning. Often, once you begin, momentum quietly returns.

Your Must is not measured by how often you feel inspired. It is measured by how often you honor your commitments, especially on uninspiring days.

WHEN YOU HIT A PLATEAU

Sometimes you are doing the work, but the results seem to stall. The scale doesn't move. The relationship feels stuck. The business numbers flatten. Plateaus can feel discouraging, but they are often where the deepest growth is happening.

On the Must path, a plateau is an invitation to refine, not a reason to resign.

When progress slows:

- Review your alignment.

    Ask, Does this goal still reflect my Must Mindset, values, standards, and purpose? If it does, stay the course. If it doesn't, adjust the goal—not your worth.

- Adjust the process, not your identity.

    Instead of concluding, I'm failing, ask, What tiny adjustment would move me forward? Change the frequency, intensity, or method while keeping the Must intact.

- Look for invisible gains.

    Some progress is internal before it becomes visible: better self-talk, stronger discipline, clearer boundaries. Name those wins. They are not extra; they are the foundation.

Plateaus are not proof that nothing is happening. They are proof that growth has moved below the surface for a season. Stay aligned, keep acting, and the surface will catch up.

WHEN LIFE GETS BUSY

There will be seasons when life feels full to overflowing: caregiving, illness, deadlines, parenting, transitions. In those times, it can feel impossible to maintain your Must Goals—and tempting to abandon them entirely.

On the Must path, busy seasons are when your alignment matters most.

When life is crowded:

- Move from expansion to maintenance.

    You may not be able to push hard in every domain, but you can choose one or two Must Goals to continue moving forward and shift others into "maintenance mode" rather than "abandonment mode."

- Simplify your Must Habits.

    Reduce duration without breaking the chain. Ten minutes instead of thirty. One weekly check-in instead of three. The goal is continuity, not perfection.

- Let your Must guide your "no."

    Use your Must Standards and values as filters. Ask, Does this commitment support or sabotage my Must? Say no more often, so your yes remains meaningful.

Busy seasons will come and go. When you protect even a small expression of your Must during those times, you preserve your identity and make it easier to accelerate again when the load lightens.

WHEN YOU FALL OFF TRACK

At some point, you will miss more than one day. You will break a streak. You will abandon a habit for a week, a month, or longer. Old patterns will resurface. This does not disqualify you from living your Must. It simply places you at a decision point.

On the Must path, "failure" is feedback.

When you fall off track:

- Tell the truth without shame.

    Acknowledge what happened—clearly and kindly. Shame says, I am the problem. Must says, I made choices that did not honor my identity, and I can choose again.

- Return to the next right step.

    You do not need to make up for all lost time in one heroic push. Take the smallest next aligned action today. Restart the habit with a lighter version. Revisit your Must Goal and reaffirm it.

- Learn the lesson.

    Ask, What made it easier to drift? Lack of rest? Overcommitment? No accountability? Use the answer to adjust your environment, schedule, or support system so returning becomes easier than repeating the old pattern.

Your Must does not disappear when you fall. It waits at the place where you choose to rise.

WHEN YOU FEEL OVERWHELMED BY TOO MANY GOALS

As you work through the Must Circle of Life, it's easy to generate more goals than any human could pursue at once. Enthusiasm can quietly turn into overwhelm. When everything feels urgent, nothing moves.

MUST GOALS

On the Must path, focus is an act of integrity.

When you feel stretched thin:

- Choose your "Vital Few."

    From your list, select one or two Must Goals that would create the greatest positive ripple in this season. Let the others become "Future Musts" rather than current demands.

- Sequence, don't stack.

    Decide what comes first, what comes next, and what can wait. A strong health habit may need to precede an ambitious career push. A relationship repair may need to precede a new community commitment.

- Accept seasonal trade-offs.

    You can have a rich, multi-dimensional life—but not all at the same level, all at once. Align your focus with your current season, then review and re-balance regularly.

You honor your Must not by trying to do everything, but by doing the right things for who you are and where you are now.

USING THIS SECTION WITH YOUR DOMAIN GOALS

Whenever you hit one of these obstacles in a specific area—health, relationships, career, finances, growth, spirituality, or community—start here first. Then, apply the principles to that domain:

- For health-related struggles, adapt the tools to movement, rest, and nourishment.
- For relationship struggles, adapt them to communication, presence, and boundaries.
- For financial struggles, adapt them to planning, spending, saving, and earning.

- For spiritual or community struggles, adapt them to connection, service, and meaning.

Your Must is one integrated identity expressed through many domains. The obstacles feel different in each area, but the way through is the same: alignment, small steps, honest reflection, and the courage to begin again.

You will face motivation dips, plateaus, busy seasons, setbacks, and overwhelm. Expect them. Prepare for them. And when they come, remember: you are not alone, you are not behind, and you are not done.

You are on the Must path. And every time you return to it, you strengthen the person you are becoming.

CONCLUSION

The Must Goal-Setting Journey Towards Becoming

"Life isn't about finding yourself. Life is about creating yourself."
—Attribu ted to George Bernard Shaw, Irish pl ay w right and philosopher

Living Your Must in the World**

There comes a moment in every meaningful journey when knowledge must turn into embodiment—when what once felt like a quiet hope becomes the very fabric of your life. If you've moved through these pages with honesty and courage, you've already taken the most important step: you've begun to see yourself not as someone chasing goals, but as someone becoming aligned with who you truly are.

You are no longer working from the outside in. You are building your life from the inside out—identity first, action second, outcome last. That shift is everything. It is what separates temporary enthusiasm from lasting transformation. It is what turns effort into devotion, and goals into a life that reflects your deepest values.

This is the power of Must.

Your Must is not a demand. It is not pressure. It is clarity. It is the steady truth inside you that says, "This matters. This is who I am. This is what I will honor."

It's the voice that says, "I must protect my health, not because I'm afraid of illness, but because I must show up for my family."

It's the voice that says, "I must grow in my career, not to prove my worth, but because I must serve my purpose."

When you make decisions from that place, your goals stop feeling like obligations—they become expressions of your authentic self.

You've clarified your beliefs, values, standards, narrative, and purpose. You've defined who you are becoming. And now, you stand at the turning point every great transformation reaches: the moment when thought must become action.

Because identity without action is potential.

Identity with action is power.

And power, lived consistently, becomes legacy.

The world will not always make your Must convenient. There will be seasons that test your commitment, distract your focus, or tempt you back into old habits. But you now know something that cannot be unlearned: you are capable of building a life that reflects who you truly are. You can choose alignment over drift. You can choose the long game over the quick fix. You can choose to honor the values and standards that define you—especially on the days when it feels hardest.

That is what separates a goal-setter from a Must-liver.

MUST GOALS

A Must-liver chooses truth over approval.

Action over avoidance.

Discipline over distraction.

Growth over protection.

Identity over impulse.

You are capable of extraordinary things, not because of luck or talent or circumstance, but because you have taken the time to align your inner world with your outer commitments. Alignment is the great multiplier. When it is present, momentum becomes effortless. When it is absent, even small tasks feel impossible.

Your goals, your habits, your systems—these are no longer disconnected tasks. They are the daily votes you cast for the person you are becoming. And the more consistently you cast those votes, the faster your identity strengthens, until living your Must becomes natural, automatic, and deeply rewarding.

Remember this truth:

You do not rise to the level of your dreams.

You rise to the level of your alignment.

And now, you have the tools to create that alignment every single day.

As you step forward, choose one Must Goal to walk with you. Let it be the one that speaks the loudest, the one that feels like both an invitation and a responsibility. Break it into steps. Turn those steps into habits. Let your habits shape your days, and let your days shape your identity. This is the quiet architecture of genuine transformation.

And when you stumble—and you will—return to your Must. Not with shame, but with clarity. Your Must is not fragile. It does not disappear when you fall. It is waiting for you each time you rise.

You are not here to chase someone else's version of success.

You are here to become the fullest expression of who you were created to be.

That is the heart of Must.

That is the work of a lifetime.

And that is the invitation standing before you now.

If there is one message that stays with you long after this book is closed, let it be this:

You are the author of your life.

Your goals are your tools.

Your identity is your foundation.

And your Must is your compass.

Build the life that reflects your deepest truth.

Take the smallest next step.

Honor the values that matter.

Live intentionally, courageously, and without apology.

Your future is not waiting for a perfect moment.

It is waiting for your commitment—today.

You already have everything you need.

Now go live your Must.

And if this book has helped you, share it with one person who is also ready to become who they're meant to be.

With my deepest admiration and encouragement, Your Friend,

Stephen Rue

ABOUT THE AUTHOR

STEPHEN RUE is a multifaceted individual whose diverse life experiences and professional achievements have shaped his mission to inspire and uplift others. Stephen, a renowned lawyer and counselor-at-law licensed in multiple states, has academic credentials that include a BBA from Southern Methodist University, a law degree, and an MBA from Loyola University, Harvard Law School leadership training, and ongoing doctoral work at National University. Voted "Best Attorney" in New Orleans, his true passion lies in personal growth and helping others overcome adversity.

Certified as a trauma recovery life coach, Stephen draws from his own triumphs over family tragedies and personal challenges. Through law and personal development, he has helped thousands to flourish and thrive in their lives. His zest for life extends to being a Mardi Gras king, author, motivational speaker, artist, sculptor, and marathon runner.

For over three decades, Stephen has immersed himself in various endeavors, studies, and deep research, culminating in this masterpiece book—*Must*. Synthesizing insights from luminaries in psychology, neuroscience, philosophy, and personal development, he offers a practical and effective roadmap for personal transformation. His unique approach combines academic rigor with real-world application, making complex concepts accessible and actionable.

STEPHEN RUE

Through this book, Stephen shares wisdom gained from overcoming adversity, providing readers with tools to navigate life's challenges and emerge stronger, more resilient, and aligned with their true selves as the person they are meant to be.

CONNECT AND GROW TOGETHER: STAY IN TOUCH WITH ME AND OUR MUST BOOK COMMUNITY

Discover Stephen Rue's acclaimed flagship books:

Must: Becoming the Person You Are Meant to Be,

and

Must Book Guided Journal: Daily Prompts for Personal Development, Self-Improvement, and Growth for Success,

available at bookstores and online retailers.

To **join our growing #mustbook community,** <u>**take a picture of yourself with your journal and share it**</u> on Instagram, Facebook, X, or your favorite social platform using the hashtag **#mustbook**. Your photo might be featured in future posts—let's inspire each other on this journey!

Book Website: MustGoals.com
Must Book Personal Development Series: MustBook.net
Author/Speaker Website: **StephenRue.Live**
Instagram: SouthernFriedLawyer

Facebook: Stephen Rue Official Facebook Page

YouTube: TheStephenRue

X (Twitter): **StephenRue**

Mail: 416 N. Vermont Street, Covington, LA 70433

Email: Stephen@StephenRue.com

Feel free to reach out through any of the methods above for further resources, encouragement, or to connect with the *Must* **community**.

Please check out our updated bibliography and resources for continued growth at ***MustGoals.com/Resources.***

HOW TO STAY IN TOUCH WITH ME

StephenRue.Live

StephenRue.com

Instagram @SouthernFriedLawyer

Facebook: Stephen Rue Official Facebook Page

YouTube @TheStephenRue

X @StephenRue

Mail: 416 N. Vermont Street, Covington, LA 70433

Stephen@StephenRue.com

KEY MUST CONCEPTS (AT A GLANCE)

Core Identity and Foundations

Must

"Must" is your deepest inner commitment—what you know you are called to be and do, not what others expect of you. It is the difference between living by pressure and living by authentic conviction, turning every important choice into an expression of who you truly are.

Must Mindset

The Must Mindset is the mental foundation that moves you from passive intention to active identity. It is the choice to see yourself as capable of growth, alignment, and purposeful action, even when circumstances or past stories suggest otherwise.

Must Core Beliefs

Must Core Beliefs are the fundamental ideas you hold about yourself, others, and the world that either limit or empower your potential. In this system, you learn to identify, challenge, and rewrite limiting beliefs so they support your Must identity and goals.

Must Core Values

Must Core Values are the non-negotiable principles that define what truly matters to you in each life domain. They act like "personal search terms" that guide your decisions, filter your goals, and ensure your achievements feel meaningful, not hollow.

Must Personal Narrative

Your Must Personal Narrative is the story you tell yourself about who you are, where you have been, and where you are going. Reframing this story turns past pain and limitation into a source of strength, aligning your goals with a more empowering identity.

Must Standards

Must Standards are the minimum levels of behavior, effort, and integrity you choose to uphold in every area of your life. They protect your progress by defining what you will and will not tolerate from yourself as you live your Must.

Must Purpose

Must Purpose is your core "why"—the larger contribution and meaning that tie your identity, values, and story together. It directs your long-term goals so they serve not only personal success, but also impact, service, and legacy.

Must Identity Map (My "I AM")

The Must Identity Map is your written "I am..." picture of who you are becoming at your best. It gathers your mindset, beliefs, values, narrative, standards, and purpose into a single, coherent identity statement that anchors every Must Goal you set.

System Maps and Visuals

Must Inside-Out Flowchart (Identity → Outcomes)

The Must Inside-Out Flowchart shows how inner life and outer results are connected: Identity → Mindset → Beliefs → Values → Personal Narrative → Standards → Purpose → Goals → Must Actions in the Must Zone → Habits → Tenacity, Perseverance & Grit → Outcomes. It is the backbone of this book, guiding you from who you are to what you achieve.

Must Alignment Map

The Must Alignment Map links your inner foundations (beliefs, values, narrative, standards, purpose) directly to your goals, actions, habits, and results. It helps you see, on a single page, whether each goal truly reflects your authentic identity or needs to be realigned.

Must Circle of Life

The Must Circle of Life is a visual framework of your key life domains: Health & Vitality, Relationships, Career, Financial Well-Being, Personal Growth, Spirituality, and Community & Legacy. It ensures your goals create whole-life flourishing instead of lopsided success in just one area.

Goals, Actions, and Habits

Must Goal

A Must Goal is a clear, measurable objective that arises from your authentic identity rather than external pressure. It is aligned with your Must Mindset, Core Beliefs, Core Values, Personal Narrative, Standards, and Purpose, so achieving it helps you become who you are meant to be.

Must Micro-Goal

A Must Micro-Goal is the smallest meaningful step you can take today toward a Must Goal. It is concrete, doable, and tightly focused, using the science of "small wins" to build momentum, confidence, and neuroplastic change.

Must Habit

A Must Habit is a simple, repeatable behavior you practice daily or weekly that keeps you moving automatically toward your Must Goals. Each repetition is a "vote" for your chosen identity, training your self-control and making aligned action easier over time.

Must Zone (and Must Actions in the Must Zone)

The Must Zone is the mental and behavioral space where you consistently act in line with your identity, values, and purpose. Must Actions in the Must Zone are the specific, disciplined behaviors you return to—especially when motivation dips or obstacles appear.

I AM SMART TO ACT™ Goals Method

I AM SMART TO ACT™ Goals Method

The I AM SMART TO ACT™ Goals Method is your identity-first upgrade to classic SMART goals. It begins with "I AM" (who you are becoming), then walks through SMART criteria, and ends with committed action, so every goal is both structured and deeply aligned with your Must.

I – Identity

Every Must Goal starts with an "I am…" declaration that reflects your authentic, evolving self. This step ensures you are not just chasing outcomes, but reinforcing who you are choosing to become.

A – Aligned

Aligned means your goal fits your Must identity—your mindset, core beliefs, values, personal narrative, standards, and purpose. If a goal is not aligned, you refine or release it instead of forcing yourself into someone else's agenda.

M – Meaningful

Meaningful goals express your Must Purpose and what matters most in this season of life. They energize you because they are connected to contribution, growth, and identity—not just appearance or approval.

S – Specific

Specific goals state exactly what you will do and how. Clear, concrete wording removes ambiguity and makes it obvious whether you are moving closer to or further from your Must.

M – Measurable

Measurable goals include visible indicators—numbers, frequencies, or clear yes/no outcomes. This allows you to track progress, celebrate small wins, and adjust your approach without losing your way.

A – Achievable

Achievable goals stretch you beyond your comfort zone while remaining realistically within your control. They honor your current season, resources, and constraints, preventing both under-reach and burnout.

R – Relevant

Relevant goals fit your current priorities and life context. They support your most important Must Goals instead of distracting you with impressive but misaligned pursuits.

T – Time-bound

Time-bound goals include a deadline and, when useful, interim milestones. Time frames create urgency, focus, and pacing so that meaningful change happens now, not "someday."

TO ACT

"TO ACT" is your reminder that identity-aligned goals only matter when you live them. It calls you to consistent, courageous steps—Must Micro-Goals, Must Habits, and Must Actions in the Must Zone—until your desired outcomes become your new normal.

Paths and Process

Exploration (Part One)

Exploration is the phase where you clarify your identity: Must Mindset, Core Beliefs, Core Values, Personal Narrative, Standards, and Purpose. Here you build the inner architecture that makes later goals authentic and sustainable.

Implementation (Part Two)

Implementation is where you translate inner clarity into concrete goals, actions, systems, and habits across every life domain. You use tools like the I AM SMART TO ACT™ Goals Method, Must Micro-Goals, Must Habits, and the Must Zone to create measurable results.

Integration (Beyond the Book / Ongoing)

Integration is the lifelong process of living your Must every day, revisiting your identity work, updating goals, and maintaining habits. It is how you turn this book from a project into a personal operating system.

Quick Start Path

The Quick Start Path gives you immediate traction: you choose one life domain, set a single Must Goal, define a Must Micro-Goal, and create one Must Habit so you start acting today. You can then circle back to deeper identity work as needed.

Deep Alignment Journey

The Deep Alignment Journey invites you to move through the book in sequence, completing the inner work in Part One before fully building out your goals in Part Two. It is the path for readers who want not just productivity, but profound identity-level transformation.

Key Science Anchors

Growth Mindset

A growth mindset is the belief that abilities can be developed through effort, strategies, and support. In the Must system, it undergirds the Must Mindset and keeps you experimenting, learning, and adjusting instead of labeling yourself as fixed.

Self-Determination Theory

Self-Determination Theory highlights three needs that fuel lasting motivation: autonomy, competence, and relatedness. Must Goals are designed to honor your freedom, grow your capabilities, and strengthen your connections, so motivation becomes sustainable.

Small Wins and Micro-Goals

Research on small wins shows that tiny, consistent successes create outsized boosts in motivation, confidence, and habit formation. Must Micro-Goals and Must Habits harness this effect to rewire your brain and identity through frequent, doable actions.

Visualization and Mental Rehearsal

Visualization is the practice of mentally rehearsing your desired future and the steps to reach it. Combined with the I AM SMART TO ACT™ Goals Method, it makes your Must Goals feel more familiar and attainable, priming your mind and attention to notice opportunities.

Reticular Activating System (RAS)

The Reticular Activating System is a filter in your brain that decides which information gets your attention. When you repeatedly focus on aligned Must Goals and identity statements, your RAS helps you notice patterns, resources, and possibilities that support them.

REFERENCES & ONGOING RESEARCH UPDATES

This book draws from decades of psychological research, behavioral science, leadership theory, human performance studies, and spiritual development literature. The works listed in the References section represent many of the foundational books, peer-reviewed studies, and theoretical frameworks that support the principles of identity-based goal setting, habit formation, motivation, and personal transformation presented in *Must Goals*.

Because science evolves, and because new studies continue to refine what we know about human behavior, habit formation, resilience, implementation intentions, purpose, identity, and motivation, **updated research—along with expanded reading recommendations, new models, and supplemental tools—will be maintained at:**

MustGoals.com/Resources

There you will find:

- Updated studies in psychology, neuroscience, and behavioral change
- Expanded reading lists for identity work, habit formation, and resilience

- Downloadable worksheets and templates
- Visual models and diagrams from the book
- Supplemental exercises and case studies
- Bonus content that continues to grow over time

This ensures that *Must Goals* remains a **living, evolving system**, grounded in the most current research and best practices.

process. That is real transformation.

If you doubt this, flip through your own writing. The evidence is there.

Who You Are Now

This book was never about becoming a flawless version of yourself. It was about becoming more *fully* yourself:

- Someone who can see clearly and still choose hope.
- Someone who can set a boundary without shutting down love.
- Someone who can handle money, health, work, and faith with more honesty and less shame.
- Someone who can fail, apologize, reset, and still remember their worth.

You are not finished.

You are *more awake*.

Your Must identity is not a destination.

It is a way you walk now.

Where You Go From Here

There is no rule that says you must "start over" tomorrow. But you may choose to. You now have several paths:

- **Repeat the year with new eyes.**

    The same questions will meet a different you.

- **Create your own Must rhythm.**

    Revisit domains monthly—health, money, love, rest, purpose.

- **Translate reflection into plans.**

    Let what you've learned shape concrete changes in the coming months.

- **Share Must with safe people.**

    Without revealing private writing, bring key questions into your relationships.

You no longer need a book to know how to ask yourself honest questions.

You have practiced that for 365 days.

A Promise Forward

The most important commitment now is not to a specific goal but to a way of relating to your life:

- To tell yourself the truth, kindly.
- To adjust your days to match what you value.
- To treat your time, body, gifts, and relationships as things that matter.
- To live as if your life is a Must—because it is.

STEPHEN RUE

This book has been a companion along the way.
Close the cover knowing the companion now lives inside you.

Every day from here is not just another date on a calendar.
It is another line in the story of your Must life.

And *you* hold the pen.

THANK YOU, AND NEXT STEPS

If this book has encouraged or helped you, **would you take a moment to leave a review?**

Your feedback makes a real difference and helps other readers discover this work. You can share your thoughts on Amazon.com, Goodreads.com, Barnes & Noble, or your preferred bookseller, and consider sharing or gifting this book to someone who might benefit from it. To continue your journey, visit **MustGoals.com** and **StephenRue.Live** for more resources, events, and tools in the Must Personal Development series.

Thank you for being part of this work and for supporting these books.

www.ingramcontent.com/pod-product-compliance
Lightning Source LLC
Chambersburg PA
CBHW032059090426
42743CB00007B/168